RECONSTRUCTION
OF
CULTURE AND ISLAM

RECONSTRUCTION OF CULTURE AND ISLAM

Prof. MOHAMMAD TAQI AMINI

Formerly The Dean
Faculty of Theology
Aligarh Muslim University
Aligarh

Translated by:

Z.A. USMANI

KITAB BHAVAN
New Delhi-110002

KITAB BHAVAN
1784, Kalan Mahal
Darya Ganj, New Delhi-110 002

FIRST EDITION : 1988

Published by Nusrat Ali Nasri for Kitab Bhavan.
Phototype Set by the Ad-Setters, 2622, Kucha Chellan, Darya Ganj, Delhi-2 & Printed at Lahooti Fine Art Press, Sui Walan, Delhi-110 006

PRINTED IN INDIA

Dedicated

to

All Valuable Patrons

FOREWORD

I have had the occassion, through, thanks to the author's courtesy, to go through his erudite and thought-provoking book "*Tabzeeb ki Tashkeel—i—Jadid*" which I would translate as '*Civilisation Reconstructed*'. The book was first published in 1973. It is but appropriate that it has been translated into English. The translation would increase its readership manifold and spark a meaningful discussion on a subject that touches humankind so intimately.

Maulana Hafiz Mohammad Taqi Amini, Professor of Theology in Aligarh Muslim University 'is widely respected not only as a profound scholar but also as an original thinker. His orthodoxy is not hide-bound. His is an inquisitive spirit. Not for him the docile acceptance of whatever has been handed down by tradition. His irresistible habit is to question. He goes behind what finds facile acceptance among the faithful. He goes back in time and delves into man's efforts to arrive at the truth and to know the why and wherefore of things? What is the essence of reality? What lies hidden underneath the facade of material well being? What does human nature consist of? How, during the ages has man endeavoured to subdue his animal instincts? From paganism to revealed religion what domains of experience have been traversed by man in different climes and countries? How revealed religion, time and again 'failed to retain its pristine purity and got mixed with the rites and customs it had endeavoured to replace and the passions and desires it had sought to curb? How the carnal,-the corporeal and the physical infiltrated into the spiritual and the austere? What relationship should exist between crime and purnishment? How can a permissive society contain the consequences of an untrammelled behaviour which inevitably becomes lewd, coarse and uncouth spelling the gravest danger to all that civilization stands for?

These are some of the questions that the author asks himself and proceeds to answer. The extensive and relevant quotations that one finds strewn in the book reveal that the author has wandered far and wide in search of the truth. These quotations are neither pedantic nor decorative. They serve to widen the horizon in the manner the portrayal of the historical background does. They also serve as desiderata for the argument and springboard for a perceptive discussion of the subject at issue. They do not interrupt either the narrative or the argument but advance either. They indicate that what is being said does not stem from the caprice of an isolated author but has behind it the weight of the probings and questionings of the human soul in different countries and at different times

Professor Amini has made Islam his sheet-anchor. He has tried to prove that the reconstruction of civilization that Islam — the last revealed Word of God — has essayed, seeks to strike a balance between the physical and the spiritual forces inherent in man.

The style of discussion adopted in this book steers clear of tame acquiescence on the one hand and aggressive rejection on the other. The author's approach is rational. He reasons out the tenets of what he has come to believe. This is the culmination of a life-long study of the evolution of, what for want of a better term may be called, man's moral phyche. It is the story of the Pilgrim's Progress that is narrated here on a collective plane and a wider canvas.

While going through the book one gets the impression that the author's intellectual quiver is full of arrows. One idea follows another in quick succession. One could wish for a more detailed discussion of the issues raised. The author himself would have preferred it. But constraints of space intervened and deprived the readers of a more copious dissertation on many an issue. But Prof. Aminis' career as an author, happily, is nowhere near its end. Come to think of it, the very fact that an Alim brought up in the orthodox Madarsa tradition has claimed evolution of civilization as his province, is itself a welcome break from erudite insularity.

S. HAMID
Former Vice-Chancellor,
Aligarh Muslim University

CONTENTS

INTRODUCTION

The encyclopaedists of western culture usually get divided into two groups. One group is that which would not bear any kind of intrusion of the East into the West. The other group is that which recognizes the operative influence of the East in every cultural construct. Scholars have given various reasons for the two extreme positions. Among them are national prejudice, the after-effects of the crusades, the lack of knowledge and research, sentimentality and superficiality.

With any fairness, it cannot be denied that the West has greatly benefitted from the East in matters of cultural build-up. But the psychological foundations for this build-up have been transplanted directly from Greek and Roman culture. Speaking of the benefit the West has derived from the East, Robert Brefault says that the fire that lighted once again the lamp of culture had not arisen from the embers that were smouldering in the ruins of Europe. In fact the fire had not come from the north; it had come with the southern invaders of the empire: the Arabs (*Making of Humanity*).

At another place Brefault observes that the power that changed the shape of the physical and the intellectual world was the product of the close inter-relationship that obtained among the astronomers, alchemists and members of the medical institutions of the later Middle ages; and this inter-relationship was the result only of the impact of Arab culture. All the scientific achievements in Europe till the end of the fifteenth century had been derived from the knowledge and learning of the Arabs. The writer is aware that he has spoken rather in detail on the contribution of Arab culture towards the cultural awakening of Europe. But misrepresentations of our time have grown to such an extent that to eliminate them he thinks this detail was necessary.

Toynbee has also spoken again and again of the beneficial influence of the Muslims on the westerners. He says that the western Christians derived full benefit from the researches of contemporary Muslim scholars and intellectuals. They derived full benefit even from that system of numerical science which is popularly called Arabic system — though it originated from India. Toynbee goes on to say that the West has advanced far beyond what it inherited from Muslims in the field of science. But the influences of the Syriac culture on the impressionable western Christianity cannot be ignored.

Psychological Foundations Imported from Greece and Rome

With regard to the psychological foundations of western culture the following observations have been made:

The lineage of western culture goes back to the clear and well-argued manner of the ancient Greeks.

Western culture has the same relation to Greek culture as the child has to the father.

Essentially, what lies at the back of the western mind is ancient Greek culture, which chose for its manifestation the human body.

The European mind is different from the oriental and Islamic mind in that it has at its back Greece and Rome. This is the most prominent feature of its structure and functioning. The liberalism of the Greeks and the Romans; their concept of freedom; their system of medical treatment; their spirit of enquiry; their secular and worldly-minded outlook; their critical attitude; and their unflinching and free mode of critical assessment of the works of human intellect — all these things have made the western world possible.

The above observations give importance to Greece and not to Rome because in science, philosophy, poetry and literature Rome was subservient to Greece. It was the consequence of this subservience of Roman culture to Greece that Rome was able to partake of the economic and political development which was characteristic of the Greek states or their satellites. Roman went through all the phases of this development; but it always lagged behind Athens by a span of almost 150 years.

For comprehending the psychological moorings of western culture it would not be irrelevant to have a survey of the religions and moral climate of the Graeco-Rome culture of pre-Christian times.

The Religious and Moral Ethos of the Greeks

Before the philosophical era in Greece and even for a long period after its emergence we do not find evidence of any religious belief directly emanating from revelation and being capable of providing moral and social guidance to the Greeks.

The religion of the ancient Greeks like that of the Indian Aryans was a religion of the worship of nature and gods and godesses related to them. Alongwith the worship of the sky, the earth, the sun, the moon and the stars etc. there was also the cult of phallic worship. Among the phallic deities Dionysous was particularly important. In his name a great Greek festival called Dionysia was held, and on the eve of this festival men and women had the licence of indulging freely in sexual orgy. Similarly towards the beginning of April a big festival was held in the honour of Venus Aphrodite the godess that represented the female sex. Those who participated in it had also a licence of sexual indulgence. Besides phallic deities there was a long pantheon of various deities who were supposed to live on Olympus and precide over various activities and functions.

According to the Greek belief Greek deities were not self-created, but were children of the Earth and the Sky. This is why among the Greeks there was no deity having the status of 'the Lord and Cherisher of the Worlds'. Though Zeus was the chief of the deities, he too could not acquire that status.

Religion is usually directed to the purification of moral sense and the setting of norms in the field of thought and action; but it is the consensus of the scholars that Greek religion had spoiled the moral of the people by giving them licence. The kind of moral education conducted in cities like Athens show that the above mentioned Pantheon of gods and goddess and nothing to do with that moral education. It was due to consolidated effort of some philosophers of the early Greek civilization and of some jurists and some priests of the temple of Delphi.

Greek Philosophy Lacked the Capability of Guidance

Around 400 B.C when there occurred a spurt of intellectual activity in Greece the nature of the established religion was also changed with the new advancements in science and philosophy. Thus the intellectual feats of Socrates (469 B.C. - 399 B.C.), Plato (b. 427 B.C.), Aristotle (b. 384 B.C.) etc. introduced the Greeks to a religion which had its basis in philosophy instead of superstition. As is usual, these philosophers at first met with great hostility and the established religious dispensation condemned them as irreligious; but in course of time the hostility decreased, and by virtue of the influence of their philosophy the Greeks turned to believe in one God. As this philosophy spread, the Greeks tried to make it their guide in life. But philosophy, on account of its basic limitations as philosophy, could not become a substitute for religion, nor could it develop the capability of social and moral guidance. To mention some of these basic limitations:

(1) Philosophy cannot be charged with passionate feelings, spiritual vision and faith; nor can it provide spiritual appeasement.

(2) The appeasement provided by philosophy is intellectual, and therefore, reductive; it cannot be of help in enabling man to bear the unpleasantness of life, nor can it bless him with any hope for future.

(3) Philosophy has no attraction for the common people and its area of appeal does not extend beyond a particular, elitistic class.

The Romans Welcomed the Influence of Greece

After the decline of the Greek civilisation (around 146 B.C.) the Romans took the place of the Greeks in the cultural world. In spite of their decline the greatest cultural conquest of the Greeks was the fact that their culture was adopted by the Romans. Thus we find that before the Romans adopted Christianity their religion seems to be very much full of Greek influence.Many of their deities seem to be imported from Greece and behave like the Greek deities in being in charge of certain functions. Similarly in matters of science and philosophy, literature and poetry, civilisation and culture, Rome drew upon Greece.

The highest deity of the Romans who was the patron of Rome and the king of all the gods and goddesses was called Jupiter. He was the king of heaven and the other deities occupied a subordinate position as his ministers.

Scholars are of the view that beliefs formed a comparatively small part of the Roman religion, and that more emphasis was laid on rituals than on belief or faith. It was for this reason that the ritualistic religion remained insulated against the formative influences of philosophy and even survived these influences. Thus many intellectuals kept observing the rituals in spite of their liberal thinking and emancipation from religious beliefs. As scholars have pointed out, Roman religion did not inculcate any moral sense — their deities were not associated with any moral concept either; rather, the immoral stories prevalent about various pagan deities had become part of the Roman religious tradition.

In respect of religion the Roman intellectuals were divided into two groups. One of these groups was theistic. Reaction against polytheism was developing in it as it had developed in the case of Greek intellectuals, which reaction ultimately made the Romans turn to belief in One God. The Roman intellectuals had reached this belief through the concept of monism. In those days monism was an effort to reach out to a rationalistic understanding of God and of His relation to Universe. Many monistic intellectuals justified idol worship in spite of this belief in One God— because they thought that for the common people it was a means of arriving at the conception of the One God.

The second group did not believe in religion and was even against it. What is deemed to be their great achievement is that they were the first to enquire into the origin of religion. For example Lucretius came to the conclusion that religion was the product of fear, dread and awe. To quote other examples, some intellectuals were of the opinion that the various deities represented the various manifestations of nature or the various powers of God. Other intellectuals were of the opinion that the gods were actually kings of some past age and that they were defied after their death.

However, the fact remains that after the light of philosophy had gone out in Greece it was rekindled in Rome. But as it happened in Rome, philosophy could not become a substitute for religion, nor could it succeed in providing moral and social guidance to the people.

First Attempts at the Formulation of Secular Laws

The achievement of the Romans in the formulation of laws was so important that it could not be matched by the other nations of the time including the Greeks. A few words about it would not be out of place.

At first the legal system of the Romans, like that of other nations, was based on religious rites and rituals.

Around 448-51 B.C. a legislative assembly was formed. It framed a set of laws, which is popularly known as Twelve Tablets. Later on this set of laws formed the basis of the Roman constitution and legal system. It contained laws concerning business affairs, social affairs and governmental administration, and also the conventions which already have the status of law in Rome. In framing this set of laws all possible efforts were made to keep the law dissociated from religious rites and rituals and to give them a secular basis. These efforts were not met with full success in the beginning but it cannot be denied that they were the first efforts to devise secular laws. The work of interpreting laws was carried on intermittently and by various individuals in subsequent times. Thus history tells us of several law books written by Gaius and others and also of several legislative assemblies that were formed. The next important legislative activity emerged after a period of one thousand years when in 527 A.D. the emperor Justinian turned his attention towards a systemic formulation of laws. After seven or eight years it resulted in the legal system that is known all over the world by the name of 'Roman Law'.

Sadistic Practices of the Romans

In spite of their religion, philosophy and law it was a practice of the Romans to derive pleasure from the infliction of torture on human beings, and even from the spectacle of this torture, and, of course, from murder and bloodshed. Thus they made certain men called 'gladiators' fight wild animals in the arena, and took sadistic pleasure in the sight of these bleeding human beings in their death throes. At first this 'entertainment' was religious ritual, performed for the appeasement of the souls of the dead in graveyards; but later on it became so popular as to be performed on all occasions of social importance, like those of triumph, marriage, death, public rejoicing or public grief. Certain Roman rulers tried to put restrictions on the common prevalence of this practice. For example Emperor Augustus promulgated a law forbidding more than 120 gladiators to fight at a time, and also forbidding a person to invite more than two of these shows in a year.

Religions of Western Civilization

The religions that have contributed towards the advancement of western culture are four. They are: Graeco-Roman religion, Christianity, Protestant Christianity, and Natural Religions.

Religion of the Greeks and Romans

The religion of the Greeks and Romans which came down to the Europeans as a cultural heritage has been discussed above. It has been rightly observed that the Greek dramatists present Zeus as the Lord of the gods in a way that suggests that the Greeks were either acquainted with the revealed religion of Moses or had access to some kind of revelation themselves. Another conjecture is that, since moral law (or natural law) was a part of the Graeco-Roman legal system, the Greeks and the Romans had some intimation of revelation which was reflected in this moral law.

But these are conjectures after all; and they are not sufficient for establishing any evidence of the existence of revealed religion among the Greeks and the Romans, particularly in view of their modes of life, which we have discussed above.

Christianity

Christianity is the religion which is ascribed to Jesus Christ. He was born in Palestine in the age of the Emperor Augustus. Historians have shifted his birth to 4-6 years earlier than the established year of his birth.

After the death of Christ Christianity was weakened for the time being, but soon, within a period of thirty years it spread in various parts of Europe. Among those who adopted this religion a large number belonged to the Greek colonies. These people were originally Jews, but they belonged to regions where the influence of Greek culture — in matters of language, thought and belief etc. — was most powerful. An as for the Roman Jews who adopted Christianity, they too had Greek culture in their bones.

In Roman empire the first centre of Christianity was established in Antakia (Constantinople). Then Christianity began to spread rapidly, so much so that it became the state religion of the Roman Empire by the order of Emperor Constantine in the year 313 A.D. Rome itself came to be regarded as one of the important religious centres in Christendom. After Christianity had become the state religion many worldly people who were idolators and polytheists at heart became its zealous supporters simply for the sake of worldy gains of rank and wealth and power.

Christianity Disfigured

Scholars are of the opinon that owing to the influences of Greek philosophy and polytheistic ideas the original form of Christian religion was very much disfigured. It has been pointed out that even the concept of Trinity is something that was borrowed from the ancient Egyptians, Greeks and Romans.

For instance, the ancient Egyptians had the celebrated trinity of Isiris, Isis and Oris; the Greeks had the trinity of Zeus, Poseidon and Hades; and the Romans that of Jupiter, Neptune and Pluto, which corresponded to the Greek trinity.

Besides approving of the concept of Trinity, constantine had approved of the revival and the continuation of many idolatorous practices out of political expediency. The Christians had compromised with them in spite of their political supremacy. In the beginning such things were done in the name of tolerance and national integration, but later on they went to form a new religion.

Idolatory Combined with Christianity to Form a New Religion

The new religion that was formed was a combination of Christianity and idolatory or paganism. Idolatorous practices and pagan rites were assimilated to Christianity. Showy methods of worship were adopted. The priests began to wear showy dresses, caps and crowns. Camphor candles, and gold and silver pots became accessories of Church Service. The Church Service acquired the gaudy look of a marriage ceremony. Sacrificial rituals were emphasized as means of purification. With the relics of saints whether geniune or faked, preodical fairs were instituted. Starvation came to be regarded as the most important means of appeasing the wrath of God and of exorcising evil spirits. People would travel thousands of miles for a pilgrimage to Jerusalem and to the tombs of saints. From Jerusalem these people, called 'Palmers', would bring maunds of earth and sell it at the price of jewels. This earth was believed to have the power of exorcising the devil. Seances were held to call up the souls of the redeemed Christians, for it was supposed that these souls kept wandering around in the universe or hanging around the places assigned to them etc.

Regarding this new Christian religion a Christian theologian (Bishop Newton) has made some very pertinent observations. He asks: Does not the worship of saints and angels in our days resemble the worship of the devils in ancient times? It does, only names are different, he says. The pagans deified their ancestors and worshipped them; Christians have deified their saints and worship them. The people who introduced such worship in Christianity knew very well that it differed in no way from the pagan modes of worship. The new worship which has replaced the old is like old wine in new bottles. To burn incense at various alters at the same time; to sprinkle holy water (or saline water) while coming and going to the church; to light hundreds of lamps and candles at alters and before images in broad daylight; to make thanks-offerings for fulfilled vows or for relief, supposedly obtained through super-natural aid, from disease or danger; to regard pious forebears as saints or gods; to go to the tombs for worshipping the dead or their relics; to take out, now and then, garish processions of images and relics; to torture one's body by flogging for the sake of spiritual discipline; to have various sects and brotherhoods of the clergy; to have the priests shave off their heads in a particular fashion; to regard life-long abstinence as the testimony of piety—these with many other practices are an integral part of the superstitious faith of the idolatorous followers of Rome.

Commenting on this deformed Christianity Draper goes on to say that in the age of Constantine Christianity enters an era when it goes on becoming political rather than religious. From now onwards it gets concerned with empire building and worldy gains. It can be said that Christianity had degenerated into some form of polytheism and idolatory. But it is equally true to say that it had developed gradually into a modified form of Greek polytheism and idolatory. The truth that when two bodies collide both of them suffer some disfigurement applies to physics as well as to social science. Thus polytheism brought about a change in the nature of Christianity and Christianity in its turn brought about a change in the nature of polytheism.

The above observations lead to the conclusion that the religion that inspired and gave direction to cultural activity in Greece and in the Roman empire was not real Christianity; but a new religion formed by the combination of Christianity and polytheism.

Role of the New Religion in Relation to Cultural Activity

In this connexion Laiki observes that the consequence of always emphasizing the dark aspect of human history was that the Christian Fathers began to entertain an exaggerated conception of the sinfulness of human nature. The concept of Original Sin implied that man was essentially sinful by nature, that by nature he was inclined to evil. Laiki remarks that in the moral history of the world perhaps nothing else forms a more painful episode than the 'epidemic of asceticism' caused by this concept of Original Sin. It was most woeful that the people who received enlightenment from Plato and Cicero and who had as models the spotless and dignified characters of Socrates and Cato had now set as their goal a truncated and undignified existence, which was an embodiment of ignorance; which was devoid of the love for the country and the natural warmth of affections; which had devoted the whole of its life to cruel self-torture; and which, due to its intense suspicion and obsession, was afraid of its own shadow as of some monster. Let us not forget that this oppressive self-denial went on not for two or four years but for 200 years, and was all the while assumed as the sign of the highest moral virtue. Laiki goes on to observe that public morale had degenerated so much that people had no fear of dishonour and bad name. Their conscience did stand in fear of religion, but the fear would get dispelled by the belief that prayers and rituals could absolve them of all sins. Thus hypocrisy and treachery were as rampant as they had not been in the time of the Caesers.

Clarification of Some Doubts

The historians who have eulogized the spirituality of the Chris tian Church are not aware of the fact that its pristine spirituality was already disfigured when it was established in the kingdoms of Greece and Rome. Whatever spirituality remained in it was outweighed by the corruption that had sickened culture and intellect. It is difficult for one to imagine how nightmarish it was.

Some scholars and intellectuals have ascribed certain teachings to Christ, which do not conform to the spirit of his mission. For example, Rousseau is of the opinion that Christ came into the world with a mission to establish merely a spiritual 'Kingdom of God', which mission resulted in separating religion from politics and destroying the unity of the state and, therefore, in giving rise to internal factions which never allowed the Christian world to have peace!' Such a view arises on account of the distorted Gospel that has pervaded the Christian world. The division of religion and politics is not the notion of Christ but of the distorted religion that goes by the name of Christianity.

Prophets, apostles and founders of religion have always contributed to the formation of the culture of their people in the right way. But, as Joseph Haile observes, the world-wide changes that Islam rapidly brought about in the structure of human culture are without precedence. Apart from this observation, it is also true that a religion can reach us in a distorted form. In view of this distorted picture certain people would raise doubts regarding the value of religion itself. They would say, like Merseer, that religion serves only the purpose of decoration and embellishment and that it is in no way useful for society. Such remarks apply, not to religion itself, but to the distorted form of religion, which, in being pervaded by lustful desires, has lost its usefulness. As for genuine religion, nobody can deny its usefulness for life. To deny it would be to deny historical facts.

Protestant Christianity

In the wake of the Renaissance in Europe ancient arts and sciences, which were burried in oblivion, were revived and they made wonderful advancements. At the same time attention was drawn towards the reformation of established Christianity. The Reformation became a powerful movement. We shall briefly speak of certain personages associated with it.

John Wycliffe, who taught at Oxford in the fourteenth century, severely critized the established Christianity. For doing this he was dismissed by the University and excommunicated by the Pope.

Erasmus (1466—1536) exposed the corruptions and evils of the Church. In his book, *In Praise of Folly* he attacked the stem of Church government, doing great damage to the position of the Pope. Erasmus was born in Holland, but he spent most of his life in France, England, Italy and Germany.

Martin Luther did most to reform Christianity. He was born in Germany in 1483, and died in 1546. It was due to his movement that Protestant Christianity came into being. It was more progressive than the older form of Christianity which was now known as Roman Catholic Christianity.

False Impression Created by Luther's Movement

Luther's reformative movement emerged at a time when Europe was coming out of backwardness and making rapid strides towards progress in every field. His work was of a negative nature. As long as it attacked corruption the movement kept producing a great stir. It was quite easy for the followers of the movement to hit at the corrupt institutions that misrepresented religion, for they had the zeal for engaging themselves in a religious strife for the sake of truth. But when their turn came to do something positive, to formulate their own system of doctrines and to offer their own inter-pretations of truth, their weakness began to show itself. They could demolish the old system but could not construct a new and positive one. Hence, very soon they were themselves divided into two sects, the Lutherian and the Calvinian. The differences of these sects became more and more intensified, as each of them tended to distinguish and define itself through further and further specifications and regimentation. Protestanism had arisen out of various complex factors, including the racial one. The racial factor operated against Protestanism itself. It was to some extent the racial factor which was responsible after sometime for the open opposition to Protestanism by the people of Southern Europe, by people who spoke Latin, Italian, French, Spanish and Portugese. The Protestant religion was the product of Renaissance; but it could not fulfil its demands. It produced its scholars and divines; but it could not do much for the common people.

Luther himself had closer relations with aristocrats and nobles than with the common people and it was on the former that he relied for support in the beginning of his campaign. It was on them that the movement itself was progressive. This has given a false impression to some scholars that all progressive cultural activity in Europe emanated from Christianity, which was now reforming itself. Thus Delthy has argued that religion gave impetus to the scientific and intellectual development of Germany, England and France and that the new spirit of Christian religion, which is Protestantism, emerged from a wider concept of religion.

Similarly, with regard to the theory of Evolution some scholars are of the opinion that it has its basis in Christian religion in that this religion conceives of movement from the lower to the higher, the highest being God.

But researchers are not inclined to yield so much to the influence of Christian religion. They have proved that the movement of Reformation, out of its basic weaknesses, could not perform a revolutionary role in the structuring and guidance of culture. Rather it has been able only to reinvigorate, directly or indirectly, those formative forces which were already operating in the field of culture.

Certain Basic Flaws in Reformation

As H.O. Weinkin points out, at first Protestantism appeared as the external manifestation of a great moral revolution. That is, some people out of their own moral sense, revolted against the heretical and corrupt practices of the established Christian religion. Since they were impelled by a reactionary spirit their relied again in his late years. The reaction against Protestanism had begun to show itself towards the end of the sixteenth century.

The observations of A.J. Grant also testify to the basic weaknesses of the Protestan movement. He says that Luther strongly opposed the peasants through his speeches and writings (and this in the days of revolt against the oppression of the upper class). He wanted the aristocracy to crush their insurgence; he did not condemn even oppressive means used for this purpose. The peasants had sued for the support of Luther to their cause. But instead of supporting it he opposed it. Consequently his movement lost its popularity among the common people, at the grass-root level, so to say. In fact, Luther had to rely on the middle and higher classes for support. His movement had links with the ruling class, and it could never dissever these links. Religion was so much related to socio-political life that any change in religion would also involve change in socio-political life, in which change Luther did not want to involve himself. Because of certain short-comings and weaknesses of his movement its opponents had the opportunity of insinuating that it became vulnerable to influences of immorality and recklessness, and failed to reform the immoral dispensation of Roman Catholicism.

In fact the major thrust of this movement was the protest against the Pope and it manifested itself only in removing outward defects. Hence there was no question of its playing any revolutionary role in effecting changes at the deeper level, in the very psychic life of the people.

Other Reformatory Movements

Besides protestantism many other reformatory movements emerged and manifested their influence in their respective spheres. Some of these movements were the Zwingly movement, the Calvinist movement, the revivalism of Catholicism etc. All these movements emerged only as reactions to this or that brand of Christianity or as reactions to one another. They could not free themselves of controversies irrelevant to life, like that of the Last Supper.

Characteristics of Calvinism

Calvinism has comparatively more defined features. For example:

(1) It laid great emphasis on moral discipline; it also instituted a department for looking after morality.

(2) It entrusted the government of the Church to a group consisting both the priests and the laity. This group was constituted of six clergymen and twelve representatives of the laity.
(3) Calvinism favoured the separation of the Church and the State. According to it the State was not entitled to interference in the affairs of the Church.

Calivinism was also against capitalism. It would not be a mere conjecture to say that Calvin did the same kind of work against the capitalists of our time in the 'sixteenth century' as Marx did against the capitalists of his time in the nineteenth century. Certainly Calvin's field was narrow; but his tools were nonetheless dangerous.

In spite of the above characteristics Calvinism could not achieve popularity. As history indicates the development of these movements depended more on socio-political conditions and national and group interests than on their own characteristics.

Established Christianity could not play any Revolutionary Role

Established Christianity in all its forms, had the opportunity of doing its work of various dimensions for a long time. But it does not show any evidence of playing any revolutionary role in organising and directing cultural activity. Laiky rightly observes that we are compelled to say that Christianity got full opportunity to test itself, and that it has not emerged successful from this test.

Natural Religion

Natural Religion is one which is free from an external corpus of rites and rituals and traditions, and is based on human nature only. Its exponents propound the following views:

Boden, while subscribing to the belief in one God writes to a friend that he should not get confused by the various forms that religion takes. He should stick whole-heartedly to the truth that real religion is in nothing else than in having a pure soul turn itself to God. This is his own and Christ's religion. He says that if superior men were not born as ideal characters from time to time people would keep wandering about the darkness. The Jewish patriarchs and prophets and the great philosophers and gnostics of Greece and Rome were such people. Boden is of the opinion that the work that was started by Plato was completed by Christ. After Christ various men of God taught the same truth. Let us note the fact that Boden does not show a definite opposition to revelation; but it seems that his views have reduced the real stature of prophets and apostles.

Another preacher of Natural Religion, Toralba, says that the best religion is one which is also the oldest religion. At first man learnt knowledge and piety directly from God. This is the Natural Religion. Man is born into it along with his faculty of reason. When people abondoned this Natural Religion they went astrary. Natural Religion and natural law are sufficient for man. He can do without all religions other than Natural Religion. Christianity, Judaism, Islam, non-semitic religion: he can do without them all. Natural Religion does not require any particular indoctrination or religious education. Man is born into it and for it. It is inherent in man's nature. The reason that we are born with can discriminate between right and wrong, though some special human beings have more of this moral and religious sensibility than others.

According to this statement revelation is not necessary for man's guidance. Natural sensibility and reason are enough. Herbart who (who furnished Natural Religion with polemical arguments and introduced it to a wider circle) has formed an epistemological theory for the teaching of Natural Religion. To put the theory briefly, if we are able to know the truth, we must have been certainly equipped with some faculties for knowing it. These faculties correspond to the universal truths we can testify by a comparative study of various religions. Among these faculties are the external and the internal senses and reason with its dialectics. Besides these we have an instinctive faculty which makes us reach such truths as are commonly realisable by all human beings.

Five Pillars of Natural Religion

Basing Natural Religion on instinctive or innate faculties Herbart has identified five assumptions which are the pillars of Natural Religion. They are as follows:

(1) The most exalted and absolute Divine Being exists. We must worship Him, and the most important part of worship is righteousness and piety.

(2) We must turn away from criminality and hard-heartedness which are sacrilegous.

(3) There is an after-life in which we shall be rewarded or punished for all deeds.

(4) With an open mind we must believe in those teachings of various religions that do not contradict the above maxims.

(5) If certain people do not believe in established religions, it is because many false and improper notions have crept into them. Which makes them disgusted with religion, so much so that they would reject even natural religion.

Herbart goes on to say that these five pillars are not by themselves sufficient for religion. What we must do is to hold on to them firmly and to ignore controversial issues. Through nature, on which Natural Religion is based, man is endowed with perpetual revelation and inner light, by virtue of which he is liberated from the instructions of the religious partriarchs or prophets.

Religion has Dissolved into Atheism

It is evident that Natural Religion is very brief and devoid of religious specifications. The world of human life has been consigned to a passive nature which cannot provide active guidance. Yet the propagation of natural religion injected into the minds of a large number of people the notion that for the shaping of character and outlook the following of religion and the belief in its authenticity is not necessary, and that the insights given by nature and reason are sufficient for man's guidance. Thus religion itself gradually dissolved into non-religion or atheism. Religion whose function it was to exercise control over environment and feelings itself came to be regarded as the product of environment and feelings. The effects that this non-religion produced in various spheres of life are not hidden from perceptive people.

In this book an outline of the scheme of cultural reconstruction is attempted, and along with this an attempt has been made to mention at some length the effects and implications of western civilisation on modern life so that the two cultural systems may be compared for good. May God accept this humble attempt and bless me and all of us with the grace to serve the cause of Religion, knowledge and humanity.

1 RECONSTRUCTION OF CULTURE AND ISLAM

The characteristics of culture, as brought out by various scholars and thinkers, can be summed up as follows:

1. the habits and manners which produce harmony and beauty in life and constitute the 'good form'
2. the things which are products of good taste and good acts
3. the standards by which life is evaluated
4. principles and laws and social institutions
5. a set of ideals and goals in life
6. a sense of values
7. arts, sciences, crafts etc.

The Reality of Culture

For culture we, in India, use the word *tehzib*. This is originally an Arabic word, and it would be interesting to look into its etymological sense. This is how it has been defined in *Lissanul Arab*:

> The root meaning of *tahzib* is the clearing away of the better fruit of *Hanzal* of all its insides and the removing of its bitterness in order to make the seed pleasant to eat.

The seed of *Hanzal* is edible, but all else inside the fruit, which is called *shuhm*, is extremely bitter: The meaning of *tahzib* in *The Tajul'Urus* is as follows :

> The root meaning of *tahzib* (and *hizb*) was pruning the trees for the sake of beauty and proper growth. Later on the word was used in the sense of cleansing, reforming and purifying a thing of its defects, and this figurative sense became the popular meaning of the word.[2]

Thus, the essential meaning of culture, in the light of the etymology of its Hindustani equivalent *tehzib*, is removing the unpleasant elements of a thing, and shaping or moulding it into some desirable form.

The Range of Culture

The unpleasant elements are found, not in any one department of western culture, but in all its departments. Beginning from the science of psychology we can trace them in every sphere of life—in beliefs, thoughts, feelings, personal life, individual life, family life, social, economic and political life, philosophy, ethics etc. Every sphere of life needs purification, needs culture in this sense.

Since all cultural phenomena can be referred back to psychology, we can divide our discussion of culture into two parts: (1) psychological basis of culture and (2) actual construction of culture.

PSYCHOLOGICAL BASIS OF CULTURE

Western Idea of Psychological Constitution

According to the western conception of man his psychological constitution too, like his physical constitution, is a higher form of the animal. In other words, just as Evolution has developed higher forms from lower forms on the physical level, in the same way it has developed higher forms from lower forms on the psychological level.

This mechanistic conception of man does not recognize any 'energy' in man except the instincts which are supposed to be common between man and animals. For the specifically human characteristics of man there is no specifically human instinct; no inborn human trait. By nature man has neither self-consciousness, nor is he pervaded by any intelligent spirit. He is nothing but a bundle of instincts and a product of the wonderful combinations of matter and heredity.

According to this conception the 'natural constitution' of man consists of animal instincts (these instincts are supposed to be the source of all human qualities; even will and intellect exist for their appeasement and satisfaction). Hence man's essential nature is supposed to be materialistic and he is supposed to be helpless in the face of the wild forces of matter. So materialism pervades philosophy, history, religion, ethics, in fact every department of culture.

It is only an Interpretation

Unfortunately the above interpretation occupies a very important place in modern knowledge but it is only an interpretation and not an established truth. This is what William McDougall himself admits towards the end of his book, *An Outline of Psychology*. He says that his description of psychic structures and processes might have given his readers the impression of cock-sureness. But he believes this is the best possible statement, which he has been able to make after thirty years of study and contemplation. He is aware that his inferences are merely plausible conjectures. It is likely that they are based more on error than on truth. McDougali goes on to say that he would not like to create the impression that the knowledge of psychology has advanced beyond the elementary stage.

Evidence of Defects in this Interpretation

In the light of experience and observation the above interpretation suffers from the following flaws:

1. Various creative and organizing abilities of man indicate that in his psychological make-up there is some other 'energy', which is inborn and natural and is responsible for the basic distinction between the psychological constitutions of man and the animal from the very beginning.
2. Persistent spiritual phenomena indicate that this 'energy' has some eternal basis, and is not merely a product of evolution.
3. Many times it happens that religious and ethical considerations become so urgently significant for man that in

comparison to them he does not give any importance to material or physical considerations. Such phenomena are undeniable facts. But if some 'energy' other than instincts is not posited they cannot be explained.

4. There are moments in life when the guidance of intellect, senses and intution fails and man stands in dire need of some other guidance. Which points to some hidden and mysterious factors in man's psychological make-up.
5. If all that is there in man is a product of instincts, heredity and tradition, where does the criterion of likes and dislikes come from? We know that man likes some acts and dislikes others, accepts certain traditions and rejects others.

Thus the theory of instincts suffers from many flaws which go to prove that it could not get access to the truth and that there exists some 'energy' other than instincts in the human psyche, by referring to which the above phenomena can be explained. It is by recognising this 'energy' that psychology gets related to ethics, and both get related to spiritualism.

There is an Energy in Man's Natural Constitution

The Quran points to the existence of an 'energy' in man's natural constitution. It is called *fitrat* or 'God's pattern' and its essence is numinous:

> *(Establish) God's handiwork according*
> *To the pattern on which*
> *He has made mankind* (XXX-30)

Hence the Holy Prophet says:

Every child is born according to God's pattern, then his parents make of him, a Jew, a Christian or a Zoroastrian. (*Bukhari; Muslim* — 'Mishkat Kitabul Qadr')

He goes on to illustrate this pattern by an example:

It is like the case of kid which is born whole and normal; it does not have the defect of being 'ear-lopped'. *(Ibid).*

Indeed, man is born immaculate, according to God's pattern or *fitrat.*

The root meaning of *fitrat* is 'kneading flour into a dough and making bread from it before it rises' (*Lughatul Quran*). Hence the following entry in the *Qamus*:

We say *taftaratul ajain* when flour is kneaded into a dough and bread is made from to before it rises.

Later on, by a figurative extension of meaning, the word came to mean 'shaping and moulding of a thing according to a particular pattern (*Majma'ul Bihar*). Thus *fatarallahul Khalg* means:

Shaping a thing into such a pattern as to enable it to perform the function for which it is created. (Imam Raghib, *Mufradatul Quran*, 'Fitrat')

Fatarullah in the above Verse of the Quran should be understood in the light of the following explication:

The 'pattern of God' implies the potentiality with which the creature has been endowed for the comprehension of Faith. (*Ibid.*)

This Energy has a Transcendental Source

The 'energy' we have been talking about is not he product of the combinatin of instincts and of particles of matter. Its source transcends matter. This is what the Quranic Verse implies:

But He fashioned him (man)
In due proportion, and breathed
Into him something of
His spirit. And He gave
You (the faculties of) hearing
And sight and feeling
(And understanding) (XXXII-9)

Indeed, this 'energy' gives to man his specific characteristics and also the ability of bringing the universe under his subjection. Hence God said to the angels:

When I have fashioned him
(In due proportion) and breathed
Into him of My Spirit,
Fall ye down in obeisance
Unto him, (XV-29)

A Tradition of the Holy Prophet elucidates further the specific position of man:

The creature whom I made with my own hands and into whom I breathed of my spirit — I am not going to put him on equal terms with creatures which came into being when I said: 'Be'. (*Mishkat*)

This Energy Manifests Itself in Psychological Constitution

According to our conception of cultural reconstruction the psychological constitution is God's pattern manifesting itself. Which implies that man's psychological make-up acquires a numinous character, and that life is freed from being a mere product of matter, and its transcendental essence is recognized. This numinous conception of psychological constitution does not deny matter. It simply recognizes the permeation of the spirit in matter, because of which the wild crudity of matter is dispelled and man is enabled to bring it to subjection and maintain his selfhood at the same time. Thus matter itself is transformed into energy and its transcendental reality is established. This provides a firm basis for ethics, and once this basis is established there is no difficulty in relating ethics to psychology.

Nature is a Combination of the Numinous and the Animalistic

When we recognise the factor of the numinous in the natural constitution of man we are led to the recognition of two psychological elements in man: (1) The numinous, and (2) The animalistic. The numinous is the product of God's pattern, and the animalistic emerges from the combinations of matter. The two elements go to make human nature.

According to the Western view of man the inborn traits and dispositions are the products of instincts, and it is from instincts that the intellectual faculties emerge. These intellectual faculties are actually the product of the conflict of opposite forces. They emerge from this conflict and become the source of man's thought and intellection, and in this way they sustain his social life.

Disadvantages of Denying the Combination of the Numinous and the Animalistic

If the combination of conflicting forces — the numinous and the animalistic — is not recognised and if man is supposed to have the same instincts as are found in an animal, it becomes difficult to trace the source of the conflicting forces. Which means that the source of the whole dialectic of human nature is obscured. But it is on these conflicting forces and dialectical elements that the superiority of man over other creatures depends.

Of course books of psychology speak of a nature which gradually evolved from the raw material of animal instincts but this nature is not recognised as a spiritual energy and it is not supposed to have anything to do with the constitution of instincts. For this reason this nature has no effective implication for the existence of conflicting qualities in man and for the distinction between man and animal.

Primitive Man in Western Thinking

The way in which primitive man has been studied in Western thinking confirms the above fallacy. Thus it is said that man is of two type (1) natural man, and (2) civilized man. By natural man is meant the primitive man who has evolved from the animal and reached the status of man but remains still unaffected by the traditions of civilization. The civilized man is one who is a product of industry and traditional knowledge. Beliefs, feelings and thoughts have been accumulated in him.

According to William McDougall the natural man would be having all the sensible qualities that we have. His faculty of sensing would be quite developed, as it is often the case with savages. He would be having all the instincts that are common to higher mammals, to which category he is supposed to belong. On sensing things and situations he too would be impelled to achieve the natural end of his instincts; experiences the hunger of demands and the motive impulses characteristic of these instincts; and is satisfied or appeased at the success of his impulsive efforts and dissatisfied or unappeased at their failure. All these things he would be having; but for language he would be having nothing but some emotional cries, sounds and signs.[2]

The natural man would not possess the specific civilized characteristics of man. Hence in his kind of life reason, moral principles, conscience, duties — all these things are lacking. In it there is no quest for happiness for the sake of happiness. It does not have a series of unappeased states. It is the life of instinctive impulse and desire.

We do not know anything about the habitat and the way of life of the natural man. We cannot say whether he, being what we have conceived of him, lived on trees or on the ground. But his life, thinks McDougall, was the kind of life he has visualized: a life dominated by instinctive impulses, which were similar to the instinctive impulses of other higher mammals. If there was any difference between their mode of living and that of man it was that the latter was marked by foresight and organization.

McDougall goes on to visualize man's gradual evolution. He thinks that in comparison with other animals man should have possessed very superior mental powers. It is because the light of his previous experiences he has greater capacity for foresight and for planning and preparing himself for responding to coming events. In carrying out their plans the human creatures should have co-operated in such effective ways and with such variety of responses as was not possible for any other mammals to do. The superior mental powers of man are also evinced by the fact that he is more self-dependent, can act with greater initiative, and can persist in his efforts for a longer time.

In view of this psychological make up of the primitive man William James observes that man is just an imitating animal and that his ability to learn and make cultural progress proceeds from his imitative character.

Loyd Morgan says that man is a powerfully thinking animal, one who sets goals for his behaviour.

But if the operation of the spiritual energy in man is recognised, the picture of the primitive man changes so much as to include civilised human characteristics. self-consciousness and intelligence in his natural constitution.

Primitive Man in the Reconstruction of Culture

According to our conception of the reconstruction of culture primitive man manifests himself as Adam and his life tells us that all the specific human qualities were present in him from the very beginning.

Thus it is said that when the angels became sceptical of about the potentialities of Adam they made the following submission to God:

Wilt Thou place therein one who will make
Mischief therein and shed blood? (II-30)

At this God said:

I know what ye know not (II-30)

But the matter was not left at that. God manifested the truth of His saying by putting man and the angels to a practical test. The angels had to admit:

"Glory to Thee: of knowledge
We have none save what Thou
Hast taught us: in truth it is Thou
Who is perfect in knowledge and wisdom". (II-32)

Man has Both Self-Consciousness and Intelligence in Him

It is obvious that the earliest life of man was not lost in instinctive experiences and desires. On the other hand Adam had self-consciousness as well as intelligence in him, owing to which he spoke to God, and even his wife did so.

We said: "O Adam! dwell thou
And thy wife in the Garden (II - 35)

Both of them had earlier received the following commandment from God:

... but approach not this tree,
Or ye run into harm and transgression (II - 35)

In spite of this commandment they approached the tree with the result that their shame became manifest. Their consciousness or sensibility could not bear it and they began to try to cover themselves:

... when they tasted of the tree,
Their shame became manifest
To them, and they began
To sew together the leaves
Of the garden over their bodies. (VII - 22)

Their self-consciousness and intelligence was also manifested by the fact that they could not persist in their disobedience for long. On the other hand they bowed themselves in all humility and said:

They said: 'Our Lord!
We have wronged our souls:
If Thou forgive us not
And bestow not upon us
Thy Mercy, we shall
Certainly be lost'. (VII - 23)

In Western Thinking Religion is Man's Invention

According to the Western conception of human psychology

religion has no place in the natural constitution of man, nor is its invention indebted to any supernatural power. It is, on the other hand, an invention of man and a product of the animal instincts in man. Its genesis is described by McDougall.[3] He says that as consciousness emerged in man he saw amazing and dreadful things around him and, therefore, he was filled with feelings of wonder and fear. He was concerned to protect himself against these things. After a good deal of deliberation he hits upon the idea of placating these things or powers for this purpose. This gave rise to prayer and religious worship and ritual.

As human consciousness and intellect developed the significance of the objects of nature went on changing till, seeking ways of protection, man reached the present form of religion and came to believe in a God who is the Creator and the Lord of all phenomena. In this picture of the genesis of religion the question of its relation of God's pattern does not arise. However, the utmost that can be said when it is linked up with instincts is that it is not related to any one instinct but is the most complex and strange result of the interaction of various instincts.

It implies that initially the instincts were not of a religious nature, nor were they specific to man. They were found both in man and in animals. But owing to gradual evolution they began to manifest some sensibility which led to the emergence of religious sentiment and to its inclusion in the instinctive nature of man.

The above opinion is expressed by those scholars and thinkers who recognize the operation of metaphysical factors in evolution. The argument is that evolution means progress from the lower to the higher, and that the highest is God.

But the reality is that metaphysical factors have no place in the theory of evolution. Hence religion is supposed to be the product of human superstitions and fancies, and God Himself the invention of an evolved human mind.

In the Islamic Scheme of Cultural Reconstruction Religion is Related to Natural Constitution

In the Islamic scheme of cultural reconstruction religion is related to the natural constitution of man and is regarded as the voice of God's created nature or *fitrat.* In its manifestation and development there works an Intelligent Power. Thus the instructions that God gave to the First Man are as follows:

1. *Man must be beware of the antagonistic forces (instinctive impulses and Satan) — for there is 'enmity between yourselves'.* (II-36)
2. *Man has to live in this world for a determined period — 'on earth will be your dwelling place'* (II-36)
3. *Man must derive benefit from the things of the earth where are 'your means of livelihood — for a time'* (II-36)

Besides these, some other instructions were also given to the First Man:

Then learnt Adam from his Lord
Words of inspiration, and his Lord
Turned towards him (II-37)

It was also pointed out that the work of instruction or Guidance will continue and a system of judgment will be established:

And if, as is sure, there comes to you
Guidance from Me, whosoever
Follows My Guidance, on them
Shall be no fear, nor shall they grieve.
But those who reject Faith
And belie Our Signs,
They shall be Companions of the Fire:
They shall abide therein. (II. - 38-39)

Recognition of an Intelligent Power Necessary for Understanding the Workings of the Unconscious

In our inner being there are certain hidden 'chords'; they are directly related to an Intelligent Power, which plays on them, as it were. Unless we recognize this power we cannot understand the notes it sounds. Nor can we have any access to the reality of religion.

Western culture has no idea of this Intelligent Power. This is why the real nature of the unconscious could not be known, and the 'spider's web' that had appeared in the inner being later on was mistaken for the 'chords'. It would be interesting to note what the gnostic saints say about it:

> The heart is like a lily. It has two sides, and both the sides are the landing places of the tempting Satan. Spider-like, he has woven a web around the heart and suspended its curtains. He lurks behind these curtains. The heart itself has layers like the petals of the lily. Satan dwells under them.[4]

Freud has divided the human psyche into two parts: the conscious and the unconscious. The conscious is that part of the psyche which is responsible for cognition, thinking, understanding, manipulation etc. The unconscious is the hidden part lying under the conscious, and is the source of all urges and feelings.

The enquiry into the unconscious is based on dreams, falterings, humour, irrationalities and, above all, neurosis. The analysis of these phenomena indicates that the unconscious is constituted of the sex urge. Further enquiry leads to the idea that knowledge, philosophy, ethics etc. are simply ways of the appeasement of the insatiable and suppressed sex urge. In other words, when human nature does not find satisfaction in sex, it seeks satisfaction in knowledge, philosophy, ethics etc.

This enquiry subjects religion to the following explanation:

1. As the child grows up and feels that his parents are unable to look after him, he begins to wish for a heavenly Father. This heavenly Father takes the place of the actual father and issues commandments.

2. Man does not get peace in life unless he sacrifices personal interests for the sake of others. This sacrifice cannot be ensured without some kind of reward. But real reward was not possible in this world, and so a fanciful reward from God was visualized, and the idea of such a reward developed to take the form of religion.

An Incomplete Discovery

The idea of the unconscious is not a definite and complete discovery. McDougall forcefully denies it. Jung considers it lop-sided and attempts to complete it. Adler proposes to replace the sex urge by the urge for superiority. Even Freud had to admit that his theory did not claim to cover the whole life, and that it seeks to explain only that aspect of life which had been ignored by all other theories.

Some Intelligent Power Existing from the Beginning

In our concept of cultural reconstruction there exists some Intelligent Power from the very beginning. Deep down in his inner being, man has an innate desire to worship and obey it. Hence God says:

> *I have only created*
> *Jinns and men, that*
> *They may serve Me.* (L1 - 56)

If the unconscious were constituted only of sex desire or desire for superiority, man would have achieved peace from the free satisfaction of either or both the desires. But experience and observation testify that the freedom to satisfy these desires enkindles lustful passions and leads man to greater uneasiness, while prayer and obedience to God leads him to peace. The achievement of peace in this way is so certain that even Freud recognizes the fact of psychic reorganization or reintegration through prayer in the case of the pious and the devoted. He admits that some classes of people can get satisfaction through things other than sex. And this is what the Quran says in this regard:

... for without doubt
In the rememberance of God
Do hearts find satisfaction. (XIII-28)

It is because prayer and remembrance of God and obedience to Him bring the 'chords' of the inner being into relation with the Intelligent Power, and no other mode of satisfaction can do so. For the establishment of this relation the Covenant mentioned in the following Verse is also an operative factor:

When thy Lord drew forth
From the children of Adam—
From their loins—
Their descendants, and made them
Testify concerning themselves, (saying):
'Am I not your Lord.
(Who cherishes and sustains you)?'—
They said: 'Yea!...' (VII-172)

Domination of Lustful Desire

The sex desire is related to the animal instincts. But the human psyche reaches a state in which this desire becomes so dominant that doubts arise regarding the essential nature of the psyche itself. This state is pointed out by the Quran:

Then seest thou such
A one as takes
As his god his own
Vain desire? (XLV-23)

This desire invents its own permanent religion:

These are nothing but names
Which ye have devised,—

Ye and your fathers,—
For which God has sent
Down no authority (whatever). (LIII-23)

The deeds done in this state seem very pleasing to the doers—

Satan has made their deeds
Seem pleasing in their eyes. (XXVII-24)

But the springs of human life get dried up, and animal life prevails over the being, and manifests itself even in dreams and through the nerves. Regarding this condition the Quran says:

God hath set a seal
On their hearts and on their hearing,
And on their eyes is a veil (II-7)

And at another place it says:

God hath set a seal on their hearts
For their blasphemy, (IV-155)

Perhaps Freud has been concerned with the study of the same animal state in which a point comes where knowledge, philosophy, ethics etc. become means for the appeasement of sex desire.

Without the Concept of the Spirit Human Psychology Would Remain Incomplete and the Position of Man Undefined

The West has failed to acquire the knowledge of the real nature not only of the unconscious but also of life and of the spirit. Without such knowledge neither the psychological constitution of man nor his place in the universe can be properly determined.

The enquiry, as we know, began with matter. Now, after about four hundred years, an 'energy' that transcends the world of matter is being conceived. But since no way of going beyond the world of matter is known the conception of this Energy is not clear, and , therefore, many areas of man's psychic life are lying obscure.

The human psyche is like a dark room. Unless it is lit up our sight cannot do much. If research is done without light certain things will be apprehended, but others will not be apprehended in spite of all attempts. Again, out of the things that are apprehended the real nature of some will be known while the real nature of others will remain unknown —either they will be conceived as things without reality or as things against reality.

Divine Energy as the Source of both the Known and the Unknown

Our conception of cultural reconstruction recognizes the Energy we have been talking of as living and eternal. It is none other but the Almighty Spirit, who is our Creator and Lord and who does whatever He wills; He is the beginning and the end of all things and He is infinite. The way towards Him is definite. He has himself arranged to light up the dark room of the human psyche. He is the source of all life. He is called Allah. Thus the Quran speaks of Him:

> *He Who created Death*
> *And Life* (LXVII - 2)

Again:

> *Say: 'He will give them*
> *Life Who created them*
> *For the first time* (XXXVI - 79)

This Almighty Spirit functions not only as Creator but also as Guide. When Pharoah asked Moses:

> ... *'Who, then,*
> *Oh Moses, is the Lord*
> *Of you two.* (XX - 49)

Moses spoke in reply particularly of two attributes of the Lord:

He said: and our Lord is
He Who gave to each
(Created) thing its form
And nature, and further,
Gave (it) guidance' (XXII - 50)

And as for Abraham, he said that it is God

'Who created me, and
It is He Who guides me' (XXVI - 78)

At another place the Quran says that it is God:

Who hath created,
And further, given
Order and proportion;
Who hath ordained laws.
And granted guidance (LXXXVII-2-3)

About the spirit of life the Quran says:

But He fashioned him
In due proportion, and breathed
Into him something of
His spirit. And He gave
You (the faculties of) hearing
And sight and feeling
(and understanding) (XXII - 9)

At another place it is said:

'When I have fashioned him
(in due proportion) and breathed
Into him of My spirit,

Fall ye down, in obeisence
Unto him'. (XV - 29)

God's Pattern is the Manifestation of Divine Energy Who has created Man's Essence as Numinous

After the discovery of the unconscious and the spirit of life the operation of some Energy in the Psyche becomes an established fact, and it does not remain difficult to determine the real place of man in the universe.

God's pattern or *fitrat* is in fact the manifestation of His Energy which has made man numinous in essence and has created his nature basically different from animals. This concept of Divine Energy implies that the means of knowledge do not remain limited to experience and observation but lead us further into another department of knowledge, the knowledge of secret or invisible things. According to gnostics man has access to three kinds of knowledge: (1) Knowledge of sensible realities; (2) Knowledge which proceeds from the known to the unknown; and (3) Knowledge of the secret or invisible things.[5]

God has Appointed Man as the Leader of All Creatures

According to this conception of Divine energy man acquires highest position in creation; no creature is His co-equal. Just as God has no co-equal, in the same way His image, man, has no co-equal. He has been appointed to the position of vicegerency of God and the leadership of all creatures:

I will create
A vicegerent on earth. (II - 30)

The capability required for deserving this status is not found in any other creature. This is why the whole creation except man refused to undertake God's offer Trust:

We did indeed offer
The Trust to the Heavens
And the Earth

And the mountains; but they refused
To undertake it,
Being afraid thereof;
But man undertook it. (XXXIII - 72)

According to gnostics 'The right of man for the vicegerency of God is on the basis of his capabilities. He possesses contradictory qualities which he can utilise for the material and spiritual rehabilitation of the world so that they become the manifestation of God's contradictory Names.' (*Akhlaq-i-Jalali*)

In the Mirror of the West the Image of Man is Distorted

After determining the real place of man in the universe man needs a mirror which can show the image not only of material things but also of realities that transcend matter.

The West does have a mirror, but it is concerned only with material realities; it does not show the image of transcendental realities. The image of man in this mirror implies that we need not go beyond matter for determining the standard of the capabilities of existence and survival. Thus according to the theory of the survival of the fittest only material capabilities are needed for survival. Similarly, for becoming virtuous moral values are of no significance. On the other hand, the virtuous person is he who is successful and able to survive because of his material capability, no matter if his character is like that of a beast. In the same way the non-virtuous person is one who has failed in his aims, no matter if his character is angelic.

According to this western conception similarity is shown between man and animal. But it has not been unanimously decided whether man falls down to resemble the animal or the animal rises up to resemble man; in other words, whether the superior includes the inferior or vice-versa. This is rather interesting.

The people who believe that man is like an animal derive human characteristics and values from the psychological behaviour and organic structure of the animals. This is done to such an extent that even mental capabilities and faculties are also derived from the animals, and are supposed to be the result of gradual evolution.

Those who suppose that the animal is like man try to prove that animals have human qualities. They go to the extent of supposing that even religious feelings exist in dogs and monkeys and flies.

Cultural Reconstruction Recognizes Transcendence of Matter

Since in our mirror of cultural reconstruction transcendental realities are also reflected it is thought that going beyond matter is a capability which gives us the standard of survival. This transcendental capability has been recognized from the beginning. Hence: (1) All souls made a Covenant with God in the spiritual world. (2) In the natural constitution of every man a numinous energy exists, by the help of which he can overcome animal or lustful desires and can transcend matter.

Transcendence has been Underscored in God's Address to Primitive Generations of Man

(3) In God's address to the primitive human generations transcendence has been particularly emphasised. Thus the Quran savs:

> *O ye children of Adam!*
> *We have bestowed raiment*
> *Upon you to cover*
> *Your shame, as well*
> *To be an adornment to you.*
> *But the raiment of righteousness,—*
> *That is the best.* (VII -26)

The particular mention of raiment in the above Verse suggests that the rational and moral consciousness of man had emerged from the very beginning. Here is another Verse pointing to the same truth:

O ye Children of Adam:
Let not Satan seduce you,
In the same manner as
He got your parents out
of the Garden, stripping them
of their raiment, to expose
Their shame: for he
And his tribe watch you
From a position where ye
Cannot see them. (VII-27)

Since by transcending material existence peace is achieved and the right relation with the unconscious established the earlier address of God to man insisted on removing the obstacles in the way of transcendence and overcoming animal and lustful desires. Also, it was pointed out that special attempts should be made to manipulate and transform the environment into a desirable pattern. This is record by the Quran:

O ye Children of Adam!
Whenever there come to you
Apostles from amongst you,
Rehearsing My Signs unto you,—
Those who are righteous
And mend (their lives),—
On them shall be no fear
Nor shall they grive. (VII-35)

In Western Culture Evolution Stops at the Human Body

In western culture man is supposed to have emerged from the lower forms of life. Previously, he was an ape, and through gradual evolution spanning millions of years he has acquired the present human form.

Mental evolution has proceeded on similar lines. Thus the mind of the man living three thousand years ago was like that of a child: it lacked in the power of intellect. It was through a process of gradual evolution that man became worthy of being called a rational and speech-possessing creature.

In this conception of man there is no place for spirituality; nor is there any idea of subsequent evolution in any other dimension. Evolution stops at the human body. Beyond it there is no dimension for evolution to proceed in.

Cultural Reconstruction Begins with the Human Body

Our conception of cultural reconstruction recognizes that man's evolution begins with the body. But it says that a subsequent and never-ending process of spiritual evolution continues. In other words, cultural reconstruction begins where the West ends.

Our conception finds support in various evidences.
For example:

1. Man has been gifted with the guidance of Reason and experience and with the knowledge of the nature of things:

And he taught Adam the names
of all things; (II-31)

Exegists have offered various explanations of *al Asma* ('the names of things'). The most plausible one takes the phrase to mean 'the nature of things'. 'Taught' implies man's capability of Knowledge, and, as it should be, this 'Knowledge means intutive knowledge and not discursive knowledge'.[7]

Owing to Knowledge and the guidance of Reason and experience all things in the universe have been subjected to man, by Divine Providence.

And he has subjected
To you, as from Him,
All that is in the heavens
And on earth: (XLV-13)

Agency for Senses Not Enough for Apprehending the Supersensible World

2. Intimations have been given to us of another world, for the apprehension of which the agency of the senses is not enough. This is the supersensible world—

God is He......
Who knows (all things)
Both secret and open (LIV-22)

The things of the supersensible world are not contradictory to reason; they simply transcend reason. In other words, it is no wonder if reason, which is grounded on knowledge derived from the senses, is unable to apprehend the realities of the supersensible world. Indeed, inability to apprehend something does not go to disprove its existence.

To deny the existence of a thing which cannot be apprehended is a human weakness. But there are many things which are beyond the reach of human reason, and even those things that are within the reach of human reason are not apprehended by a particular person or by the intellectual calibre of a particular age, while some other person of some other age may be able to apprehend them as undeniable truths.

If such is the state of affairs, it would be a self-deception to regard the inapprehensibility of a thing as an evidence of its non-existence. The Quran speaks of people who fell into this error:

Nay, they charge with falsehood
That whose knowledge they
Cannot compass, even before
The elucidation thereof
Hath reached them: thus
Did those before them
Make charges of falsehood: (X-39)

Faith in the Supersensible is Necessary

In order to establish relation with the supersensible world it is necessary to have faith in its realities. The most important of these realities is Divine Energy. This Divine Energy partakes of our psychological constitution. Owing to it infinite possibilities of evolution are opened, and the correspondence between psychological constitution and actual reconstruction of culture is established.

All Depend on Divine Energy

This Divine Energy has always been there and will always be there. It is none other than God whose Knowledge encompasses all things and whose Mercy embraces all creation. His Power is supreme and His Sovereignty is over all the worlds. His Justice is equal for every creature and His Providence works equally in the whole creation:

Praise be to God
The Cherisher and Sustainer of the Worlds;
Most Gracious, Most Merciful;
Master of the Day of Judgment. (II-4)

All depend on Him, and He depends on none. He is Absolute Act and Absolute Being, and He has no equal or partner:

Say: He is God,
The One and Only;
God, the Eternal, Absolute;
He begetteth not,
Nor is He begotten;
And there is none
Like unto Him. (CXII 1-4)

He is unique in His Essence and Attributes, and there is no one like Him.

.....there is nothing
Whatever like unto Him. (XLII -11)

Through Faith in Divine Energy Man Achieves Self-realization

Man achieves self-realization through faith in Divine Energy. He finds his own self which he could not find even after seeking for it for thousands of years. And after he has found his Self his field of activity does not remain limited to the world of matter but extends beyond it. He ascends into the transcendental world, in comparison to which this world of matter is inferior and less valuable.

In Western Culture Worldly Life is the Goal of Evolution

In western culture worldly life is regarded as the last phase or goal of the evolution of life. After it there is death and mere annihilation. The result of such a view is that beliefs, goals, ideals and values are confined to this world of matter. Neither any other world is supposed to exist nor is there any way of ascent into it. This means that as regards his own self man is where he was 1400 years ago, and that the light of knowledge has not been able to dispel the darkness of ignorance about himself. The Arabs of the Days of Ignorance also held a similar, materialistic view of life:

And they (sometimes) say:
'There is nothing except
Our life on this earth,
And never shall we be
Raised up again.' (VI-29)

At another place the Quran speaks of people holding this view:

They say: 'What;
When we are reduced

To bones and dust,
Should we really be raised up
(To be) a new creation?' (XVII-49)

Evidence of Hereafter

According to our conception of cultural reconstruction it is believed that beyond death there is another life and another world which is called the Hereafter. To reach this other world one has to pass accross a bridge. This bridge is death. In this way life is a continuous process and it does not end in death. On the other hand it goes on from stage to stage.

Man is destined to reach the goal of the Hereafter sooner or later.

How can ye reject
The Faith in God?—
Seeing that ye were without life,
And He gave you life;
And again to Me will ye return. (II-28)

This goal is not a material goal; it is the goal of transcendental and ultimate realities. In the Hereafter the consequences of man's deeds—good or bad—will be manifested in the same way as effects follow causes in this world. There is:

A reward for their deeds (XXXII-17)

The good and the bad deeds of man are recorded and their consequences are manifested:

But verily over you
(Are appointed angels)
To protect you,—kind and honourable,—
Writing down (your deeds):
They know (and understand)
All that ye do. (LXXXII—10-12)

The Means of Knowledge of the West are Confined to the Senses

Unfortunately the West does not possess any means of knowing the reality after death. After death nobody comes back to tell of his condition either.

The means of knowledge of the West are related only to the senses, but the world of the Hereafter is related to what is beyond the senses. This is why in spite of all the material advancement the West has ignored the realities of the Hereafter.

Man is very fickle-minded. When he does not know anything or is not able to know it, he jumps to the conclusion that it does not exist. Though the same thing may turn up as an established reality later on.

If the judgement of the West regarding transcendental realities were acceptable, the progress of knowledge would have stopped long ago and those hundreds of things which were unbelieveable before would not have been discovered as realities now. Just as the impossibilities of yesterday are the possibilities of today, in the same way it would be no wonder if the impossibilities of today become the possibilities (like C.E.M. Joad). These thinkers are seeking the next phase of the evolution of life and they have gone to the extent of saying that the next phase of human life is not material but spiritual.

Knowledge of Transcendental Realities in the Islamic Scheme of Cultural Reconstruction

In the Islamic scheme of cultural reconstruction there is a means of knowledge which can throw light on the next phase of man's life and which can have access to transcendental realities. This means of knowledge is revelation. It is necessary for us to have faith in it, for its guidance goes beyond the sensible world. The knowledge acquired through revelation is not quantified knowledge. It is intitutive knowledge. Through it the inhabitants of the world get into the secrets of transcendental realities:

> *..... say:*
> *'the Guidance of God,—that*

Is the (only) Guidance'.
Wert Thou ., to follow their desires
After the knowledge
Which hath reached thee,
Then wouldst thou find
Neither Protector nor Helper
Against God. (II-120)

The real subject of Divine revelation is man and its argument is concerned only with human life which continues after death.

Without Transcendental Knowledge the Puzzle of the Universe Remains Unsolved

If our life is devoid ot the guidance of transcendental knowledge the puzzle of the universe will not be solved, nor will the problems of mankind be resolved. This is why God has given this knowledge to man from the very beginning:

And if, as assured, there comes to you
Guidance from Me, whosoever
Follows My Guidance, on them
Shall be no fear, nor shall they grieve.
But those who reject Faith
And belie our Signs,
They shall be Companions of the Fire:
They shall abide therein. (II— 38-9)

Through Revelation Man Gets Scientific Knowledge

Through revelation the secrets of life are known and man is led to acquire scientific knowledge. But the materialistic attitude associated with science has created a very unfortunate situation and made life meaninglass and futile. The secret of life lies hidden in the inner being of man.

Science has been trying to relate this inner being to some Intelligent Power. To have access to both the inner being and the Intelligent Power is impossible for the man who is merely a creature of reason and selfish desire and who has been further mutilated by industry and the advances of science and technology.

Revelational Knowledge Recognises The Natural Constitution of Man

The culture which has been built up according to revelational knowledge emphasises the shaping of personality according to the natural constitution of man and also the use of the things of the world for human benefit.

Since man is a combination of the material and the transcendental and since in matters related to his own self, his abilities are usually unable to function properly, it is necessary to have such a guidance for the development of personality as may reach beyond reason and sense experience and may encompass both the material and the transcendental. If the guidance of the reason and sense experience is regarded as sufficient only the material part of man's being will be dealt with. The transcendental part will be misunderstood or not understood at all with the result that man will get sick of life, and culture will reach the point of self-destruction. This is being observed in the case of western culture nowadays. But in this case, we may note, even the material part of man's being will not be fully dealt with. The greater part of human life passes in the darkness of passion, and in this state the guidance of reason does not work and sense experience does not yield any fruit. Moreover, reason and modes of sense experience are always subject to change. In such a situation if we rely upon reason and sense experience the state of life and culture will become chaotic. This will be particularly so because there will be no distinction between reason and lustful desire and every human experience will get coloured according to an individual's personal inclination.

The Universe is Easier to Manipulate than Man

In comparison to man the manipulation of the Universe is

easier. For man is himself the manipulator and the newer phases of his progress are products of his infinite desires and necessities. As for the manipulation of the Universe, the above mentioned guidance is not needed. In this case reason and sense experience can do the job and progress can continue —

Say: and I do admonish you
On one point: that ye
Do stand up before God, —
(it may be) in pairs,
Or (it may be) single, —
And reflect (within yourself):
Your Companion is not
Possessed: (XXXIV - 46)

The Source of Revelation is Divine Energy

The source of revelation is Divine Energy and for deriving benefit from it the transcendental part of man has to be tuned up. The person to whom the revelation comes is not merely a messenger; he has an insight in the transcendental part of his being, through which he can apprehend super-sensible realities.

Two Kinds of Means of Knowledge

The means of knowledge are of two kinds: (1) Material (2) Transcendental. The material means are those which are related to the body and the transcendental means are those which are related to what is beyond the body. Pertaining to the first kind of knowledge we have sense perception, axiomatic truths and reason, and to the second kind is revelation and intution.

The second kind of knowledge begins where the first kind ends and the end of the second kind is the beginning of the Absolute. It means that the end of the first kind is reason, which is related to the physical but is very close to what lies beyond it.

The end of the second kind is revelation which is related to the transcendental but is very close to the Absolute.

Revelation is the Highest Form of Non-physical Means of Knowledge

It means that revelation is the highest form of non-physical means of knowledge. It operates on the ultimate frontiers of human consciousness and is a divine gift to man (we shall speak more about it later on):

Such is the Bounty of God,
Which He bestows
On whom He will. (LXII - 4)

Again:

God knoweth best where
(And how) to carry out
His mission: (VI - 124)

For receiving the divine gift of revelation a particular capability is needed, which is to be trained. Thus the Quran speaks of Moses:

And We tried
The invarious ways.
Then didst thou tarry
A number of years
With the people of Midian.
Then didst thou come hither
As ordained, O Moses!
And I have prepared thee
For Myself (for service) (XX — 40-41)

In this verse by *qadar* ('as ordained') is implied the prophetic capability of receiving divine revelation. Exegetes have explained this word as follows:

We have determined for the way of knowledge and guidance and also it is proper time. Thou hast come up to our standard. (*Tafsir 'Araisul Bayan'*)

Another interpretation is as follows:

Thou hast reached the highest destiny according to thy capability. (*Tafsir Mohiuddin Ibn-i-'Arabi*)

For the training of capability the Prophet passes through circumstances that do not befall ordinary man or are beyond their toleration. The Holy Prophet Mohammad (peace be upon him) was asked: "Who is subject to the greatest test" He replied: 'the Prophet, then he who is close in status to him, and then he who is close in status to the later and so on'. (*Tirmizi; Ibn-i-Majah; Mishkat: 'Ayadatul Mariz wa Thawabul Maraz*)

The ascent of Moses to mount Sinai in the state of fast; the state of Jesus in the wilderness in the state of fast; and the medidation and the prayers of Prophet Mohammad (p.b.u.h.) in the cave of Hira—all these things were meant for the training of their respective capabilities.

Various Forms of Guidance From the Absolute

The Guidance from the Absolute comes according to a particular pattern. For achieving this Guidance material means do not count. The various forms of Guidance are mentioned in the Quran:

It is not fitting
For a man that God
Should speak to him
Except by inspiration,
Or from behind a veil,
Or by the sending
Of a Message
To reveal, With God's permission,
What God wills: for He
Is Most High, Most Wise. (XLII - 51)

It is this Guidance that we spoke about in connection with God's address to the primitive generations of man. Without this Guidance there can be no harmony between man and the Universe, nor can there be a balance between materialism and transcendentalism. The Quran says:

> *Do they seek*
> *For other than the Religion*
> *Of God? — while all creatures*
> *In the heavens and on earth*
> *Have, willing or unwilling,*
> *Bowed to His Will*
> *(Accepted Islam),*
> *And to Him shall they*
> *All be brought back.* (III - 83)

The process of Guidance has continued in human history and it has been available to every community and every people. Through this Divine Guidance the Right Way has been pointed out and the construction of culture has been taken place —

> ... *and to every people*
> *A guide.* (XIII - 7)

At another place it is said:

> *And there never was*
> *A people, without a warner*
> *Having lived among them*
> *(in the past).* (XXXV - 24)

There is Continuity and Evolution in the Matter of Guidance

There is continuity and evolution in the matter of Divine Guidance. Thus the Quran says:

Then sent We Our apostle
In succession: (XXIII - 44)

Again it is said:

None of Our revelation
Do We abrogate
Or cause to be forgotten,
But we substitute
Something better or similar: (II - 106)

The Guidance Aims at Perfect Enlightenment of Mankind

The continuous process and Guidance was stopped, as it was necessary, after mankind reached perfect enlightenment. Thus a limit was set to the perfection of humanity. The Quran says:

Muhammad is not
The father of any
Of your men, but (he is)
The Apostle of God,
And the seal of the Prophets: (XXXIII -40)

The perfection of enlightenment, which is revelation, is achieved in every sense:

The Word of thy Lord
Doth find its fulfilment
In truth and in justice: (VI - 115)

There is no question of changing His words:

None can change His word (VI - 115)

In fact the change can be towards the superior or towards the inferior. It cannot be towards the superior because the Words are spoken at the frontiers of human consciousness. It can not be towards the inferior because after this stage of evolution there is no question of retrogression.

The Perfection of Enlightenment is the Last Phase of Human Consciousness

There is no doubt that the Guidance of revelation comes in the last evolutionary phase of human consciousness. The Guidance itself has its stages, the last stage being the perfection of revelation. But every apostle to whom revelation comes is a human being. He is not a partner of the Divine Being, nor is he transformed into a creature other than man:

Their apostles said to them:
And truth, we are human
Like yourself, but God
Doth grant His grace
To such of His servants
As He pleases. (XIV - 11)

Prophet Muhammad (p.b.u.h.) is ordained to clarify his position:

Say: 'I am but a man
Like yourself, (but)
The inspiration has come
To me, that your God is
One God.' (XVIII - 110)

Again:

Say thou; 'I am
But a man like you:
It is revealed to me
By inspiration, that your God,
Is one God: so stand

True to Him, and ask
For His forgiveness. (XLI - 6)

This state of revelation in the history of mankind is as sensitive as it is invitable. If the apostles were not human beings, they would not be able to guide human beings according to the demands of their nature; and if revelation had not been the last phase of human consciousness, lasting benefits could not be derived from the Guidance.

As regards the sensitivity of the state of revelation, it may be noted that in every period of human history various misunderstandings have arisen about it. Sometimes the Prophet is apotheosized into a partner of God or His Manifestation or Autar or even His son. Sometimes the status of apostlehood is so much degraded that every seer has been given the status of the Prophet, no matter if he is not innocent and pure of character.

This is a Very Sensitive and Delicate State

This last phase of the evolution of mankind is so lofty that, let alone mortal beings, even etherial being can not reach there. A Tradition of the Holy Prophet says: 'I was made to ascend to the Last Lote Tree'. The Lote Tree is the place where any other creature has not reached.

Except Muhammad (p.b.u.h.) nobody else reached this place. (*Bukhari, Vol.II, Hadith Isra*)

In spite of all this it signifies a state of humanity and creaturehood, one which does not partake of the Divine at all. The Quran speaks about it:

Glory to (God)
Who did take His Servant
For a journey by night
From the Sacred Mosque
To the Farthest Mosque,
Whose precincts We did

Bless, — in order that We
Might show him some
Of Our Signs. (XVII - 1)

The following Verse speaks of nearness to the Absolute:

And was at a distance
Of but two bow - lengths
Or (even) nearer;
So did (God) convey
The inspiration to His Servants —
(conveyed) what He (meant)
To Convey. (LIII — 9-10)

The laws of the numinous world are different from those of the world of matter. In the case of nearness to the Numinous or Absolute the law of the material world dissolved. So do the categories of space and time. The ultimate reality is revealed, and man becomes a direct receipient of blessings from the Divine Being.

It is obvious that for the apprehension of this state material means are not enough. If attempt is made to reach there by means of material means it would result in fallacy in the same way as fallacy results when the intellect of man is approached through the concept of animal psychology. Perhaps it is for this reason that the Quran clinches the argument by saying:

... in order that We
Might show him some
Of Our Signs. (XVII - 1)

At another place it is said:

For truly did he see,
All the Signs of His Lord,
The Greatest! (LIII - 18)

The Need of Guidance has been There in Every Age

After the last phase of the evolution of human consciousness the process of revelation came to an end. But its need has always been there and will always be there. For man is inclined towards his physical nature and is easily entangled in naturalism. Sometimes this entanglement becomes so intense that his intution and senses are affected and what is sweet and good for him becomes unsavoury. Hence it is very necessary to have some systematic programme of promoting his higher nature and of maintaining a balance between the higher nature and the lower or animal nature. Unless both the higher and the lower chords of his being are struck the desirable music cannot be produced.

In fact it is for the sake of producing this music that the Guidance of God is needed. It will be needed as long as man exists on this earth. Thus the Quran says:

It is He who has sent
Amongst the unlettered
An apostle from among
Themselves, to rehearse
To them His Signs,
To sanctify them, and
To instruct them in Scripture
And Wisdom (LII-2)

God did confer
A great favour
On the Believers
When He sent among them
A apostle from among
Themselves, rehearsing
Unto them the Signs

Of God, sanctifying them,
And instructing them
In Scripture and Wisdom. (III - 164)

At another place God says:

We sent aforetime
Our apostles with Clear Signs
And sent down with them
The Book and the Balance
(Of Right and Wrong), that men
May stand forth in justice; (LVII - 25)

Special Protection for Divine Revelation

The last Guidance of God is valid for ever and ever, and for this reason God himself has undertaken to protect it. The Quran says:

We have, without doubt,
Sent down the Message:
And We will assuredly
Guard it (from corruption) (XV - 9)

Then for translating this Message into a practical form the Holy Prophet's life was presented as a model and God saw to it that it was so:

Ye have indeed
In the Apostle of God
A beautiful pattern (of conduct)
For anyone whose hope is
In God and the Final Day
And who engages much
In the praise of God. (XXXIII - 21)

Those who assimilated this model or pattern in their own lives were set as models for their successors:

That the Apostle May be
A witness for you,
And ye be witnesses for mankind! (XXII - 78)

At another place the Quran says:

These have We made a few
An ummat justly balance
That ye might be witnessed
Over the nations,
And the Apostle a witness
Over yourselves; (II - 143)

Even After the Last Phase the Guidance Continues

After the last Message the Guidance still continues. This is why the Quran says:

Ye are the best
Of Peoples, evolved
For mankind
Enjoining what is right,
Forbidding what is wrong,
And believing in God. (III - 110)

Consequences of Deprivation From Guidance

If man is deprived from Guidance his life achieves no harmony. Rather it degenerates into self-hatred and self-revulsion. Similarly, if cultural reconstruction is not done man will not be able to establish relation with the Absolute, nor will it be possible for him to manifest the transcendental dimensions of his life. His culture will be lacking in justice and his civilization will be led to self-destruction.

WORK OF CULTURAL RECONSTRUCTION

Man Holds the Most Important Place in the Scheme of in Cultural Reconstruction

According to revelational knowledge the place of man is of foremost importance in the scheme of the reconstruction of culture. The next importance is given to the understanding of the constitutive principles of culture. After this one can talk about man's individual, social, economic and political life and about philosophy and ethics.

For the understanding of man's place in the universe four things should be considered:

1. The essence of man;
2. His competence;
3. The nature of his work; and
4. The field of his striving.

The first and the second topics have been discussed under psychological constitution. We shall now discuss the 'nature of man's work' and 'the field of his striving'.

On account of man's competence and essence the Creator has made him His vicegerent and the leader of the universe. Thus the Quran says:

I will create
A vicegerent on earth (II - 30)

At another place it is said:

O David! we did indeed
Make thee a vicegerent
On earth: so judge thou
Between men in truth (and justice):
Nor follow thou the lust
(of thy heart), though they will
Mislead thee from the Path
Of God (XXXVIII - 26)

The implication is that the nature of man's work is such that through it should be manifested the nature of the Creator and His Wisdom. On the one hand man reflects the attributes of God, and on the other he performs creative works and works of subjecting nature to himself, and these works manifest God and His power —

His manifestation is thy manifestation, and thy manifestation is His manifestation. Thou shouldst manifest God and God should manifest thee.

For man's striving two fields have been set: (1) His self, (2) the universe.

The Quran speaks of these fields. Thus it is said that there are God's Signs on the earth—

As also in your own
Selves: will ye not
Then see? (LI - 21)

And again:

And He has subjected
To you, as from Me,
All that is in the heavens
And on earth (XLV - 13)

Relations between the Human Self and the Universe

The relation between the human self and the universe is a mutual relation. It is from both the sides. If anyone side is neglected the result will be destruction. In other words if an exclusive emphasis is laid on man's exploitation of the universe and higher values are neglected, civilization will be committing suicide. Similarly, if all emphasis is laid on higher values and the scientific and progressive process of comprehending and exploiting nature stops, the survival of man will be in danger.

For the sake of maintaining a balance between striving for higher values and exploiting nature God has sent Guidance through his apostles. With regard to one field of human striving, i.e. the self, detailed instructions were sent down from God.

Regarding the other field, i.e. the universe, only fundamentals were determined.

Man's own self is more complex than the universe. In this matter human faculties do not work. This is why detailed Guidance was necessary in this regard. But the universe is not so complex. Man is its master and his exploitation of the universe arises from his own desires and necessities. For this reason detailed Guidance in this regard was not necessary, nor would this Guidance keep pace with changes in the universe. It is understandable why God sent down a series of detailed instructions with regard to the human self and pointed out only the fundamentals with regard to man's relation to the universe. The apostles of God performed their work with regard to both the fields of human striving. With regard to the first field, the human self, they tried to educate man in character building; and with regard to the second field, the universe, they performed some miracles, so as to point to the direction of the exploitation of nature, and left the rest to the Guidance of human reason and experience.

The Teachings of Prophet Mohammad are More Comprehensive

Since Mohammad (peace be upon him) comes at the last phase of the evolution of humanity his teachings are more comprehensive. Thus, on the one hand the Quran gives detailed instructions regarding the education of the human self, and the Traditions provide us with a record of the life of the Holy Prophet, and on the other the Quran mentions the physical realities of life, the beauties of the universe, the objects of nature and man's conception of the universe, and the Holy Prophet's life tells us of certain miracles through which he has pointed to modern discoveries and advances of culture.

Western culture is unfortunate in one respect. It has carried the exploitation of nature to higher and higher stages of advancement but, for certain reason, it has neglected the education and character building (the real psychological constitution of man and the proper development of his personality), with the result that it is cursed with revulsion and hatred of life itself and its civilization is an enemy of civilization itself.

The Gnostics' Way of Knowing the Place of Man

The gnostics have defined the place of man in a different way and have taken a different approach to this subject. Their discussion is brief but very interesting. They say that in the essential being of man there is something which is called *heart*. This is the place where gnosis of God is found like a pearl in an oyster. The relation of the *heart* to the physical heart is like the relation of the content to the vessel or that of the dweller to the house (we are going to discuss this subject later on).

The *heart* is the centre of numinous energy in man; it is the dwelling place of love and faith and consciousness. Owing to it man has his distinctive place in creation, and he has become, so to say, the cream of creation and the very purpose of the universe. Again it is owing to the *heart* that he is worthy of the vicegerency of God. Sheikh Sharfuddin Yahya Muniri observes:

> There were all kinds of created beings, but with man it was a different matter. When God willed to bring this creature of clay into existence and to exalt him to the place of vicegerency the angels said: wilt thou bless therein one who will make mischief therein...? The Eternal Love replied: Love does not recognise advice and logic. If we did not accept them what would be the value of all your prayers. And if we are willing to show mercy and forgiveness to man what harm can his sin do to us? You see that in the affairs of life man has relation with Us, but you do not see that in the matter of love we have relation with him". A Poet has rightly said: 'When the beloved commits some mistake or lapse, her beauty pleads in a thousands ways'. (*Epistle 38*)

In another Epistle Sheikh Sharfuddin Yahya Muniri says:

> Do not look down on (this creature of) water and clay (man) all the excellencies are there in him and whatever you find in the world has come here along with him. Except him everything else is a shadow on the wall. The gnostics have said that the bird of love took its flight from the nest of Grace. It came near the highest heaven, saw Majesty and passed by. It came near the throne of God, saw infinitude and passed by. It reached heaven, saw loftiness and passed by. Then it reached the dust (man) saw toil and striving and descended there. (*Epistle* 50)

Abu Ali Daqaq says:

If the sun of love had not shone on the being and the *heart* of man his case too would have been like that of other creatures. (Sheikh Muniri, *Epistle* 46)

Man Deserves his Exaltation Because of the Heart

According to the gnostics the exaltation of man is owing to his *heart*. Regarding its value it has been said by Sheikh Muniri:

God created the Empyrean and put it under the charge of the highest angels. He created Paradise and put it under the charge of Rizwan. He created Hell and put it under the charge of the Angel of Hell. But when He created the *heart* of the believer He said: 'The heart, in fact, lies between the two fingers of the Benevolent One.' (*Epistle* 43)

At another place the Gnostic observes:

If anything dearer than the heart had been there I (God) would have placed my Gnosis there. (*Epistle* 38)

There is a Tradition of the Holy Prophet which is hadith-e-Qudsi: 'I cannot be contained by the heavens, nor by the earth, it is only in the heart of the believer that I can be contained.'

Another Tradition says:

I can be contained in no other place except in the heart of the believer.

The essence of the Heart cannot be conceived even by Angels

Sheikh Muniri goes on to say that the heart has an essence which is so noble and so much beyond comprehension that, not to speak of material being, even angels can not conceive of it—

Brother! it is a very big thing that thou hast been made the object of prostration for the angels and of jealousy for the heavens. However, clouded in his physical being man may be, he is so numinous and holy in his essential being that the intelligence of the angels and the speculation of man are unable to comprehend his reality. When his essential being blazes forth the angels are amazed and the heavens become dizzy. They courtsey to him and are overpowered with awe.

Western culture recognizes its helplessness with regard to the understanding of the essential being of man, in spite of modern psychological researches. It has not been able to explore the *heart* of man. For westerners the *heart* of man is the physical organ, which is merely a pump to supply blood to the various parts of the body. But the above argument brings out that the *heart* is the source of human life and energy and that its influence permeates every department of culture.

The Three Constituent Principles of Western Culture

After understanding the place of man in the universe it is necessary to understand the constituent principles of culture, for without such an understanding the ideals and goals of life cannot be determined, nor can any plan of character building be conceived.

The Constitutive Principles of Western Culture Are

(1) Freedom of thought and consciousness;
(2) Materialistic tendency;
(3) Test for beauty and the good things of life.

These constitutive principles have been derived from Greeco-Roman culture. They have their potential for good as well as for evil. If they are allowed to operate without any check they can lead to the most appalling manifestations of beastliness and lust; but if certain limits are observed they can be most beneficial for mankind.

Unfortunately, in western culture these constitutive principles have been allowed to operate unchecked. In the beginning the evil consequences were not so prominent because people were more concerned with constructive activity.But later on their power of striving and resistance was weakened and the riot of profligate thought and action broke out to work destruction on humanity. Attempts were made to check it by means of philosophy. But philosophy was bound to fail where only Faith would have succeeded.

The Three Constitutive Principles of Cultural Reconstruction

The three constitutive principles of cultural reconstruction are: (1) the state of Faith, (2) transcendental concerns, and (3) relation with the Absolute.

These constitutive principles have been derived from the natural constitution of man. If they are allowed to do their proper function in the building up of culture, the spiritual essence of man will be manifested, and the synthesis of reason and the *heart,* of materialism and spiritualism, and of this-worldliness and other-worldliness will be achieved. The achievement of this harmony will help man bring his passions under the control of reason, and enable him to lead his life in a way worthy of his place in creation.

On the other hand, if lust for power and sensual enjoyment prevails, mankind will suffer stagnation and degeneration, and will be led to stain with blood-shed even the Holy places of worship, which has been observed in the case of people in a state of decline.

Let us consider each constitutive principle in some detail.

THE STATE OF FAITH

The State of Faith is the Result of Synthesis

The state of Faith does not emerge from dead evidence and rigid belief. It is the product of the synthesis of Knowledge and conviction, gnosis and love. After achieving this synthesis man resigns his will to the Will of God. He purifies his *heart* and engages it in devotion to God.

The state of Faith is the source of motive power It is there behind all revolutionary movements. Through it culture is built up and the elements that promote life are activated. For it is directly related to the psychic life of man, where ideas are born and the seeds of revolution are sown.

What has been Said about Faith

It has been said that 'owing to Faith the strength of a person is magnified ten times'. The Bible rightly observes that the power of Faith can move mountains. Those who have caused revolutions in history were certain ill-equipped but sincere persons whose Faith was extremely powerful. That which makes one army victorious over another is not merely physical factors (which also count) but an internal power. Think, it was the power of Faith that made the militarily ill-equipped Arabs, those 'backward inhabitants of the desert', victorious over the immensely large and well-equipped armies of Khosro and Caesar.

All the consequences and effects of Faith that the Quran speaks of follow from the state mentioned above. For mere dead evidence and rigid belief cannot produce any change in the human psyche or in life. It would only give some sentimental satisfaction and perpetuate certain empty rituals. This is testified by certain Verses of the Quran which we shall quote.

The Effect of Faith is Love

The Quran says:

> *But those of Faith are*
> *Over-flowing in their love*
> *For God.* (II-165)

It means that the heart is purified of the love of everything other than God, the love of idols so to say, and it is engaged fully in the love of God only, valuing no other love before it; neither the love for relations and friends nor the love for power and glory.

In this state of love for the Absolute man does not care for any worldly considerations or relations.

Thus the Quran says:

> *Say: if it be that your fathers,*
> *Your sons, or brothers,*

or maids or your kindred.
The commerce in which ye fear
A decline; or the dwellings
In which ye delight—
Are dearer to you than God,
Or His Apostle or the striving
In His cause;—then wait
Until God brings about His Decision. (IX-24)

If the heart is turned from God's loe, the Decision of God is manifested in the f rm of humiliations for a whole people. It must also be noted that the manifestation of the Decision has various phases corresponding to the degree of the presence or the absence of love for God. The Quran says:

Thou wilt not find
Any people who believe
In God and the Last Day
Loving those who resist
God and His Apostle,
Even though they were
Their fathers or their sons,
Or their brothers, or
Their kindred.
For such,
He has retained Faith
In their hearts, and strengthened
Them with a spirit
From Himself. (LVIII-22)

The implication is that the love induced in man as a result of Faith prevails over his will, thought and action and over all his relations with others. In fact this Love can be identified by those of pervading quality.

The Philosophy of Love Resolves the Tangles of Life

The philosophy of love as gnostics have presented it resolves the tangles of life and psychic complexes. Sheikh Yahya Muniri has rightly observed:

> The monotony and unanimity that you see in the works of angels is there because they are unaware of the lore of love; and the ups and downs that you see in the lives of men are there because they are concerned with love (God loves them and they love God). (*Epistle* 46)

At another place the Sheikh says:

> "Brother! a broken thing carries no value, but it is a different matter with the heart; the more broken it is the more valuable it becomes. Moses in one of his prayers asked God where he could seek him. God answered: "I am with those whose hearts are broken (because of Me)". (*Epistle* 6)

And this is what Iqbal says:

> Keep it not secure: let it break. Know that
> this mirror of thine—
> The more broken it is the more valuable does
> it become in its Maker's Eye.

History is Explained Through Love of God

The love of God testifies to the realities of the suffering and trails of the prophets. Their sufferings and trials are meant to show that no other love, even the love of the dearest thing or person is more valuable than the love of God.

Why Setting Partners of God is An Unpardonable Offence

In the light of love it becomes understandable why setting partners of God is such an unpardonable offence:

> *God forgiveth not*
> *(the sin of) joining other gods*
> *With Him; but He forgiveth*

Whom He pleaseth other sins
Than this; one who joins
Other god with God,
Had strayed far, far away
(from the Right). (IV-116)

Indeed, it is all because of love. For if the heart which God has made for an exclusive attachment to Himself joins others with God in its love it is an unforgivable sin.

According to Gnostics Love Encompasses the Whole Universe

The gnostics regard love as all inclusive and eternal. For them it encompasses the whole universe. Such a conception of love leads to the resolution of all problems. Sheikh Sharfuddin Yahya Muniri observes:

> The lore of love encompasses every age, the beginning and the end of all time. It is a love that has been and is and will be the same in future. Seekers of Truth have said that this world and the other world both are the worlds of desire. If somebody says that the other world is not the world of desire it is not true. Of course on Doomsday prayer and fasting will not be there and all commandments (of the *shariah*) shall be obliterated, but two things will always remain: (1) the love of God, (2) the praise of God. (*Epistle* 46)

Faith Demands Sacrifice of Love and Property

It is necessary to present the philosophy of love in modern terms and to consider it as a permanent subject of enquiry. Only after such an attempt its full form will become manifest:

God has purchased of the Believers
Their persons and their goods:
For their's (in return)
Is the garden (of Paradise):

They Fight in His Cause,
And slay and are slain:
A promise binding on Him
In Truth, through the Law,
The Gospel, and the Quran:
And who is more faithful
To his Covenant than God?
Then rejoice in the bargain
Which ye have concluded:
That is the achievement supreme. (IX-III)

After achieving Faith in God neither life nor property belongs to the Believer. He resigns them to God, and regards himself only as a trustee of the things that he can dispose only according to the commandment of God.

Self-exile, Holy War and Giving Aid are Obligatory

For this state of Faith self-exile (*hijrat*), Holy war and striving (*jihad*) and giving aid (*nusrat*) to the Believers who have exiled themselves or are fighting in the cause of God are obligatory:

Those who believe,
And fight for the Faith,
In the Cause of God,
As well as those
Who give (them) asylum
And aid—these are (all)
In very truth the Believers: (VIII-74)

At another place it has been said:

Only those are Believers
Who have believed in God

And His Apostle, and have
Never since doubted, but
Have striven with their
Belongings and their persons
In the Cause of God:
Such are the sincere ones. (XLIX-15)

At still another place the Quran proclaims:

Those who believe, and suffer
Exile and strive with might
And main, in God's cause,
With their goods and their persons,
Have the highest rank
In the sight of God:
They are the people
Who will achieve (salvation) (IX-20)

In these Verses the phrases: 'these are (all) in very truth the Believers', 'such are the sincere ones', and 'they are the people who will achieve (salvation)' testify that without self-exile, striving and fighting in the Cause of God, and giving aid to the Believers who have exiled themselves and are striving and fighting in the Cause of God Quranic Faith cannot be achieved, nor can success in this world and in the next world be achieved by a Muslim.

All the Three Duties are Natural

1. *Self-exile*

Self-exile or *Hijrat* is abandoning all things for the sake of Faith — all things that come in the way of Faith and its demands: even if one has to leave his home and family.

2. *Striving or Jihad*

It means striving in every way for the cause of Faith—striving in the physical sense, by means of the tongue and the pen, by means of intellectual abilities. Striving implies all means and modes of human activity; it implies facing every kind of obstacle and not hesitating in making the greatest sacrifice, even the sacrifice of one's own life.

3. *Giving Aid to Believers or Nusrat*

It means helping one another and standing by one another in the face of difficulties and hardships. It, therefore, implies mutual cooperation and the spirit of sacrifice.[8] These three factors are the natural modes of progress of all nations. The difference between the Muslims and other nations is that the other nations follow these modes for the sake of power and conquest of lands, but in the cultural reconstruction programme carried out by the Muslims the three modes are followed for the sake of God.

There is no difficulty about understanding the concepts of Hijrat and Nusrat, but the concept of Jihad has been misinterpreted by some bigoted historians as a manifestation of barbarism. In reply to these historians it would be enough to refer to the French author Sadeaux. He says that these people have gone deaf to the voice of truth and they are devoid of imaginative insight.[9]

It has happened in history that wars among nations have been devoid of moral considerations. As regards western culture this freedom has taken an extreme form, such as has no precedent in history.

It Was the Quran that First Laid Down a Code of War

In the context of cultural reconstruction it can be claimed that the Quran is the first Book that laid down a code of war and brought war under the control of moral principles.[10] It made it clear to the world that the purpose of war should be the removing of corruption and injustice and the propagation of

God's message of mercy, and not power or materialistic expansion. Thus the Quran says:

> *And fight them on*
> *Untill there is no more*
> *Tumult or oppression*
> *And there prevail*
> *Justice and Faith in God* (II - 193)

The Holy Prophet also said: 'strive and fight till God prevails'. Since a detailed discussion of the subject is beyond our scope we shall content ourselves with quoting the statement of certain non-Muslims. In the last days of the Caliphate of Omar or the early days of the Caliphate of Osman a Nestorian Priest recorded his impression as follows:

> These Tais (Arabs) whom God has made rulers, these Tais have also become our masters. But they are not at all hostile to Christian religion. On the other hand they protect our religion, give regard to our priests and saints and make donations of land and property for our churches.[11]

Walker in the History of International Law says that it is a common phenomenon in history that barbarous people attack civilized states and conquer them. But in comparison to the Teutonic and Tartarian barbarians the Bedouins of Arabia who spilled over into other lands cannot be categorised as barbarian conquerors at all. For these Bedouins conquerers manifested superior culture and morality than the "Civilized people" they conquered."[12]

In the history of the law of nations a Roman Catholic priest says that even the Jacobite Christians welcomed the Muslim Arabs as their redeemers. The greatest innovation of these Muslim Arabs was that they regarded the followers of every other religion as an autonomous entity and also appointed the priests of other religions to prestigious posts.[13]

Faith is the Essence of Social Organization

It must be noted that it is the Islamic concept of cultural

reconstruction that first recognized religious and ethnic minorities as an autonomous entity. According to this concept the essence of social organization is Faith. Thus the Quran says:

But no, by Thy Lord
They can have
No (real) Faith,
Until they make thee judge
In all disputes between them,
And find in their souls
No resistence against
Thy decision, but accept
Them with fullest conviction. (IV - 65)

At another place it is said:

It is not fitting
For a believer,
Man or woman
When a matter has been decided
By God and His Apostle,
To have any option
About their decision: (XXXIII - 36)

For the believers the Quran comments:

And hold fast
All together, by the Rope
Which God (stretches out
For you), and be not divided
Among yourselves; (III - 103)

Again:

And obey God and His Apostle:
And fall into no disputes,
Lest ye boose heart
And your power depart:
And be patient and persevering:
For God is with those
Who patiently persevere: (VIII - 46)

Such Verses indicate that all the three constituents of social organization, allegiance, centrality and unity, emanate from Faith. Psychologists are of the opinion that the following factors are essential for a higher kind of social organization:

1. The members of the community must love one another, and there must be mutual love between them and their leader.
2. They must regard the good of all as the very aim of their life.
3. They must regard consideration for one another as their duty.

The social organization that partakes of these factors will certainly improve moral qualities and prevail over everything else.[14]

Good Deeds Alongwith Faith

The Quran has repeatedly insisted on the value of good deed alongwith Faith. This combination will certainly result in the vicegerency of man and his mastery in the world. The Quran says:

So lose not heart
Nor fall into despair:
For ye must gain mastery
If ye are true in Faith (III - 139)

Again it is said:

God has promised,
To those
Among you who believe
And work righteous deeds,
That He will, of surety grant them
In the land, inherent
(of power), as He granted it
To those before them: that
He will establish in authority
Their religion — one
Which He has chosen for them:
And that He will change
(their state), after the fear
In which they (lived), to one
Of security and peace: (XXIV - 55)

These Verses go to prove that without good deeds there can be neither the construction of culture nor the surety of its survival.

Meaning of Good Deeds

Regarding the heading of good deeds we get the following entry in Arabic dictionaries (like *Qamus, Sirah, Lissanul Arab*):

"*Salaah* is the opposite of *Fasaad* and *Salaah* is the opposite of *Fassad.* One who properly carries out ones duties is *Saaleh.* Hence *Salehal kaza* is said when a person has the ability of carrying out some act. *Salahiyat* is the state which produces what is *Saaleh.*"

Let us look at some Arabic idioms in this connection:

(1) Such and such a person's condition has become *Saaleh*, which means that the germs of corruption have been eliminated in him.

(2) Such and such a thing is *Saaleh* for thee which means it suits thee.
(3) The thing which was spoiled (*Afsad*) by hail has been restored to good condition by rain (this is said when somebody restores to good conditions what has been spoiled by another person).
(4) The thing which is not right and suitable (*layaslah*). It is better and more proper to abandon it.
(5) Reform (*Aslah*) yourself: People will be in your favour.
(6) He has accomplished sufficient gains (*Saaleh*) out of literature.
(7) A great gift has been obtained (*Saalehata*) from such and such a person.

Except no. 6-7 (where *Saaleh* has been used figuratively) all the above idioms go to prove that in the arabic language *Saaleh* is used in the sense of capability and suitability of accomplishment.

The Quran and the sayings of the Holy Prophet and the interpretations of exegetes also testify to the above mentioned general meaning of the word *Saaleh*. The Quran says:

> *'If Thou givest us*
> *A goodly child*
> *We vow we shall*
> *(ever) be grateful'*
> *But when He giveth them*
> *A goodly child, they ascribe*
> *To others a share in the gift*
> *They have received.'* (VII - 189-90)

Before a child is born the parents wish that their child may be healthy and comely in every respect. The Quran has used the word *Saaleh* for these qualities, and the exegetes have interpreted accordingly.[15]

At another place the Quran says:

Do not mischief on the earth,
After it hath been
Set in order, (VII - 56)

Here for setting in order the word *Islah* has been used, and the setting in order implies setting in order through invitation to the gospel, through which invitation the *hearts* are sown with spiritual capabilities and sensibility and good deeds appear as the fruits of this process. On one occasion the Holy Prophet saw a weary and hungry camel and used the word Saaleh for the animal in a healthy condition. Thus the Tradition says:

Fear God with respect to what you do to these speechless animals. Ride them when they are healthy and strong, and leave riding them in that condition. (*Mishkat*)

It means that you should not leave riding them when they are worn out and not suitable for riding or carrying loads.

In another Tradition it is said:

In the body of man there is a lump of flesh. When it is healthy and in working order the whole body is healthy and in working order. When it goes out of order the whole body goes out of order. This lump of flesh is the heart of man. (*Bukhari*, Kitabul Iman)

In this Tradition the health and the right working condition of the heart has been called *Salaah* and the opposite of it is called *Fasaad*. Regarding the word *Saaleh* exegetes have made the following observations:

By *Saalehaat* those deeds are implied that are right from the point of view of the Book and the Sunnah. (*Madarik*, p.127)

By *Saalehaat* are implied all those deeds that the shariah has approved and appreciated. (*Baizawi*, p. 47)

Fasaad means transgression or the going beyond limits of something, and *Salaah* is its opposit. These (concepts) respectively refer to all that is harmful and all that is beneficial. (*Baizawi*, p.29)

Regarding the deeds that are good or Saaleh Sheik Mohammad Abduhu Misri says:

By them we mean those good deeds which are spelled out in detail in the

Quran and are beneficial for oneself, family, community, and for all people in general. (Tafsir Sura *Wal' Asr*)

The above explanations indicate that for the manifestation of Faith and the construction of culture the good deeds that are necessary are not merely rituals, and conventional or outward virtues. Good deeds, in fact, comprehend both the inner and the outward life of man: they comprehend the whole being of man. But the inner life comes first; for without it a healthy community cannot come into existence, nor can man's use of nature yield any common benefit.

General Effects of Faith

Faith gives rise to a mode of behaviour that combines conviction with good deeds. Through this behaviour man accomplishes what is essential for a progressive society. For one thing this mode of behaviour implies the attitude of right and scrupulous action in every sphere of life. For this attitude the Quran uses the comprehensive term *taqwa* (for which the word 'piety' would be a bad translation).

Taqwa is a pious state, one which is related to the *heart*. It enables a man to distinguish between right and wrong, and to feel pangs of conscience if he goes astray. An episode from Islamic history would bring out the meaning of *taqwa*.

The following dialogue took place between Hazrat Omar and Hazrat Abi bin Ka'ab:

Omar: What is *taqwa*?
Abi bin Ka'ab: Have you ever walked along a thorny way?
Omar: I have.
Abi bin Ka'ab: What did you do on that occasion?
Omar: I gathered up my garments and tried to save myself from thorns.
Abi bin Ka'ab: Well, this is what *Taqwa*

In other words, *taqwa* is saving oneself from dangers of temptation.

2 TRANSCENDENTALISM

Transcendentalism Recognizes the Guidance of Reason, Heart and Revelation

In western civilization materialism dominates, and materialism recognises reason as the only source of knowledge. But in our concept of cultural reconstruction transcendentalism is the basis of everything, and transcendentalism recognises the combined guidance of reason, *heart* and revelation for the acquisition of knowledge. In all sphere of life such a combined guidance is necessary. The guidance of only one faculty is not enough.

Definition and Importance of Reason

(1) For materialists reason is the ultimate means of knowledge. Regarding reason scholars have made the following observations:

Imam Ahmad is of the opinion that "reason is a sustaining power". [1]

Imam Ghazali observes

> Reason is a sustaining power, by means of which man prepares himself for acquiring discursive knowledge. Life itself is a sustaining power, for by the help of life man prepares himself for voluntary actions and sense perception"[2].

Abul Hasan Tamimi says:

> "Reason is neither a body, nor a form, nor an essence: It is only light".[3]

In our concept of cultural reconstruction reason holds a position of great importance. Thus the Quran emphasizes the need for thinking over the realities of existence, the order of the universe, and the phenomena of nature, and it also emphasizes the need for making use of reason. The purpose is that man should exploit nature according to his needs and desires, and not only this, he should also mould it through his innovation according to the demands of his evolution, for the purpose of embellishing the garden of this world, in which task he should prove his worth as much as possible.

The Holy Prophet has also spoken of the importance and excellence of reason, regarding which we need not go into details. Although Imam Ghazali has mentioned certain Traditions dealing with this subject, the evidences of these Traditions are rather weak. After quoting certain Traditions concerning the importance of reason Shah Waliullah says:

"Although scholars of *hadith* have doubts regarding the authenticity of these Traditions their evidences are such as to give support to one another.

Ibn Taimiya has refused many of those Traditions regarding reason that go to support the theory of "the ten intellectual faculties" of the ancient philosophers. But the Traditions that affirm the psychic importance of reason are not questioned by anybody.

Flaw in the Accessibility and Guidance of Reason

For every group of thinkers the accessibility and guidance of reason is not without flaw, notwithstanding the fact that the importance of reason is acceptable to all. It is because reason has access only to material things and to things related to sense experience. Such things do not comprise the whole of life. The following observations make it clear:

Through reason we do not arrive at a things as it is itself in reality (this implies a negation not of the Whole, but of the part)[5]

Another observation is as follows:

Sometimes it happens that because of the interference of contingent obscurity and also because of the fallacy of its method reason fails to take us to the desired truth".[6]

The Observation of Shah Waliullah Regarding Contingent Obscurities

Regarding contingent obscurities Shah Walliullah observes:

"Many times it happens that demands of nature prevail upon man, and then he frees himself of all conventional and rational considerations and becomes bold and unscrupulous. Such a state is called "obscurity of the ego".[7]

At another place Shah Waliullah observes:

Human nature dominates the *heart* and mind and makes them its servants. From this many low entities emerge. The sum total of these low entities is called the 'ego'.[8]

The individuals who are able to dispel the obscurities of the ego in order to make their reason strong, such individuals are called "the virtuous through knowledge" by Shah Waliullah. Thus he says: the civilized individuals whose reason is strong are *called* "The virtuous through knowledge".[9]

Kant on Sense Experience

Kant has entered into a detailed discussion on sense experience. He is the first Philosopher in western culture, who has determined the limits of reason through his philosophical critiques and who has shown the superiority of reason over impure knowledge. In his philosophy the validity of reason is examined first of all in order to determine what subjects are accessible to reason and what are not. Opposed to this Kantian philosophy is the philosophy that makes a priori assertions and starts making use of reason without examining its validity.[10]

In his book *The Critique of Pure Reason* Kant has not actually discussed pure reason, as the title of the book would suggest, but he has defined the limits of reason and shows its superiority over impure knowledge. According to Kant the knowledge derived from reason is of two kinds: (1) impure and (2) pure.

Pure knowledge is the knowledge acquired by virtue of the essential structure of the mind and its innate nature. It does not recognise the interference of senses. Impure knowledge is one that comes through the distorting senses and is inseparable from sense experience. Kant says that experience is not the only field to which our cognition is limited. Experience does tell us about what *is*. But it does not tell us about what *ought to be*. Hence through experience we can never get at the knowledge of general truths and our reason, which is concerned specially with general truths, is not satisfied by experience, but becomes unappeased. Kant goes on to say that general truths, which are also in the nature of axioms, must be independent of experience. They should be what they are before experience and even after it.

Kant's Criticism of Locke and Hume

Criticising Locke, Kant says that he saw purely rational concepts in experience and therefore he thought that they were derived from experience. Further, Locke is also inconsequently tried to obtain with their aid knowledge which far transcends all limits of experience. Kant also criticises Hume. He says that Hume recognizes that for making use of rational concepts in the case of knowledge beyond experience it is necessary that these concepts should have an *a priori* origin. But Hume cannot explain why understanding regards these concepts as necessarily connected in the objects of experience when these concepts are not connected in understanding itself. He failed to grasp the point that through these concepts understanding itself shapes the experience in which objects are manifested, and thus he was constrained to think that the concepts were derived from experience. Kant goes on to say that the empirical derivation of rational concepts in which Locke and Hume got stuck up does not reconcile with the scientific *a priori* knowledge that we actually possess, namely pure Mathematics and general science of nature; and this fact, therefore, suffices to disprove such derivation".

For Kant Religion and Faith are Beyond Reason

Regarding religion and faith Kant says that they should be kept beyond the realm of reason. But it also implies that the moral basis of religion should be absolute and that it should not be derived from sense experience which may be subject to controversies. Religion should not be contaminated with our fallacious reason. It should be derived from intution and immediate experience of the inner being. We must prove that even pure reason can by empirical which means that it can be itself determine the will without the help of any experiential reality. In other words the moral sense in man is innate and is not derived from experience. The moral imperative, which we need for the basis of religion should be an absolute imperative.

Here we do not propose to offer any critical review on Kant's theories. We just want to show that even for this great western philosopher the knowledge derived from reason is not always pure, nor do the interference of reason encompass the whole of life.[11]

The Definition of Heart

(2) The *heart* is the basic means of non rational knowledge. Gnostics have made the following observations regarding the nature of the *heart*.

"The *heart* is a refined, spiritual inner force".[12]

Again it is said:

"By *heart* is meant a spiritual essence (as distinguished from the lump of flesh) which is the ground of the gnosis of God".[13]

Another observation is as follows:

"By *Heart* we mean that refined part of our being which coordinates all essences".[14]

Knowledge Through Hearts According to the Quran

In our conception of cultural reconstruction the *heart* holds a position of great importance. It is regarded as the super sensible means of knowledge. Thus the Quran says:

They have hearts wherewith they
Understand not, (VII - 179)

Or are
Their hearts locked up
By them? (XLVII - 24)

God hath set a seal
On their hearts ... (II - 7)

The above Verses refer to the lack of understanding which is related to the heart; they do not reject reason at all.

Evidence from Traditions

The various Traditions of the Holy Prophet also testify to the same truth regarding the heart. For example:

"When Allah wills the good of His servant He sets up a preacher in his *heart*".[15]

Another Tradition says:

"Allah keeps His guard for the person in whose *heart* there is a preacher".[16]

"The *heart* of the Believer is pure. A lamp shines in it".[17]

On one occasion the Holy Prophet was asked about the purity of heart. He said:

"It is a light which God introduces in the heart".[18]

Testimony from the Sayings of Saints and Gnostics

The gnostics and Saints have also testified to this truth. For example Imam Malik says:

"Knowledge is not the multiplicity of information. It is a light which God introduces into the heart of His servants". (*Abat,* Abqa 9)

Imam Ghazali has called this light a "key". He says:

"And this light is the key to most of the secrets". (*Al Munqaz minal Zalal*)

Doctrinalists call it, metaphorical, the 'inward eye'.[19] Gnostics regard it as the essential reality of man. They say that 'the refined element (called *heart*) is the essential reality of man'.[20] At another place the *heart* is compared to the throne of God.

"The heart is the sanctum of God and the inner being is His Throne. In the heart of the believer the light of God is like a lamp burning in a niche".[21]

Sheikh Ahmad Sarhindi writes:

It seems that the Seeker has not traversed even ¼th of the journey of the *Heart*. All the stages of this journey have to be gone through so that the first reality of the spiritual world may be manifested.[22]

Relation of Heart to the Physical Organ

The relation of the *Heart* to the physical organ has been described in various ways. For example, it is said:

"The relation of the *heart* to the physical organ called heart is similar to the relation of the accidents to the bodies, of the attributes to the person, of the instruments to their user, and of the dweller to the dwelling place".[23]

Another observations is as follows:

"The special and foremost relation of the refined element, the *heart*, to the physical organ called heart is of course there. Then there is its relation to the whole body. It means that it is the ground of the physical organ called heart; it is its realm; its kingdom and its medium".[24]

Shah Waliullah says:

"The spiritual faculty called the *heart* dwells in the conical lump of flesh" (*Altaful Quds*, Chapter III, p. 23)

In fact an enquiry into the heart and its associated matters becomes difficult for those whose range of cognition is illuminated by reason.

The relations between the physical heart and the (spiritual) heart is baffling for the minds of most people.[24]

It is because the relation is concerned with revelational knowledge.[25]

The Heart is the Consciousness of Divine Friendship

The heart is the consciousness of Friendship with the Divine. It has many stages:

(1) *Comprehension:* This is the first stage of consciousness of the Divine. In this stage man gets insight into reality by

observing certain external manifestations. The Holy Prophet says:

"Take care of the comprehension of the believer, for he sees with the light of Allah". (*Tirmizi; Tabrani*)

(2) Discovery (*Kashf*). This is the stage of consciousness of the Divine in which the spiritual states of man and other hidden realities are discovered. Gnostics have divided it into two parts:[26]

(i) *Phenomenal Discovery*: Through it the invisible realities of the phenomenal world are discovered. Similarly the realities belonging to the past or future are also discovered.

(ii) *Noumenal Discovery*: Through it the seeker comes to know of his own spiritual states and of the spiritual states of other Seekers. Also the degree of one's relation to God is known. Knowledge regarding the Essence and Attributes of God also belongs to this category of Discovery.

(3) *Revelation:* This is the stage of consciousness in which knowledge is revealed to man through a secret and mysterious agency.

And its enlightenment
As to its wrong
And its right. (XCI - 8)

Qazi Thanaullah Panipati says: 'Among other things revelation is the enlightenment that God bestows on the heart of the mystic'.[27]

The Range of the Conscience of the Divine is Far-Reaching

Gnostics have recognized that the range of the conscience of the Divine is far-reaching. For example:

(1) It guards the essential abode of the spirit.
(2) It shows the reality through faith and intution.
(3) It amends those damages of life about which reason is helpless.

(4) It acts as a medium between the Intellect and the Action and keeps up a right relation between them.
(5) It establishes a higher consciousness of relations between mind and the universe.
(6) It assimilates Divine Names and the reflection of their Attributes.
(7) It gives access to certain invisible realities.
(8) Sometimes it elevates man to a state where physical laws are suspended and the boundaries of space and time cease to exist and man begins to perform miracles.

Evidence from the Savings of the Saints

The evidence of the above is provided by the sayings of certain Saints.

Khwaja Fariduddin Masood says:

By the remembrance of the Manifest the mirror of the *heart* is extended. The *heart* has seven aspects and one of these aspects contains the "Pearl" (of gnosis).[28]

Sheikh Shahabuddin Suharwardi says:

Because of piety the selves of the gnostics are purified and because of austerity their *hearts* become clean. When these people give up worldly interests their inner being is activated and they begin to hear by the *heart*.[29]

After this activation of the inner being it sometimes happens that miracles are manifested through the gnostics, which knowledge fails to understand. Mysteries of the heart are beyond the knowledge of the senses, for the heart itself is beyond this knowledge.[30]

Qazi Thanaullah says the same thing in a different way:

Among other things there is a mysterious influence which is of two kinds: (1) Influence is created by the Saint in the inner being of the disciple and in this way the disciple is made to turn to God. (2) Influence is created in the phenomenal world and in this way God fulfils the prayer and will of the Saint.

A gnostic puts the same thing in a couplet which may be translated as follows:

There is no difficulty except that of the complexity of the *heart*. Reason is baffled in understanding the *heart*.

The Consciousness of the Divine Friendship does not Comprehened Every Dimension Nor does it Ignore Reason

The consciousness of the Diving Friendship has a very wide range, but it does not comprehend every dimension of being, nor does it do away with reason. The *heart* is greater than reason, but it does not comprehend all dimensions of being.[31]

Ibn-i-Rushd says:

This mode of knowledge the consciousness of Divine (Friendship) is not common among people. (*Sharh Irshadat-i-Tusi*)

Then many times conventional obscurities and hindering circumstances so predominating that the real knowledge of the consciousness of Divine Friendship is suppressed and its truth is distorted.

Evidence of Obscuring Veils From the Quran

(1) The obscuring veils have been mentioned in the Quran. For example it is said:

By no means:
But on their hearts
Is the stain of the (ill)
Which they do. (LXXXIII-14)

At another place the Quran says:

... and seal up
Their hearts so that they
Could not hear (VII-100)

Al Ghazali explains the "stain" (and the "seal") as follows:

Base influences are like dusky smoke which ascends towards the mirror of the heart and is deposited there layer upon layer, with the result that the mirror of the heart is darkened and obscured in relation to God. The Quran calls this state 'stain' and 'seal'. (*Ahya, Jam'e Ausafil Qalb*)

Further Explanations of the Obscuring Veils

The obscuring veils have been explained is various ways. Fariuddin Masood says: "the heart is like a lily. It has two sides, and both the sides are the landing places for the Devil. The tempting Devil has woven up a web, spider like, around the heart and has suspended curtains of these webs. The Devil lurks behind these curtains. The heart itself has curtains, just as the lily has petals. The tempting Devil dwells behind these curtains". (*Ganjul Asrar,* Fasl III, Dar Sharh-i-Dil)

In western culture Freud is able to reach these curtains. This is why he has recognised sexuality as the constituent of the unconscious. We have already discussed it above.

Shah Ismael Shaheed speaks of weakness and interference in the consciousness of the Divine Friendship as follows:

> Interference occurs in the Discovery in the following ways: (1) Diabolical temptations come. (2) The internal enemy conspires. (3) Weakness occurs from every direction in the Discoverer. Besides these there are other factors which we shall deal with later on. (*'Abqaat,* Abqa, p. 6)

Some gnostics have observed that because of weakness and the interference of diabolical temptation the heart does not stand in surity of purity.[32]

Ibn Khaldun discusses the subject. His discussion can be summarised as follows:

> Discovery is right and perfect only when the doctrines of the shariah are followed. It also occurs to certain persons which have purified their hearts through discipline and strife, without following the shariah. But the two kinds of persons differ from one another, and the difference is like the difference of two mirrors, one having a level surface and the other a rough surface. Evidently the latter would give a distorted image and the former a clear and proper image. (*Muqaddama,* p. 392)

The Heart is Like a Mirror

Gnostics have defined the *heart* (the consciousness of Divine Friendship) by the example of a mirror. Just as the reflection of the mirror may be hindered in various ways, so that the proper image is not obtained, in the same way the heart meets with hindrances or obstacles and so the authenticity of its perception is interfered with. The hindrances in the case of the mirror are as follows: (1) The polish has not been properly done; (2) the mirror is stained; (3) In spite of being clean there may be no object of reflection before it; (4) In spite of an object before it there may come some obstacle between it and the mirror; (5) the direction of receiving the reflection may be unknown.

The hindrances of the *heart* are as follows: (1) It may not have developed the full ability of reflection because of weakness; (2) it may be enveloped in darkness because of sins; (3) in spite of cleanness attention to reflection may not have been given; (4) In spite of attention false belief and thoughts may form an obscurity over it; (5) Consideration may not have been given to proper order at the time of reflection.

The civilized persons who are able to remove these hindrances and to purify the heart and make it capable of reflection—such persons are called by gnostics Siddiqeen, Shohada, Abbaad. (*Altaful Quds,* Chapter IV)

Rousseau on Resultant Conditions

Rousseau has spoken at length about resultant conditions (which are due to obscuring veils). Although his views could not become a constituent of culture at any stage, he is the first thinker of the west who has examined critically the philosophy of illumination and the resultant conditions in an age of crisis and has formed a basis for showing the contradiction between human nature and modern civilization. Regarding modern social life he says that the needs of the body and the spirit are different. The needs of the body are the basis of society, but the needs of the spirit are its ornament. In modern social life there is an exhibition of artificial morality. Real morality is badly lacking. Rousseau says that affectation has moulded our behaviour and has taught our feelings an artificial language. Originally our morals were rough but they were natural and genuine. There are many evils which are given the status of moral good. Adopting them or at least assuming them is regarded necessary. Regarding the progress of art and Science Rousseau observes that the more we progressed made in science and arts the more dirty our morals became. Whenever knowledge and arts made their appearance in history, virtue flew away. This phenomenon has happened without exception in every country and in every time. The existence of knowledge is more dangerous in its effects than it is futile in its aim. Rousseau points out that the progress of science and arts has not added to our real happiness: it has on the other hand spoiled our morals and our tastes. Today the question is not whether man is honest but whether he is clever.

Rousseau on Virtue

Regarding virture Rousseau says that it is a spiritual energy. Its nature is free from all embelishment. The virtue of man is like a wrestler who likes to be naked at the time of wrestling and looks down on gaudy dresses which would interfere in the free display of his skill.

Virtue is the highest knowledge for the simple ones. Is any labour needed for knowing it? Are not its simple rules engraved on every human heart? What else is needed for knowing its rules than self-assessment and the attention to the voice of the conscience after passions have been silenced? Virture is the true philosophy which teaches us contentment.

Rousseau on Religion

Regarding religion Rousseau says that religious feeling should not be injected into the child from outside. His heart must develop his own religion according to his needs. To a friend Rousseau writes that the source of faith is in the inner being. The faithful person does not believe in God because everything is good. No' it is the other way round: he sees good in everything because he believes in God.

Rousseau actually believes in natural religion about which we have spoken earlier. He thinks that if people accepted the dictates of their hearts there could be no other religion except the natural one. But how to make the heart receptive to such dictates and instructions and how to save it from the domination of contingent circumstances—regarding these things Rousseau's philosophy is silent.

Here it is beyond our scope to go into the views of Rousseau or to attempt in critique of these views. We only want to point out that for Rousseau the domination of contingent circumstances suppresses the inner voice or distorts its truth.

Definition of Revelation

For man in his material condition the non-material means of knowledge are the highest agency. Regarding it scholars have made the following observations:

> In the Shariah revelation is the word of God, which has been sent down to any of his Prophets.[33]

Again it is said:

> Revelation means the message of the shariah, or something resembling it, sent by God to one of his Prophets.[34]

Regarding the *last revelation* it is said:

> The Quran is a discourse from God in the form of a clear revelation.[35]

Revelation Implies the Consciousness of Prophethood

Revelation implies the consciousness of Prophethood which has many phases. In every phase revelation was complete in view of the needs of the time. The Quran says:

> *Those apostles*
> *We endowed with gifts,*
> *Some above others:*
> *To one of them God spoke;*
> *Others he raised*
> *To decrees (of honour);* (II-253)

Moreover, we gave Moses
A Book, completing
(Our favour) to those
Who would do right,
And explaining all things
In detail, (VI-154)

... We sent him
The Gospel: therein
Was guidance and light, (V-49)

The Last Phase of Revelation is the Last Prophethood

The last phase of the consciousness of revelation is the Last Prophethood, which occurs at the last stage of the evolution of humanity. It is indeed attunded to the perfection of religious consciousness. The Quran says:

Mohammad is not
The father of any
Of your men, but (he is)
The Apostle of God,
And the Seal of the Prophets:
And God has full knowledge
Of all things. (XXXIII-40)

This day have I
Perfected your religion
For you, completed
My favour upon you,
And have chosen for you
Islam as your religion. (V-4)

Features of Consciousness of Prophethood

There are many features of consciousness of Prophethood, on the basis of which it has superiority over both mind and heart. For Example:

(1) It opens the door of the Abode of the Spirit and receives the reflection of Essence (and not merely of Names and Attributes).

(2) It grows in light and the rays of light always accompany it.

(3) It is always marked by numinous power and the revelationary consciousness.

(a) As the numinous power operates the selfish desires are precluded and there is an awakening of consciousness and development of the spirit.

(b) As the revelationary consciousness develops the light of reality illuminates the inner being and reveals its secrets.

(4) It is the result of the operation of Grace and of personal experience and observations, and not of any inner consciousness or intuition etc.

(5) It introduces man to the secrets of life and of his own self and teaches him to lead his life according to the natural constitution.

(6) It reveals to the dweller of the earth the secrets of the noumenal world and manifests its laws in the form of miracles.

Miracles are actually brought about by the influence of the laws of the noumenal world over our world. Since we lack knowledge of the operation of this influence we consider miracles as oddities or wonders. Otherwise they are not so, nor are they against the laws of nature.

(7) It establishes direct relationship with the secret or invisible world which is the repository of all knowledge and is free of all pollution.

(8) It protects man against error and transgression, and this can be said with certainty.

Indication of These Features in the Quran

These features have been indicated in the following Verses of the Quran:

And to promulgate it:
But when We have
Promulgated it, follow thou
Its recital (as promulgated) (LXXV—17-18)

... and We have
Rehearsed it to thee in slow,
Well-arranged stages, gradually (XXV-32)

And recite the Quran
In slow, measured rhythmic tone (LXXIII-4)

Hazrat Ali had defined *tartil,* or slow, measured rhythmic tones as 'the knowledge of the proper articulation of various Phonemes and morphemes and of the pauses.'[36] The knowledge of this articulation and of pauses means that 'every sound should be articulated in the proper manner and with its particular qualities, and every word or Verse should be articulated in such a way as to give it the proper pause, and one must know that by giving that pause the meaning is not disturbed.'[37]

This is the Book:
in its guidance sure,
without doubt (II-2)

We have, without doubt,
Sent down the Message;
And We will assuredly
Guard it (from corruption) (XV-9)

So set thou thy face
Steady and truely to the Faith:
(establish) God's handy work according
To the pattern on which
He has made mankind:
No change (let there be)
In the work (wrought)
By God: that is
The standard Religion:
But most among mankind
Understand not. (XXX-30)

Soon will We show them
Our Signs in the (furthest)
Regions (of the earth), and
In their own souls, until
It becomes manifest to them
That this is the Truth. (XLI-53)

Say: "I am no bringer
Of new-fangled doctrine
Among the apostles, nor
Do I know what will
Be done with me or
With you. I follow
But that which is revealed
To me by inspiration; (XLVI-9)

But
No change wilt thou find
In God's way (of dealing) (XXV-43)

This is part of the tidings
Of the things unseen
Which We reveal unto thee
(O Apostle!) by inspiration; (III-44)

Nor does He make anyone
Aqauinted with His mystries,—
Except an apostle
Whom He has chosen: (LXXII—26-27)

The (Prophet's) (mind and) heart
In no way falsified
That which he saw. (LIII-11)

(His) sight never swerved,
Nor did it go wrong! (LIII-17)

... if thou
After the knowledge hath reached thee,
Wert to follow their (vain)
Desires,—then wert thou
Indeed (clearly) in the wrong. (II-145)

The Saints do not Partake of the Consciousness of Prophethood

The consciousness of prophethood, and its address and its manifestation are specific to the Prophets. The Saints do not partake of it. Ibne Taimiya says:

It could not be imagined that the address and insight which is characteristics of the Prophets is also endowed to the Saints. (*Sharhul Aqidatul Isfahaniya*, pub. Kurdistan at 'Ilmiya, p. 107)

Iqbal says:

There is a sanctified place under the heaven which is nobler than the Divine Throne.

Junaid and Bayazeed come here having lost their breath.

Prophets and Angels do not Partake of the last Prophethood

The Prophethood endowed upon Mohammad (peace be upon him) in its address and manifestation, is specific to him. No other Prophet or angel partakes of it. Ibne Taimiya says:

Among the Saints the superior most are Abu bakr, Umar, Usman and Ali and those who are like them. But none of them has the observation and insight which the Holy Prophet had on the night of the *Mairaj.* Nor had the angels this observations and insight, even the angel who brought revelation to the Holy Prophet. None of these angels did ever hear the Word of God which God spoke to his Apostle on that night; nor did the other Prophets have heard this Word, what to speak of the Saints (Sharhul Aqeedatill-Asfahanya)

The poet Sadi has visualised the dialogue between the Holy Prophet and the angel Gabriel on the night of *Mi'raj.*

As they advanced further into Divine Nearness
Gabriel lagged behind Mohammad by the Lot Tree

To him said Mohammad, the guardian of the house of God: 'O bringer of Revelation go further with me. I have found thee true in friendship' Why dost thou forsake my accompany now' He replied: 'further than this I dare not go. I have stopped because my wings have no more power. If I fly further even by a hair's breadth I get my wings burnt down by the increasing intensity of Divine Glory.

Another poet has brough out the distinctive quality of Mohammad (peace be upon him) in this way:

'Moses lost senses due to one glimpse of Attributes; Thou lookest at the very Essence smiling".

Revelation is Doctrine and Transcendental Reality

In fact revelation is not a developed form of intution and inner light or the consequence of the activity of reason and heart. It is rather an external and transcendental reality and it is a form of knowledge in its own right, free of every material pollution and of physical and conventional obscurity and the influence of contingent circumstance. The following Verses of the Quran make it clear:

Verily this is a Revelation
From the Lord of the Worlds:
With it came down (XXVI-192-194)
The Spirit of Faith and Truth
To thy heart and mind (XXVI-192-94)

He doth send down His angels
With inspiration of His Command,
To such of a servants as He pleaseth... (XVI-2)
Raised high above ranks
(Or degrees), (He is) the Lord
Of the throne (of authority):
By His Command doth He
Send the spirit (of inspiration)
To any of His servants
He pleases ... (XL-15)

Say: Whoever is an enemy
To Gabriel—for he brings down
The (revelation) to thy heart
By God's will ... (II-97)

The traditions speak of the state of revelation and its Effect as follows:

"According to Aisha revelation to the Holy Prophet began as a true dream or vision. The dream that he saw at night came true the next day. Then he began to like solitude and he would carry his food to the Cave of Hira and engage himself in worship and prayers. This went on for quite some days till the Truth was revealed to him, and in the Cave of Hira itself an angel appeared and said: "*Iqra*" ("Read"). Mohammad said he was not literate. According to his description the angel pressed him to his breast in a close embrace so powerfully that it pained him. He released him and said again: "Read". Mohammad again replied that he was not literate. The angel again embraced him powerfully and again it pained him. This happened three times. Then the angel said:

> *Proclaim! (or Read!)*
> *In the name of thy Lord and Cherisher,*
> *Who created—created man, out of*
> *(mere) clot*
> *Of congealed blood:*
> *Proclaim! and thy Lord*
> *Is most Bountiful,—*
> *He Who taught*
> *(The use of) the Pen,—* (XCVI-1-4)

After this the angel disappeared and Mohammad came back home in a state of terror and with his heart pounding. He said to his wife Khodija: "Wrap me in a blanket! Wrap me in a blanket!" Khodija wrapped him in a blanket and the state of terror was dispelled after sometime. *(Bukhari, Muslim* and *Mishkat)*

According to Scholastic Interpretation Revelation is The Consequence of Inner Phenomena

Philosophers and scholastics, in their attempts to reconcile the transcendental reality of revelation with the human mind, have tried to interprete it as, to a great extent, the consequence of inner conscience and intution or of reason and *heart* on a higher level. Witness the following interpretation.

Interpretation of Ancient Philosophers

Among ancient philosophers Aristotle and his disciples have not spoken on this subject. Farabi has discussed it briefly and Ibn-i-

Sina has discussed it in detail at many places. Here we give a summary of Ibn-i-Sina's views:

That God is the Speaker of the word means that from Him Revelation is inscribed on the tablet of the heart of the Holy Prophet through the Pen (Active Intellect or Angel). Thus the word of God comprises the knowledge that is characteristic of the Holy Prophet.[38]

At another place it is said:

The Apostle of God received Secret Knowledge through the Angel and his imagination transformed it into various words and images. Then the tablet of the self which was blank till now was inscribed with these words, and as a consequence the Apostle heard rhythmic and versified discourse and saw a figure resembling human body. This is Revelation.[39]

It means that the tablet of the heart of the Apostle was clean like a mirror, so much so that it received not only the reflection of the Meaning but also that of the Divine Speaker. The reflection of Meaning was manifested sometimes in the Hebrew language and sometimes in the Arabic language. Thus the Source was one and its emanations were various. The following commentary makes it clear:

Let us talk of the reality of Revelation and Inspiration. When the speaking self becomes so powerful that its involvement with the body does not obstruct the union with the Divine Essence, and imagination becomes so powerful that it can liberate the common sense from outward senses the speaking self establishes contact in a state of awareness with absolute intellect and transcendental beings. Thus it achieves fully the knowledge of the Secret Realities, and the imagination reports in proper detail of invisible things. This report descends into the common sense and becomes objectified and palpable. And thus some persons are able to hear versified discourse or visualise some beautiful scene associated with this discourse. This discourse is related to their state and to the state of things with which they are concerned. (Maulana Akbarabadi, *Wahye Ilahi,* 'Maqasidul Marasid').

Ibn-i-Maskoya after discussing the state of revelation, brings out this distinction between the philosophers and the Prophets:

Both of them are similar in respect of the cognition of truth. But the philosopher moves from the lower to the higher, whereas the Prophet moves from the higher to the lower. The philosopher achieves knowledge through an ascending movement, but the Prophet achieves it through a descending movement. But the truth in both the cases is one and the same. (*Ali Asghar,* 'Kaifiatul Wahi')

Interpretation of Modern Philosophers

In view of the recognition of the significance of intution by modern philosophers like Burgson some scholars have regarded intution as the source of revelation. On this basis revelation is defined as follows:

Revelation is inspiration which operates, not from without, but from within the being of the Prophet. (Rashid Raza Misri, *Al Wahiul Mohammadi,* Chapter III)

Again it is said

The source of revelation is the self of the Prophet: nothing comes into it from without. The secret world which is regarded as transcending matter and nature is not empirically verifiable in our view. (*Ibid*).

The summary of anicent philosophical interpretations that Abul Baqa has made, with reference to Abi Sina, coincides to a great extent with modern philosophical interpretations. Thus regarding revelations he says:

We perceive things through the medium of the senses and the Prophet perceives them through the medium of inner faculties. We perceive before we know; the Prophet knows before he perceives. (Shibli, *Alkalam,* p. 176)

The Interpretation of Razi

Here is a summary of the interpretations of the scholastics by Razi:

The Apostle of God is the most perfect of the perfect ones and he is the most superior too. He comes in the last phase of human evolution. It has been established that the end of every lower creature is the beginning of a higher creature. Since the end of man is the beginning of the angel the apostle of God is possessed of all the qualities and characteristics of the angel. For example he is not much preoccupied with bodily concerns. In his spiritual state he achieves ecstasy and transport, which makes his insight so perfect that he is able to receive Divine Manifestation and gnosis, and his power of action is so effective that he is able to manipulate evidence in the physical world. This is what we mean by miracles. (*Matalibul 'Aalia,* 'Al Muqadmatul Khamisa)

The Interpretation of Ghazali

Regarding the features of Prophethood Ghazali says:

Prophethood had three features. One of them is under the influence of imagination, the other under that of intellect and the third under that of empirical intelligence. (*M'arijul Quds,* MS Maulana Azad Library, A.M.U., Aligarh)

He goes on to describe the function of the imagination and says:

The imagination performs the same function as it does in the state of sleep. It picks up certain evidences and formulates them mimetically. It dominates the senses so much that its forms are infused in the common sense. Afterwards various numinous forms appear and numinous discourse is heard, and these things are like revelationary knowledge. However, this state is inferior to Prophetood. The higher state is one in which the forms are so powerfully embodied as to give no chance to the imagination to picturise other things. There is a still higher state in which the imagination is always engaged in mimetic formulation, and in this case, if forms of reason and infancy do not contradict them, the forms of the imagination are preserved in memory. In this case the imagination will have such a powerful influence on the common sense that strange and novel forms will be embodied and every faculty will continue its function in its own way. This is the stage of revelation which is concerned with the intellect and thought. (*Op. Cit.,* 'Khawasul Nabuwwat')

At another place Ghazali says:

This is the distinctive quality of Prophets and Apostles that for them the mute language of reality becomes concrete and articulate, in the same way as for ordinary persons the mute language of reality is concrete and articulate in the state of sleep. These ordinary persons, in that state, hear sound and discourse. For example the dreamer sees the horse and the camel sliding or a dead man giving, holding or snatching something. The Prophets and apostles see such things in the wakeful state, and these things make discourse to them. The difference is that he who is awake cannot discriminate if the discourse is fancy or any objective sensuous reality, whereas the sleeper is able to discriminate it after he is awake. (*Al Maznun bihi 'Ala Ghair Ahlihi,* Section III)

The Interpretation of Shah Waliullah

Shah Walliullah says:

By the will of God the apostle is blessed with such Grace as to be exalted suddenly from common humanity to a state of holiness. After this he takes cognition of transcendental beings, their discourse, the ways of Divine Grace and the revelation of the good in the hearts of the people. All these experiences are then formulated in the form of a Book. (Fuyuzul Haramain, pp. 16-17)

At another place he says:

Revelation is formulated in words, phrases, and style of discourse in accordance with in the mind of the Apostle. Thus for Arabs Allah sent down His revelation in the Arabic language, and for the speakers of Syriac language Allah sent it down in Syriac.

Shah Walliullah has discussed the subject in his Persian Journal *Sat'aat.* He says:

The wisdom of God which seeks to choose a reformer demands that a perfect human being should be made its instrument so that its purpose may be fulfilled. Hence Divine Will is imaged in the nobler part of that perfect individual in the same way as the form of the sun is imaged in a mirror. At such a time the faculties of the heart and the intellect are illuminated by the light of the noble part of the *heart* and many forms of knowledge and will descend upon him.(p.11)

In the above interpretation the speaking self, the imagination, the *heart,* and the nobler part of it have a primary importance. They can be explained by referring to inner powers, intution, inner conscience, inner activity and the developed forms of intellect and *heart.*

The Ancients have Recognised Revelation As Transcendending Reason

In spite of these interpretations the ancients recognize that revelation and Prophethood transcendend reason. Thus Ibn-i-Khaldun says:

Follow the actions and beliefs of the spiritual guide, for he is a greater well-wisher of yours than you are yourself. He knows what is profitable for you, for his knowledge is superior to your knowledge and it is achieved in a way through a mode that transcends your reason. But his intellect is not opposed to reason and common cognition. On the other hand intellect is the right measure for this knowledge. His commandments are certain and free of falsehood but the measure is not such as to enable us to assess monotheism, the affairs of after-life and the truths about Prophethood and divine attributes. Making such an assessment would be impossible desire, for these things are beyond the ways of reason and rational cognition. (*Muqaddema*, Egyptian edition, p. 384)

Ibne Khaldun goes on to speak of the finitude of reason. He says:

The finitude of reason can be understood by an example. Suppose somebody wishes to weigh a mountain by using a balance for weighing silver. (When he is not able to do it) It will not be said that his balance is faulty. On the other hand it will be said that every balance has its functional limits beyond which it can not work. In the same way the balance of reason has also its functional limits, beyond which it ceases to work. Beyond these limits it can not take note of the Attributes and Essence of God. For reason is, after all, one of the particles of existence, one which God bestows on man. By the help of this example you can know the error and lack of intelligence of those people who are out to prefer reason to what is heard or formulated mimetically through revelation. (*Ibid.*)

Ghazali says:

There is a mode of experience transcending reason. In this mode the inner eye is opened and through it the secret and future things are known and also those realities are revealed regarding which reason cannot work... the intellectuals who deny this mode have no basis for doing it. Their denial is due to sheer ignorance. (*Al Munqiz minal Zalal,* Al Qaul fi Khawasul Nabuwwat).

Sheikh Ahmad Sarhindi says:

Just as the mode of reason is superior to the mode of senses, so that that which cannot be known through the senses is known through reason, in the same way the mode of Prophethood is superior to the mode of reason, so that that which can not be known by reason is known through reason. He who does not recognise any mode of experience beyond reason actually denies prophethood and is opposed to revelationary enlightenment. (*Maktubat,* vol. III).

Two Defects in the Above Interpretations

The above interpretations, in spite of their recognition of revelation and prophethood as supra-rational, suffer from two defects:

(1) The distinction between the consciousness of Saintshood (friendship of the Divine) and the consciousness of prophethood is not made clear.

(2) It becomes very difficult to draw a line of distinction between the Quran and the Hadith (Traditions).

Our Scheme of Cultural Reconstruction is Free From These Defects

But according to the view adopted in our scheme of cultural reconstruction the sources and positions of Sainthood and Prophethood are separate and distinct from one another. So the new interpretation does not suffer from the above defects. As pointed out earlier, the seed of Sainthood (Friendship of the Divine) is the *heart* and that of the consciousness of Prophethood is revelation. Revelation is of two kinds, which correspond to these two consciousnesses:

(1) One kind of revelation has its source in the *heart.*
(2) And the other has its source in inspiration.

The first kind is the word of the Prophet (Hadith), which is the product of the intution and inner consciousness of Prophethood. The second kind is the word of God (Quran), which is bestowed by God on the Last Prophet in the last phase of the evolution of humanity. Thus the difference between the consciousness of Sainthood and the consciousness of Prophethood is not merely one of quantity but also one of quality. Failure to understand this has led to various confusions. It has brought down the Quran to the level of Hadith and then the Hadith is denied. In Arabic the word *Wahi* (revelation) is common. Its senses include making gesture, writing, sending messages, communicating secretely and inducing something in the heart. (*Lissanul'Arab; Qamusul Muhit).* Hence the term *Wahi* for both kinds of consciousness.

Answer To A Dobut

According to the above interpretation the source of Hadith is the seat of the *heart.* But it does not detract from the importance and validity of Hadith. For the hearts of the prophets were always full of the light of Prophethood and consciousness of Divine manifestations, and they were always protected from the interference of Satan and lustful self. Thus Ibn-i-Taimiya says:

Anybody who has a comparative experience of the sayings of the Prophet and those of ordinary people has always found the former in the right and the latter in the wrong. Even Razi who excels everybody else in taunting hard non-rational discourse is compelled to make the following observation. He says that he pondered very much over the modes of philosophy and scholasticism but found that none of these heels the spiritually sick or satisfies the thirst of the spiritually thirsty. But the mode of the Quran comes close to doing it. For example in positive terms, there are the verses.

Anybody who goes through an experience similar to mine will realise like me. And anybody who ponders over the sayings of people who have not held on firmly to the sayings and teachings of the Prophet will find them suffering from puzzlement, doubt, loss of way and direction and manifold ignorance. (*Risail Ibn-i-Taimiya: Risala Al Furgan*, pub. in Egypt, p. 109)

Revelation is Superior Both to reason and Heart

In our scheme of cultural reconstruction revelation is superior both to reason and *heart*. Revelation does not necessarily deal with every fact; it also allows reason to fulfil its responsibility in its own sphere. The trouble arises when we regard only of one them as the sole guide. In that case neither transcendental sensibility emerges nor man is able to find his own right place. As gnostics observe:

The shariah does not necessarily deal with every fact. What it has rejected is really negative, and what it has affirmed is positively true. What it is silent about is of an ambiguous status. He who dispells the ambiguity and points to a direction will not be opposed to the shariah. Beware and take heed. (*Abqat*, 'Abqa' IV)

It would not be irrelevant to point out that the three modes of knowledge, reason *heart* and revelation do not contradict one another, as some people think. In fact contradictions appear due to internal and external pressures (obscuring veils and circumstances). They appear in those persons who are not protected against these pressures. But in those who are there is never any contradiction. As Shah Ismail Shahid puts it:

If all the three modes are secured against the disturbing factors in knowledge there is no question of contradiction among these modes. ("*Abqa*" II)

Only those who have perfect temperance in inner and outer life are protected against internal and external pressures. Such protection is the speciality of the prophets—

But the protection is the speciality of the prophets, who are protected from the cradle to the grave. (*Ibid*)

No Transcendental Absolute in Western Culture

Western culture does not recognise the existence of anything beyond matter, so in it there is no question of anything beyond matter, so in it there is no question of the transcendental absolute and man's relation to it. The materialists says: "the secret world which in the opinion of some people lies beyond matter and nature has no proof of its existence in our opinion. (Rashid Raza Misri, *Al Wahiul Mohammadi,* Chapter III)

In the Scheme of Cultural Reconstruction the Source of the Spirit is Transcendental

In our scheme of cultural reconstruction there is always existed a window called "Spirit" for taking flight into the world of transcendents. The source of the spirit is the transcendental absolute. The satisfaction of its need is not possible without the establishment of relation to the source. The Quran says:

When I have fashioned him
(in due proportion) and breathed
Into him of My spirit,
Fall ye down in obeisance
Unto him. (XV-29)

Again it is said:

But He fashioned him
In due proportion, and breathed
Into him something of
His spirit (XXII-9)

When the Holy Prophet was asked about nature of the spirit, the following Verse was revealed:

They asked thee concerning
The Spirit (of inspiration).
Say: "the Spirit (cometh)
By Command of my Lord:
Of knowledge it is only
A little that is communicated
To you, (O men!)" (XVII-85)

Ghazali has interpreted Command of Lord as follows:

It is a Divine and wonderful command. Reason is helpless with regard to understanding its reality. (*Ahya*, Part III, Al Lafz Thani)

At another place he says:

"The World of the Command means the existants which are beyond senses, thought, dimension, space and time." (*Halli Masaili Ghamiza*, p.29, MS)

Ibne Qayyam says:

By command is meant the Agency of Command. In the Arabic language and in the Quran this implied sense frequently occurs. (*Kitabul Ruh*, Zikrul Ikhtilaf fi M'anal Ruh)

Some Sayings Regarding the Reality of the Spirit

There are about 20 sayings of physicians, philosophers, mystics and scholastics with regard to reality of the spirit. Some of these sayings are given here.

Ghazali equates the spirit with the Essence. He says: "It is an essence and not an accident."[40] At another place he speaks more elaborately:

The essence is such as to be free of matter, magnitude, dimension and space. It is the power of the knowledge of things. It partakes of the Attributes of God. Its operation in the microcosm is similar to that of the operation of the Essence of God in the macrocosm.[41]

Ibne Qayyam calls it 'the etherial body'. He says: "it is an etherial and rarefied body which is alive and dynamic and which pervades the very essence of physical organs. (*Kitabul Ruh,* 'Al Qaulul Sawab fi Haqiqatil Ruh', p.220)

Two Kinds of the Spirit According to Shah Waliullah:

According to Shah Waliullah[42] Spirit is of two kinds:

(1) the airy spirit and (2) the holy spirit. Regarding the airy spirit he says: "in the body there is a rarefied vapour which is produced in the heart due to purification'. Regarding the holy spirit he says: "It is a niche towards the numinous world." The airy spirit has relation to the body,;the body is, as it were "the vehicle of the airy spirit." The holy spirit has relation to the airy spirit: "the airy spirit is the carriage of the real or (Holly) spirit". The Holy spirit is not without relation to the human body: "The primary relation of the Holy spirit is to the airy spirit and its secondary relation is to the body'.

The airy spirit partakes of the material and the transcendental or the animal and the angelic—

"That which tends towards the Holy Secret is angelic and that which tends towards the earth is animalistic."

But the holy spirit is transcendental and angelic throughout. Through its agency transcendental relatives are revealed—"through the Holy spirit all those (transcendental) realities are revealed to the airy spirit, for the revelation of which it has proper capability.

The Human Spirit has an Element of the Transcendental

From the above observations it is evident that in the constitution of the human spirit both the airy and the Holy elements take part. This is supported by the above Verses of the Quran which answer the question about nature of the Spirit: (XVII-85) it means that for the human spirit there is some element of the transcendental (which has been called "the holy spirit") or the Command of the Lord. For the understanding of this transcendental elements our equipment of knowledge is insufficient. of knowledge it is only a little that is communicated to you (O men!)" (XVII-85)

The word *'Min* (by) in XVII-85 refers to 'some part'. But by seeing it like this no flaw occurs in the sense. *As Ruhul M'aani* observes.

"In *Min Amre Rabbi,* the word *Min* has the sense of 'some'. Some scholars see it as an article having no meaning in itself.

The Treasure House of Transcendental Reality is the Numinous World Which is Beyond Matter

The transcendental reality (the Holy Spirit) has its treasure house in the numinous world which is beyond matter. The Holy Prophet says:

There is a host of spirits. The spirits which have affinity with one another join, and those which do not have it remain separate. (*Muslim,* Kitabul Bir Wal Sila)

This can be explained by an example. The real source of electricity is the power house. From this source electricity is accumulated in the supply station or transformer. From there it is supplied through various wires. In the same way the source of the transcendental reality (the Holy spirit) is the Essence of God but numerous spirits issue from their source and gather in an intermediary place (which is like a supply station). "There is a host of spirits' refers to it). From there they are supplied to various human individuals, as if through some 'wires'.

The Qualities of the Spirit After Receiving the Transcendental

After the transcendental is combined with the human spirit it aquires the following qualities: (1) The spirit becomes like a wise ruler, and the intellect and the *heart* act as ministers. (2) the operation of the spirit in the world of matter is freed from its dependence on physical phenomena. (3) Through the power of certain spirits wonderful things are performed which remain inexplicable in terms of the laws of material world (4) the spirit has a window for flight beyond matter and into the world of transcendence. (5) Relations with the transcendental absolute is established. The firmer this relation becomes the greater is the power which the spirit aquires. Thus the spirits of the prophets are most powerful. (6) Correspondence to Gabriel (the angel of the Holy spirit) is established and the spirit aquires the ability of receiving revelation from its Source.

Certain Hints Towards Evidence

The following Verses hint at these qualities of the spirit:

... for such
He has written Faith
In their hearts, and strengthens
Them with a spirit
From Himself. (LVIII-22)

... and He is
With the wheresoever ye may be (LVII-4)

... for We
Are nearer to him
Than (his) jugular vain (L-16)

Those apostles
We endowed with gifts,
Some above others (II-253)

And thus We,
By Our command, sent
Inspiration to thee (XLII-52)

Say, the Holy Spirit has brought
Revelation from thy Lord
In truth. (XVI-102)

There is a Hadith-i-Qudsi (a saying of the Prophet in which God speaks in the first person) which says:

> The creature (man) whom I created with My own Hands and breathed of My Spirit unto him——I shall never put him on a par with those creatures for whom I said: 'Be!' and they came into being. (*Mishkat*, Babo Badel Khalq)

The Means of the Satisfaction of the Spirit

Western culture is not aware of the combination of the transcendental reality in the human make-up. For this reason it has failed to cater to the spirit and its needs in spite of all its paraphernilia of material conforts. In our scheme of cultural reconstruction the needs of the spirit are satisfied through the remembrance of God and His worship. For in this way the spirit establishes contact with its Divine Source, and imbibes all that it needs from this source. As the Quran says:

... for without doubt
In the remembrance of God
Do the hearts find satisfaction (XVII-28)

The worship of God is the very purpose of the creation of man:

I have only created
Jins and man, that
They may serve Me (LI-56)

The foremost thing that every Prophet did was inviting the community to the worship of God.

... "O my people!
Worship God! ye have
No other God but Him (VII-65)

For We asuredly sent
Amongst every People an apostle,
(with the Commands), "serve
God, and eschew Evil": (XVI-36)

Not an apostle but We
Sent Before thee without

This inspiration sent by Us
To him: that there is
No God but I: therefore
Worship and serve Me (XXI-25)

God regards all people as one people in that all of them have been commanded to worship Him:

Verily, this brotherhood
Of yours is a single brotherhood,
And I am your Lord
And Cherisher: therefore
Serve Me (and no other). (XXI-92)

Then here is the Verse in which man is commanded to worship his Lord till his death:

And serve thy Lord
Until there come unto thee
The Hour that is Certain (XV-99)

Meaning of Worship

The literal meaning of worship in Arabic is the expression of lowliness and humility before God. "Worship is the extreme state of lowliness" (Iman Raghib, *Mufradat*). *Liasanul Arab* defines it as follows:

Worship (*Ibadat*) means obedience' (page 2, 3) .

In Arabic writings there is a saying: "When somebody offers prayer to God, he worships God (Lisanul Arab)" Ibne Taimiya says:

The actual meaning of worship is lowliness. Hence *Muabbad* is the way which has been trodden well. But the worship commanded by God implies both lowliness and love. That is, one should present oneself before God in a state of extreme lowliness and extreme love. (*Risalatul Ubudiya* P. 4)

The technical and doctrinal meaning of worship has been explained by Ibne Taymiya:

Worship is an all inclusive term. it includes all the outward and inward actions and words which please God. *(Op. cit.*, P. 2)

This has been elaborated as follows:

For example prayers, fasting, Zakat, Haj, righteousness, honesty, doing good to kinsfolk, obedience to parents, fulfilment of promise, enjoining the right and forbidding the wrong, jihad (striving or war) against infidles and hypocrites, doing good to neighbours, orphans, the poor, and subordinates, be they human beings or animals, orisons, remembrance of God, reciting the Quran etc—all such good deeds are included in the term "worship". In the same way the love of Allah and his apostle, the hope for Divine Mercy, the fear of punishment from God, the turning of ones being to God, purity of hearts, patience, fortitude, resignation to God and submission to His will etc. — all such virtues too are included in the term worship.

Again it has been said:

The whole religion or the whole way of life is included in the meaning of the term worship.

Some Forms of Prayers Imply States of Mind and Heart

According to the above observations the meaning of worship in the scheme of cultural construction is not limited to any one aspect of life. It encompasses the whole of religion and shariah. But in this total body of worship there are some forms which have the same status as vital organs like brain and the heart have in the totality of the human body. Hence special importance has been given to them, and they form the basis of Islam. The Holy Prophet says:

Islam is based on five pillars: (1) the testimony that there is no deity other than God and that Mohammad is His Apostle: (2) The establishment of prayer (namaz); (3) The giving of zakat (alms); The performance of Haj (the Holy pilgrimage) and (5) fasting in the month of Ramadhan. (*Bukhari; Muslim; Mishkat;* Kitabul Iman)

Just as in the marriage contract acceptance of the two parties is a decision and a convenant implying the duty of the fulfilment of the demands of domestic life, in the same way *Kalma-e-shahadat* (which says there is no deity other than Allah) is an important decision and covenant implying the worship of only one God and submission to Him. It also implies following the commandment of God and His Apostle in other spheres of life.

After such a decision and convenant Namaz, Zakat, Fast and Haj acquire the status of a training course. He who carries it out dutifully has his whole life moulded in the form of worship and submission to the Divine commandment.

Prayer Develops the Sense of Devotion

Prayer plays an important role in developing a sense of devoting towards Allah and His apostle and towards carrying out their commands. For through the various postures of prayer like sitting with folded knees, performing various movements, kneeling, prostration etc. man expresses his sense of being God's servant and of submission to Him, and in the recitation of the Quran, orisons etc. he expresses his sense of entering into a spiritual dialogue with God. The Quran says:

And establish regular prayer
For celebrating My Praise (XXII-14)

Prayer brings man close to his God:

But bow down in adoration,
And bring thyself
The closer (to God)! (XCVI-19)

The essence of prayer is that it checks man from immodest and shameful deeds:

... for prayer
Restrains from shameful
And unjust deeds (XXIX-45)

Prayer is difficult to come but for those who fear God and have faith in meeting Him it comes easy:

It is indeed hard, except

To those who bring a lowly spirit,—
Who bear in mind the certainty
That they are to meet their Lord,
And that they are to return to Him. (II-45-6)

Mohammad (peace be upon him) has defined the state of real prayer as follows:

Worship God as if you were seeing Him. If not so, then as if He was seeing you. (*Bukhari, Muslim, Mishkat,* Kitabul Iman)

Indeed when somebody offers you prayers he enters into a dialogue of whispers with his Lord. (Ibid.)

Still another Hadith says:

Allah's servant is nearest to his Lord when he is in the state of prostration (*Muslim*)

Shah Waliullah says that Namaz comprises of three elements:

(1) There should be a feeling of devotion in the heart at the time of experiencing the glory of God.

(2) Man's tongue should speak of His Glory in the most appropriate and articulate language.

(3) The various parts of the body must correspond in their movement to the feeling of devotion.[43]

Thus prayer not only fulfils the needs of the spirit it also moulds the whole of human life into a particular form, which becomes the basis of the building up of individual and social virtues.

Zakat Purifies One of Base Elements of Nature

Zakat (charity) plays a special role in purifying man of those base elements which become obstructions in the worship of God and in the following of the instructions of the Holy Prophet. For example, through zakat the human self is purified of the lust for money and property, the inordinate love of the world, selfishness and usurpation of the rights of others. Against these base element prayer cultivates virtues like sacrifice, sympathy and considerateness for others. It means that namaz and Zakat both are two positive and negative aspects of the same spiritual training. The former establishes relation with Allah and the latter prevents it from breaking. This is why the Quran juxtaposes namaz and zakat and speaks of them in the same breath. For example:

Those who believe,
and do deeds of righteousness
And establish regular prayer
And regular charity
Will have their rewards
With their Lord: (II-277)

But if they repent,
And establish regular prayers
And practise regular charity
Then open the way for them (IX-5)

But (even so), if they repent
Establish regular prayers,
And practise regular charity,—
They are your brethern in Faith. (IX-11)

Abu Bakr once said:

"By God I will certainly fight with the man who creates discrimination between namaz and zakat". (*Muslim*, Kitabul Iman)

The purpose of prayers is the purification of self, it is purgation of all base elements:

But those most devoted
To God shall be
Removed far from it,—
Those who spend their wealth
For increase in self-purification (XCII. 17-18)

Again it is said:

Of their goods take alms,
That so thou mightest
Purify and sanctify them: (IX-103)

Zakat or alms is the manifestation of love and God:

To spend your substance
Out of love for Him,
For your kin
For orphans,
For the needy
For the wayfarer
For those who ask
And for the ransom of slaves. (II-177)
And they feed, for the love,
Of God, the indigent,
The orphan, and the captive— (LXXVI-8)

Through zakat man is purged of the love of the world which is the root cause of all evils. The Holy Prophet says: "the love of the world is the root cause of all sins. (*Mishkat*, Kitabụl Riqaq) Zakat initiates man into sympathy for the poor and in this way they are provided for. The Holy Prophet says: "Allah has made zakat incumbent on people; it will be taken from the rich and distributed among the poor. (*Op. cit.*, Kitabul Zakat)

Zakat cultivates the feelings of sacrifice and charity:

They ask thee
How much
They are to spend;
Say: "What is beyond
Your needs" (II-219)

By no means shall ye
Attain righteousness unless
Ye give (freely) all that
Which ye love. (III-92)

Shah Waliullah says:

Zakat has two good reasons behind it: (1) the first reason is related to man's individual life, for through zakat the self is purified of the worst evils like miserliness and greed: (2) the second reason is related to man's social life, for through zakat the poor and the needy are provided for and thus Religion flourishes.[44]

Fasting Leads to Essential Piety

Fasting plays a special role in inculcating transcendental qualities and the very essence of piety. Through it man overcomes his selfish desires and cultivates within himself those qualities which correspond to the qualities of God, and in this way through fasting the spirit establishes contact with its Source. The Quran says:

O ye he believe!
Fasting is prescribed to you
As it was prescribed
To those before you,
That ye may (learn)
Self-restraint,— (II-183)
Ramadhan is the (month)
In which was sent down
The Quran (II-185)

According to a Tradition the Holy Prophet has spoken of the virtues of fasting as follows:

The reward of every good deed of man is from ten times to seven hundred times but as regards fasting Allah says: "it is specially for Me. It is for My sake alone that My servant gives up eating and drinking and also his lustful desires. Hence I Mvself will reward fasting infinitely. (*Bukhari, Muslim,* Kitabul Saum)

Some scholars of Hadith have read 'for me' instead of 'for my sake', which means: 'I am myself its reward.' However, it is certain that fasting is such a lofty form of worship that the highest good is of an inferior value when compared to its reward.

In the case of fasting there is a special arrangement for keeping away from carnal involvements and for achieving spiritual purification. Thus the Holy Prophet says: "The month of Ramadhan comes to you. Its fasts were made incumbent on you. In this month the gates of heaven are opened and gates of hell are closed. The feet of the rebellious devils are put in chains. In this month there is a night which is better than the nights of thousand months. He who deprives himself of (the blessings of) this month deprives himself of all good.' (*Ahmad, Nisai, Mishkat,* Kitabul Saum) Another hadith says: 'The month of Ramadhan is the month of patience and fortitude. Its reward is paradise. It is a month of imaginative sympathies'. (*Baihaqi, Mishkat,* Kitabul Saum)

Ghazali speaks of the purpose of fasting as follows:

The purpose of fasting is to invest man with one of the attributes of God, the attribute of Absolute Independence, and, by overcoming selfish desires, to achieve resemblance with the angels, as the angels are free of such desires. (*Ahya,* Vol. I, pp. 3-4)

Ibn-i-Qayyam says:

The purpose of fasting is to prevent the self from indulgance in selfish desires and to take it away from self-pleasing objects and also to establish temperance in matters of worldly desires so that man may be prepared to achieve the beatific end. (*Zadul M'aad,* Vol. II, p. 15)

At another place Ibn-i-Qayyam says:

Fasting protects the health of the heart and the bodily organs, and restores the virtues that have been lost due to following the dictates of worldly desires. (*Ibid.*)

Haj Strengthens Love

Haj plays a special role in strengthening man's love for God and in inducing self-surrender and transport. Through it sympathic links are established with those monuments of love that inspire man to sacrifice everything for the sake of God's Will.

The various rituals of haj form a comprehensive set of worship. They include the essential elements of prayer (namaz) and alms giving (zakat) and fasting. The Quran speaks of Haj:

Pilgrimage thereto is a duty
Men owe to God,—
Those who can afford
The Journey. (III-97)
God made the Ka'ba
The Sacred House, an asylum
Of security for men... (V-100)
And proclaim the Pilgrimage
Among men: they will come
To thee on foot and (mounted)
On every kind of camel,
Lean on account of journeys
Through deep and distant
Mountain highways:
That they may witness
The benefits (provided) for them, (XXI 27-28)

The Holy Prophet said:

The reward for Haj that is accepted (by God) is nothing else than Paradise. (*Bukhari, Muslim,* Kitabul Haj)

Again he said:

He who performs the Pilgrimage of this House (of Allah) and does not commit (in the meantime) any act of lust or sin will come back as innocent and pure as if he was newly born. (*Bukhari,* Kitabul Haj)

During Haj a person is always addressing his Lord as follows: 'My Lord I am at thy service, I am at thy service. None is Thy partner. I am at Thy service. Indeed thine are all praises and gifts. Thine is the Kingdom and glory. And none is Thy partner'.

Ghazali comments as follows:

The eagerness to meet God the Almighty engenders the eagerness to *meet* the Symbols that mediate this meeting. Since the lover holds dear everything associated with the Beloved, and since the Sacred House is associated with the Beloved this association is enough to arouse the eagerness of the lover to visit it, though the promise of bounteous reward for this visit is an additional factor. (*Ahya*, Vol. I, p. 24)

Shah Waliullah observes:

Very often it happens that a man is eager to see his Lord. On such occasions he feels the need of *seeing* something which might appease his eagerness. This eagerness can be appeased only through Haj. (*Hujjatullahil Baligha*, Vol. I, p. 59

It is evident from the above elucidation of the pillars of Islam that they are not only worship but also the matrix of worship. No other form of worship can mould life into worship and bring it in conformity with the teachings of the Holy Prophet to the extent that these Pillars of Islam do.

3 INDIVIDUAL AND PERSONAL LIFE

In our scheme of cultural reconstruction personal character and individual qualities are related to the essential nature of man. They all depend on the concept of the essential nature. The measure of character is determined by this concept.

In Western Culture the Measure of Character is Worldly Gain

In western culture the essential nature of man is regarded as animalistic and therefore the nature of character is determined in terms of material power and worldly gain. Only those qualities are valuable which have a direct bearing on worldly gain and material power. For example in business, honesty, forthrightness, keeping up promise, industry, dutifulness, punctuality, patriotism, social sense, national interest etc. are the criteria.

The qualities which do not have a bearing on worldly gain are not valued. On the other hand violation of these qualities is considered as a merit. But qualities like modesty, chastity, affection and regard, mutual friendship and love, caring for the family, generosity of heart, soft-heartedness, sincerity, humanity and considerateness for the rights of others are of no value.

In the Scheme of Cultural Reconstruction Divine Attributes are the Measure of Character

In our scheme of cultural reconstruction the essential nature of man is numinous. For this reason the measure of character is Divine Attributes, and only those qualities are considered valuable which are a direct reflection of Divine Attributes. The qualities that do not reflect them are discarded.

Two Dimensions of Divine Attributes

Divine Attributes have two dimensions: (1) Through them gnosis of the Essence of God is achieved; and (2) through them the measure of human character is determined.

According to the first dimension Divine Attributes can be divided into three categories: (1) those related to Eternal Beauty; (2) those related to Eternal Power and Glory; and (3) those related to Eternal Perfection. From the first kind of Attributes emanate mercy, compassion and forgiveness, love and affection. From the second kind emanate Greatness, Power and Kingship of God. From the third emanate Good, Uniqueness, perfection etc.

Four Categories of Attributes According to Second Dimension

According to the second dimension of Divine Attributes they can be divided into four categories: (1) Essential, (2) Distinctive, (3) Constructive and (4) Complementary. The first category includes the qualities which go to inculcate the realization of self and the realization of God. Under the second category come those qualities which distinguished man's nature from that of the animal. The third category comprises the qualities which go to manifest man's nature and dignity and his superiority and power and kingship. The fourth category includes the qualities which distinguish the nature of man from that of the angels.

It need not be told that for the determination of the measure of character it is sufficient to have a cumulative image or cumulative image or reflection of the Divine Attributes; it is not necessary for every Attributes to be imaged in its full form. Similarly having the image of God in man does not imply having a partner to God, nor does it imply the dissolution of the human individuality. The Divine Attributes according to the second dimension are discussed as follows:

Essential Attributes

Under the category of essential attributes those qualities are manifested which are exclusive to the Essence of God. For example *Alahad:* the One and Only; *Alwahid:* One; *AlSamad:* Eternally and Absolutely Independent of Everything; Alquoldoos; Absolutely Holy; *Alhai:* Eternally Living; *AlQadeen:* That Which Has Always Existed; *AlDaim:* Ever Lasting; *AlAwwal:* The Absolutely First; *AlAkhir:* The Last Which Endures After Everything Else Perishes; *Alwitr:* The Odd, Which Has No Match, etc.

Distinctive Attributes

Under the category of distinctive attributes are manifested those qualities which are related to beauty. For example *AlRaheem, AlAleem:* the Merciful, the Knower; *AlWahhab, AlGhaffar:* The Bestower of Infinite Bountees, Most Forgiving: *AlSalam, AlMomin:* The Source of Peace (and Perfection), The Guardian of Faith; *AlBari, AlMussawwir: The Evolver, The Bestower of Forms. AlRazzaq, AlFAttah: Sustainer, The Resolver; AlBasit, Alrafe' The Expander, The Exalter; AlLateef, AlKhabeer;* One Who understands the Finest Mysteries, The All-acquainted; *AlMoiz, AlHafeez:* Giver of Power and Honour, Giver of Protection; *AlWajid, AlMoqeet:* One Who Receives, One Who Provides Sustenance; *AlHaseeb, AlMoqsit;* One Who Calls to Account, One Who Dispenses Justice; *AlHaleem, A Kareem :* The Meek One, The Generous One; *AlWakeel, AlHameed:* The Best Dispenser of Affairs, The Most Worthy of Praise; *AlMudda, AlMoeed:* One Who Brings things Into Existence, One Who Causes things to Return; *AlMohi, AlMomeet:* Giver Of Life, Sender of Death; *AlMunim, AlMohib:* One Who Gives Rewards, One Who Loves; *AlRaoof,* AlBar, Aljameel: Most Kind, Most Good, Most Beautiful; AlMughni, AlMo'ti: Who Frees from Need, Who Bestows; *AlNafe', AlHadi:* Giver of Benefits, Giver of Guidance; *AlBadi', AlRasheed:* One Who Devises, One Who Moves along the Straight Path, *AlMojeeb, AlKafeel:* One Who accepts, One Who Provides For; *AlHannan, AlMannan:* Most Affectionate, The Greatest Doer of Good; *AlKamil-AlJawwad:* The Absolutely

Perfect, The Most Generous; *AlKafix, AlShafi:* One Who is All-Sufficient, One Who Heals; *AlWadood, Al-Shakoor:* The Greatest Lover, The Greatest Acknowledger; *AlWali, AlTawwab:* The Greatest Friend, Approver of Repentence; *AlNaseer, AlMoghees; AlMojeer:* The Greatest Helper, One who Listens to Cries of Help, One Who Gives Shelter, ZulTaul ZulFazl: One Who Has Long Reach, Bounteous.

Constructive Attributes

Amongst constructive Attributes those qualities are imaged which belong to *ÀlQabiz, Alkhafis:* One Who Covers, One Who Spreads; *Alwase', AlMomeet, AlMoeed:* One Who Spreads Infinitely, One Who Sends Death, One Who Causes Things to Return; *AlMozil, AlRaqeeb:* One Who Lays Low, One Who keeps Watch; *AlQavi, AlMateen;* AlShaheed: The Powerful, The Firm, The All-Acquainted; *AlMuntaqim, ZulJalal Wal Ikram;* The Avenger of Wrongs, The Possessor of Glory and Power and Greatness; *Al-Ma'ne', AlDhar;* One Who Prevents, One Who Dispenses Losses and Adversity; *AlSuboor, AlBaseer:* The Most Patient, The Greatest Seer; *Al'Moazzib, AlDayyan:* Dispenser of Punishments, The Judge *ZulBatsh Shadeedul Iqab:* The Most Powerful in Catching and The Giver of the Greatest Punishment.

The Complementary Attributes

Among complementary attributes the qualities related to Divine Perfection are reflected. For Example *AlRab, AlRahman;* The Lord and Sustainer, The Beneficient, *AlKhaliq, Al'Adil, AlHakim;* The Creator, the Justicer the Wise; *AlSamee', AlBaseer, AlQayyum:* One Who Listens, One Who Sees, One Who Holds Up; *AlTahir, WalBatin,* The Manifest, and The Hidden; *AlMajid, AlJame', AlBa'is:* The Glorious One, The Greatest Gatherer, One Who Causes everything; *Al-Moheet, AlMoreed, Al-Qareeb:* The All-Encompassing, One Who Wills Absolutely, One Who is Absolutely Close; *AlAli, AlRafi, AlJalil, AlKaleem;* The Exalted, the High, The Glorious, The Noble; *AlModabbir, AlMotakallim:* One Who Plans, One Who Speaks; *Malikal Mulk:* The Sovereign of All the Worlds; *Allamul Ghoyub:* The Knower of Secret Things; *Aleemo Bizzatis Sudoor:* The Knower of the Secrets of the Hearts; *Laisa Kamislehi Shaian:* There Is None Like Him.

Among the above Divine Attributes there are some which over-lap one another; but it makes no difference in respect of their reflection or imaging in man.

Virtues Emanating From Essential Attributes

The following virtues emanate from the Essential Attributes of God:

(1) Self-Respect

Owing to self-respect man is able to rise above objection and lowliness. Once he is lifted to the state of self-respect he does not bow before any worldly power or greatness. He belives that the greatest agents of power and the greatest dispensers of profit and loss themselves depend on Almighty God. The Quran says.

... that to God
Belongs all power (II-165)

... the Command
Rests with none but God (VI-57)

Verily those whom ye
Call upon besides God
Are servants like unto you (VII-194)

No aid can they give them,
Nor can they aid themselves! (VII-192)

There is no help
Except from God,
The Exalted, the Wise (III-126)

To Him belongs the Keys
Of the heavens and the earth (XLII-12)

If God do touch thee
With hurt there is none
Can remove it but He:
If He had designed some benefit
For thee, there is none
Can keep back His favour: (X-107)

(2) Comprehensive Outlook

From the Essential Attributes is derived a comprehensive outlook. By virtue of this outlook a man is able to transcendend personal, communal and national limitations so as to have his being spread over the whole universe. In all his attitudes, in his friendship and animity, his love and hatred, his regard and disregard he achieves a universal standard. Everything in the universe belongs to him simply because it belongs to his God. The Quran says:

... *While all creatures*
In the heavens and on earth
Have, willing or unwilling
Bowed to His Will
(Accepted Islam),
And to Him shall they
All be brought back. (III-83)

O mankind, we created
You from a single (pair)
Of a male and a female,
And made you into
Nations and tribes, that
Ye may know each other
(not that ye may despise

Each other). Verily
The most honoured of you
In the sight of God
Is (he who is) the most
Righteous of you.
And God has full knowledge
And is well aquainted
(with all things) (XLIX-13)

It is He Who hath created for you
All things that are on earth: (II-29)

Mohammad (peace be upon him) said: All human beings are brothers to one another. (*Muslim, Abu Daud*) At another place he said: Undoubtedly the earth belongs to God and human beings are servants of God. (*Abu Daud, Nasbul Raya*) On one occasion Ali said: Their goods (the goods of other human beings) are like our goods and their lives are like our lives. (Nasbul Raya, Vol. III, Kitabul Sair)

(3) Peace of Heart

Another virtue is peace of heart. Owing to this virtue a man does not give way to despair, even if circumstances go against him. God is always with him. This is such an invaluable virtue that all efforts of intellect and philosophy fail to achieve it. All the advancement of western civilization and all its material equipment cannot equal it in value. The Quran says:

When My servants
Ask thee concerning Me,
I am Indeed
Close (to them): I listen
To the prayer of every

Suppliant when he calleth on Me:
Let them also, with a will,
Listen to My call,
And believe in Me:
That they may walk
In the right way (II-186)

Say: "O My Servants who
Have transgressed against their souls
Despair not of the Mercy
Of God: for God forgives
All sins: for he is
Oft-forgiving, Most Merciful (XXXIX-53)

... and never
Give up hope of God's
Soothing Mercy: Truly
None despair of God's
Soothing Mercy, Except
Those who have no faith (XII-87)

(4) Patience and Fortitude

Through this virtue a man's heart becomes strong and he sees the power of God with him. He learns to bear afflictions. The Quran says:

Nay seek (God's) help
With patient perseverance
And prayer: (II-45)

... For God is with those
Who patiently perceivier (II-153)

And We appointed, from among
They, leaders,
Under Our command, so long
As they persevere with patient. (XXXII-24)

On one occasion the Holy Prophet said: 'Patient perseverence is the commander of his (somebody's) army'. Ali has brought out the psychological aspect of patience as follows:

Patience has the same relation to (the body of faith) as the head to the human body. Just as on severing the head the body becomes useless and dead, in the same way the man who has lost patience cannot attain the faith. (Ibn-i-Abi Shaibah, *Musannaf; Baihaqi*)

(5) Contentment

Owing to this virtue base emotions like lust and greed and jealousy are got rid of. For achieving benefit and avoiding harm a man abstains from adopting a method which may injure self-dignity and self-respect, for he knows that the ends of all things are in the hands of God. The Quran says:

... All bounties
Are in the hand of God.
He granteth them
To whom he pleaseth:
And God careth for all,
And He knoweth all things (III-73)

For the earth is God's
To give as a heritage

To such of His servants
As He pleaseth: (VII-128)

Thou enduest with honour
Whom Thou pleasest:
And Thou bringest Low
Whom Thou Pleasest:
In Thy hand is all Good.
Verily, over all things
Thou hast power (III-26)

(6) Humility

Owing to the virtue of humility self-respect is created, and the self-respect so created does not lead to any pride. One the other hand a man always feels himself humble and low before the power of the Almighty. The Quran says:

He is the Irrestible, (watching)
From above over his worshippers (VI-61)

But God is free of all wants
And it is ye that are needy. (XLVII-38)

And the servants of (God)
Most Gracious are those
Who walk on the earth
In humility, and when the ignorant
Addressed them, they say,
"Peace!" (XXV-63)

(7) Resignation

Through this virtue a man does not continue to have real trust in material means. His trust is established only in God. The Quran says:

The parable of those who
Take Protectors other than God
Is that of the Spider,
Who builds (to itself)
A house: but truly
The flimsilst of houses
Is the Spider's house :— (XXIX-41)

If God helps you,
None can overcome you: (III-160)

... whoever
Rejects evil and believes
In God hath grasped
The most trustworthy
Underhold, that never breaks. (II-256)

(8) Hope and Fear

Through these virtues man becomes fearless and independent of everything except God. Only with God he establishes a relation of hope and fear. In this way his life aquires a centrality and his conviction aquires a force. This attitudes makes for success and well being. We can quote the following Verses from the Quran:

(God) who begets no son
And has no partner
In (His) dominion: (XVII-111)

Who is there can intercede
In His presence except
As He permitteth? (II-255)

God forgiveth not
(The sin of) joining other gods
With Him: but He forgiveth
Whom He pleaseth other sins
Than this. (IV-116)

Do no mischief on the earth,
After it hath been
Set in order, but call
On Him with fear
And longing (in your hearts): (VII-56)

It is a strange fact in history that when the intellectuals of Greece wanted to break the yoke of their tyrinnical rulers they encouraged polytheism. They came forward with the idea that just as the universe is not ruled by one God in the same way government on earth should not be the sole monopoly of one person. The idea worked with the Greeks; they were able to dethrone their ruler from his position of autocracy.

Similarly the philosophy of history ascribes the real greatness of the Romans to two things: (1) Limited resources for the needs of life and (2) The force of Conviction, because of which an individual sacrifices his life, property, family and everything for the sake of some conviction.

(9) Bravery

This virtue inculcates realistic outlook and self-confidence in a man. He stops relying on false trust and hope and does not hesitate in making the greatest sacrifice for the sake of achieving his goal or ideal. The following Verses of the Quran throw light on the subject:

That man can have nothing
But what he strives for: (LIII-39)

And say: "work (righteousness):
Soon will God observe your work,
And His Apostle, and the Believers" (IX-105)

That (the fruit of) his striving
Will soon come in sight;
Then will he be rewarded
With a reward; (LIII-40-1)

God hath purchased of the Believers
Their persons and their goods;
For theirs (in return)
Is the garden (of Paradise):
They fight in His Cause,
And slay and are slain: (IX-111)

Virtues Emanating from Distinctive Attributes

The virtues that emanate from Distinctive Attributes are of two kinds: (1) Those that are related to the goodness and nobility of personal character; and (2) Those that are related to the well-being of other human beings. The first kind has the following implications:

Truth and Sincerity

The greatest virtue emanating from Distinctive Attributes are truth and sincerity. The Quran says:

And whose word can be
Truer than God's? (IV-87)

God's promise is the truth (IV-122)

Truth is of many kinds: the truth of the tongue, the truth of the heart and the truth of action. The truth of the tongue means that falsehood should not be spoken. The truth of the heart means that what the tongue speaks should be supported by a conviction from the heart. The truth of action means that what is expressed through the tongue and the heart should correspond to action. This last is the perfect form of truth. It is called sincerity. The Quran says:

Only those are Believers
Who have believed in God and His Apostle,
And have never things doubted, but
Have striven with their
Belongings and their persons
In the cause of God:
Such are the sincere ones. (XLIX-15)

Falsehood And Hypocrisy are the Opposites of Truth And Sincerity

Falsehood is the opposite of truth. Falsehood too is of many kinds. There is the falsehood of the tongue, which means speaking lies so that the heart does not go with what is spoken by the tongue. It may even go contrary to it and what is spoken may not be translated into action, rather the action may be contrary to what is spoken. This is called hypocrisy:

And invoke the curse
Of God on those who lie! (III-61)

... they solemnly
Invoke the curse of God
On themselves if they
Tell a lie. (XXIV-7)

To say one thing and to have another thing in the heart is hypocrites: and it is worse than a lie. For this reason the Quran harshly condemns hypocrites:

And God beareth witness
That the Hypocraites are
Indeed liers (LXIII-1)

The hypocrisy say one thing and have another thing in their hearts:

Saying with their lips
What was not in their hearts (III-167)

The hypocrisy say something and do something else:

... because
They broke their Covenant
With God, and because they
Lied (again and again). (I-77)

Once the Holy Prophet was asked if a Believer can be a coward. He said: 'Yes'. Then he was asked if a believer can be a miser. He said: 'Yes' and then he was asked if a believer can be a lier. He said: 'No' (*Moatta Iman Malik,* Chapter 'Majae Fil Sidqi Wal Kizb')

There are other forms of falsehood. For example: simultation; speaking falsehood for the sake of amusement; propagating mere hearsay. The Quran says:

And pursue not that
Of which thou hast no knowledge;

For every act of hearing
Or of seeing
Or of (feeling in) the heart
Will be enquired into
(On the Day of Reckoning). (XVII-36)

The Holy Prophet once said:

This is enough of a lie for a man if he goes reporting what he has merely heard. (*Mishkat; Muslim; Preface*)

Charity:

Charity or generosity means doing the utmost good to others. It has many forms. For example:

(1) Foregoing one's right.
(2) Giving priority to the needs of others over one's own needs.
(3) Deploying one's goods. energy and intellect for the well being of others.
(4) Undergoing loss for the sake of the benefit of others.
(5) Sacrificing one's self interest for the sake of the survival of others.

Without charity there can be neither sympathy nor love, which are of the very essence of humanity. Nor can there be any perfection of virtue,. which is the emballishment of humanity. This is why the Quran incites on spending out of what one has in the way of God:

O ye who believe!
Spend out of (the bounties)
We have provided for you,
Before the day comes
When no bargaining
(Will avail), nor friendship
Nor intercession.

Those who reject faith—they
Are the wrong doers. (II-254)

By no means shall ye
Attain righteousness unless
Ye give (freely) all that
Which ye love (III-92)

Owing to charity a man gets rid of inordinate love for material wealth, which love is the root cause of many evils:

The Evil One Threatens
You with poverty
And bids you to conduct
Unseemly. God permitteth
You His forgiveness
And bounties.
And God careth for all
And He knoweth all things (II-268)

By virtue of charity a man acquires wisdom. Hence the next Verse in the Quran:

He granteth wisdom
To whom He pleaslth:
And He to whom wisdom
Is granted receiveth
Indeed a benefit overflowing (II-269)

Wisdom is such an invaluable gift of God that it has been mentioned with reference to almost all the Prophets. Defining wisdom Imam Raghib Asfahani says: 'to reach the truth through knowledge and intellect is wisdom.'[2] In Lissanul Arab we have the following definition: "to attain knowledge of higher values through higher sciences is wisdom."

Ibne Maskoya lists the following features of the wisdom: "Sharpness of mind; power of understanding; clear headedness; intellectual acumen; aptitude for learning etc. He says : 'through these qualities the power capacity for wisdom is constituted'.[3] Exegetes have given various interpretations of wisdom which can be summarised as follows:

> Wisdom is a kind of power through which the knowledge of realities is attained, as also the ability to order experience. Furthermore after attaining wisdom a man's attention is focussed on the cultivation of moral sense and he directs his attitude towards this Holy task.[4]

The Quran states an extremely high standard of charity. For example it prescribes that (1) no useless thing should be given to the other person, none that the giver would not like to have for himself; (2) that after giving something no benefit should be obtained in return; (3) that the receiver of obligation should not be put to any uneasiness or trouble; (4) the receiver should not be taunted with the mentioning of obligation; (5) the receiver should not be made small by the reminders of obligation; (6) recompense should not be expected:

O ye who believe!
Give of the good things
Which ye have (honourably) earned
And of the fruits of the earth
Which We have produced
For you, and do not even aim
At getting anything
Which is bad, in order that
Out of it ye may give away
Something when ye yourselves
Would not receive it
Except with closed eyes (II-267)

O ye who believe!
Cancel not your charity

By reminders of your genorosity
Or by injury. (II-264)

Those who spend
Their substance in the cause
Of God, and follow not up
Their gifts with reminders
Of their genorisity
Or with injury,—for them
Their reward is with their Lord: (II-262)

Usually there are two considerations which hinder charity or genorisity: (1) Why should one give away one's things to others? (2) By giving away things to others one would suffer from scarcity and therefore it would cause trouble. The Quran repudiates the first consideration by proclaiming that Allah is the owner of everything. Man is only a trustee and the trustee is bound to the wishes of the owner in making use of the trusted goods. The second consideration is repudiated by the idea that scarcity and bounty, comfort and discomfort, are all in the power of Allah. His servant depends on him in every conditions:

And what cause have ye
Why ye should not spend
In the cause of God?
For to God belongs
The Heritage of the heavens and the earth. (LVII—10)

And spend (in charity) out of the (substance)
Whereof He has made you
Heirs. (LVII—7)

To him belong the keys
Of the heavens and the earth:

He enlarges and restricts
The Substance to whom
He will: for He knows
Full well all things. (XLII-12)

The Opposite of Charity or Genorisity is Miserliness

The Opposite of charity or genorisity is miserliness which is the source of many evils and discourtesies. For example: greed, lust, dishonesty, ingratitude, cruelty, hard-heartedness, narrow mindedness, timidity, unfair dealings, selfishness etc. This is why the Quran condemns it harshly and dwells on its evils:

and there are those
Who bury gold and silver
And spend it not in the Way
Of God: announce unto them
A most grievous penalty—
On the Day when heat
Will be produced out of
That (wealth) in the fire
Of Hell, and with it will be
Branded their foreheads,
Their flanks, and their backs,
—"This is the (treasures) which ye
Buried for yourselves: taste ye
Then, (treasures) ye buried!" (IX—34-5)
By no means! for it would be
The fire of hell!—
Plucking out (his being)
Right to the skull!—
Inviting (all) such

As turn their backs
And turn away their faces
(From the Right) (LXX—15-18)

Seest thou one
Who denies the Judgement
(To come)?
Then such is the (man)
Who repulses the orphan
(With harshness), and encourages not
The feeding of the indigent. (CVII—1-3)

Who pileth up wealth
And layeth it by
Thinking that his wealth
Would make him last
For ever!
By no means! he will
Be sure to be thrown into
That which Breaks the Pieces. (CIV—1-4)

Nay Nay! but ye
Honour not the orphan!
Nor do ye encourage
One another
To feed the poor!—
And ye devour inheritance—
All will greed,
And ye love wealth
with inordinate love! (LXXX IX—17-20)

For God loveth not
The arrogant, the vainglorious,
(Nor) those who are niggardly
Or enjoin niggardliness on others,
Or hide the bounties
Which God bestowed
On them, (IV—36-7)

The harm of miserliness or niggardliness is not restricted to an individual or a few individuals only; it encompasses the whole society. For this reason very often it happens that the increase of miserliness destroys faith and degrades the whole society:

Behold, ye are those
Invited to spend
(Of your substance)
In the Way of God:
But among you are some
That are niggardly. But any
Who are niggardly are so
At the expense of
Their own souls.
But God is free
Of all wants,
And it is ye that are needy
If ye turn back
(From the Path) He will
Substitute in your stead
Another people; then they
Would not be like you! (XLVII-38)

According to one of the Quranic Verses the consequence of niggardliness is hypocrisy which destroys faith:

So He hath put as a consequence
Hypocris into their hearts,
(To last) till the Day Whereon
They shall meet Him: (IX-77)

And spend of your substance
In the course of God,
And make not your own hands
Contribute to (your) destruction; (II-195)

For all these reasons Mohammad (peace be upon him) has always prayed for refuge against niggardliness. He says: "I seek refuge with God against niggardliness." It would not be irrelevant to mention that niggardliness is not found only in matters of wealth or goods: it applies to knowledge and power as well as to material wealth. Whatever God has bestowed upon man is meant for giving away to othrers, and the question of niggardliness arises in relation to every gift of God. One who is niggardly of knowledge and power also deserves punishment from God.

Chastity

Chastity is the soul of all virture and the very essence of humanity. It enlightens one's life and makes for the distinction between man and animal. In Western civilization the measure of character is worldly benefit and therefore chastity is not very much valued, nor does anybody bother to protect it and keep it up. But in the Islamic scheme of cultural reconstruction the measure of character is Divine Attributes. So the virture of charity aquires a great salience and special attention is given to its protection and maintenance. Chastity is the integral part of Prophethood. It is the distinctive characteristic of the family of the Holy Prophet and of the saints and the godly. In the Quranic Verse there is the evidence of the wife of the Governor of Egypt in favour of Joseph:

I did seek to seduce him
From his (true) self but he did
Firmly save himself
Guitness!... (XII-32)

Earlier it has been said of Joseph:

... thus
(Did We order) that We
Might turn away from him
(All evil and shameful deeds:
For he was one of Our servants,
Sincere and purified. (XII-24)

Regarding Yahya the Quran say:

... and (be
Besides) noble, chaste,
And a Prophet,—
Of the (godly) company
And the righteous (III-39)

After mentioning the stories of many other Prophets. The Quran Quran says:

They were, in Our sight,
Truly, of the company
Of the Elect and the Good. (XXXVII-47)

Regarding the members of the family of the Holy Prophet the Quran observes:

These are not affected
By what people say (XXIV-26)

Regarding the Saints and the godly the Quran says:

Those who invoke not,
With God, any other god,
Nor slay such life as God
Has made sacred, except
For just cause, nor commit
Fornication; (XXV-68)

There is very strict punishment for one who falsely accuses somebody of fornication, which implies the special importance of chastity:

And those who launch
A charge against the chaste women,
And produce not four witnesses
(To support their allegation),—
Flog them with eighty stripes;
And reject their evidence
Ever after: for such men
Are wicked transgressors;— (XX IV-4)

Lewdness is the Opposite of Chastity

Although the word 'lewdness' covers all kinds of evils, but it is mostly used for shamelessness and promiscuity (or adultery)—the Quran says:

If any of your women
Are guilty of lewdness, (IV-15)

... except
Where they have been guilty
Of open lewdness: (IV-19)

Encouragement of Lewdness in Western Civilization

Western Civilization has a paraphernelia which serves to deprive man of chastity and to encourage in him lewdness both on the level of thought and action. On the level of thought there are "isms" which condemn the suppression or concealment of sex desires. Then there is a hedonistic philosophy which says that man is as free to gratify his desires of sex as he is to gratify his desire for water; any interference in this matter is deemed as an interference in personal or private matters. On the level of action there are nude pictures of women, parties of dance and music, free mix up of sex, night clubs, blue films, dresses exposing or involving nakedness, exhibition of beauty and even beauty contests, dances charged with sexuality, sexy music and art, different types of female friends, for example, girl freind, call girl, company girl, party girl etc.

Encoragement of Chastity in the Scheme of Cultural Reconstruction

In our scheme of cultural reconstruction arrangements are made to prevent lewdness and to encourage chastity. Hence all things that directly or indirectly lead to lewdness have been rejected and disapproved of. For example the human eye takes precedence in conveying messages of lewdness and therefore a check is put on the aberration of the eyes. The Quran says:

Say to the believing men
That they should lower
Their gaze and guard
Their modesty: that will make
For greater purity for them:

And God is well aquainted
With all that they do. (XXIV-30)

They slight carelessness and forwardness on the part of women may create misunderstanding in a man and may encourage them to take liberties with them. For this reason special checks are put on women. The Quran says:

And say to the believing women
That they should lower
Their gaze and guard
Their modesty: that they
should not display their
beauty and ornaments except
What (must ordinarily) appear
Thereof; and they should
Draw their veils over
Their bosoms ... (XXIV-31)

O Prophet! tell
Thy wives and daughters,
And the believing women,
That they should cast
Their outer garment over
Their persons (when abroad):
That is most convenient,
That they should be known
(as such) and not molested. (XXXIII-51)

In the Traditions there are various instructions regarding keeping away from lewdness and maintaining chastity. Once the daughter of Abu Bakr, Asma, came into the presence of the Holy

Prophet wearing a very thin piece of clothing. The Holy Prophet said:

Asma, when a girl attains puberty, it is not decent to look at any part of her body except her face and palms. (*Abu Daud, Mishkat: Kitabul Libas*)

As regards looking at women, the Holy Prophet said:

After the first glance, which is accidental, do not cast another glance. The first glance is alright for you but the second glance is not so. (*Tirmizi*, Kitabul Istizan, Bab 'Maja-afi Nazratil Fuja-ah)

It means that if one happens to cast a glance on a woman, he must not cast the glance the second time. Jarir b. Abdullah said: 'I asked the Holy Prophet regarding the casting of accidental glance. He instructed that one should turn away one's glance'.

Extreme Care Commanded

Besides this there is prohibition against all those things that interfere with the maintenance of chastity—improper dresses and manners, immodesty of behaviour, use of perfumes, exhibition of body or dress or ornaments.

In Western Culture there are No Strict Laws Against Lewdness

One way of depriving man from chastity and encouraging lewdness in him is to have leniency in laws and punishment regarding lewdness. In Western culture lewdness is divided into "with consent" and "without consent" and thus rape is regarded as a form of amusement. But even in the case of the evidence of an assault on woman there is no very severe punishment, such as may set an example for the society and bring correction in it.

At first the freedom of the West in these matters looked very commandable, particularly when it was seen as non-interference in personal matters. But when things went too far and the violation of chastity became common and open proposals like the following came up: "the habitual sex criminals, should be castarated through surgery instead of being kept in prison for years and years." (*London,* 14 April, quoted by *Sidq-e-Jadid,* 30 April 1965). In 1965 Mary Stock, an eminent

British Gynaecologist, proposed that such a law should be promulgated. It exists in Denmark where sex crimes have very much decreased, she said.

Severe Punishment in the Scheme of Cultural Reconstruction

In the scheme of cultural reconstruction the crime of lewdness is punished very severely and there are very strict laws against it. Thus, on the one hand, criminals get their due and on the other the whole society learns a lesson. For example, for women with whom adultery is a first offence the following punishment has been prescribed:

If any of your women
Are guilty of lewdness,
Take the evidence of four
(Reliable) witnesses from amongst you
Against them; and if they testify,
Confine them to houses until
Death do claim them,
Or God ordain for them
Some (other) way. (IV-15)

This commandment applies to the situation of first offence. The last phrase of the Verse has the same implication otherwise strictures against this crime would have been mentioned at one place. For men the punishment is prescribed as follows:

If two men among you
Are guilty of lewdness,
Punish them both.
If they repent and amend,
Leave them alone; (IV-16)

Corporeal Punishment for men and imprisonment for women are prescribed probably in view of the physical weakness of the latter. Another reason for the punishment of imprisonment in the case of women is that their immodesty creates greater mischief and therefore by shutting them up this mischief can be prevented. These punishments cover all forms of lewdness and promiscuity, be they hetero-sexual or homosexual. Regarding the next phase of the crime of lewdness. which is one of hardened criminality, the following punishment is prescribed for both the man and the woman guilty of lewdness:

The woman and the man
Guilty of adultery or fornication,—
Flog each of them
With a hundred stripes:
Let not compassion move you
In their case, in a matter
Prescribed by God, if ye believe
In God and the Last Day:
And let a party
Of the Believers
Witness their punishment. (XX IV-2)

Punishment For Marital Lewdness

The above punishment was meant for unmarried persons. For married persons guilty of lewdness the Holy Prophet has ordained stoning to death. Thus a Tradition says:

A man called Ma'iz came to the Holy Prophet and confessed his adultery four times. The Holy Prophet gave orders for the stoning of the man to death (*Abu Daud; Mishkat*). The punishment for lewdness is very severe. This is why there are very strict conditions laid down for the establishment of the crime. These details are found in books of Islamic Jurisprudence.

Punishment Like Bitter Medicine

To modern civilised man these punishments appear not only severe but savage. It is because he is not very much aware of the value of chastity and the bad influences of lewdness on society, when in his society he sees lewdness being encouraged. The culture having this awareness would make severeness of punishment in such matters inevitable. In that case severeness of punishment would be considered like some bitter medicine necessary for the health of the society.

Western Culture Not Aware of the Monstrosity of Lewdness

In fact Western culture lacks the awareness of the monstrosity of the offence of lewdness. It is for this reason that it does not feel need of having strict laws against it, laws that may prescribe very severe punishments. If the awareness had been there, western society would not have hesitated in prescribing such punishments against this offence, punishments similar to those it prescribes for offences like treason or spying—in which case the victim is subjected to death by various kinds of torture, electirc shocks and all. If the occurence of sex crimes continues as such and if chastity is commonly violated in western culture, the day is not far off when western society would take recourse to very severe punishment for habitual criminals.

Monstrosity of Lewdness Realised in the Scheme of Cultural Reconstruction

In our scheme of cultural reconstruction the monstrosity of lewdness is realised fully. This is testified by the following Traditions of the Holy Prophet:

Nobody commits the act of lewdness in the state of faith (*Mishkat*).

It means that purity and nobility of faith and the monstrosity and corruption of lewdness are incompatible. On one occasion, the Holy Prophet listed the activities of certain organs as lewdness, for these organs act as instruments of this crime:

The lewdness of both the eyes is looking at private of forbidden parts. The lewdness of the ear is listening to forbidden voices. The lewdness of the tongue is uttering forbidden discourse. The lewdness of the hand is to make use of the hands for forbidden actions. The lewdness of the feet is walking in forbidden ways. (*Mishkat*, Babul Qadr).

This gives an idea of the awareness of the monstrosity of lewdness in Islamic culture. Thus even 'going near this deed' has been forbidden—

Nor come nigh to Adultery,
For it is a shameful (deed)
And evil... (XVII-32)

Once the Holy Prophet was asked: 'which sin is the greatest?' He replied: Regarding somebody as equal to God, though it is God Who has created thee. Then he was asked: 'Which sin is next in greatness ?' He replied: Slaying one's child for fear of sharing one's food with him or her.' Then he was asked: 'Which sin is next in greatness?' He replied: "Committing adultery with the wife of one's neighbourer" (*Mishkat*, Babul Kabair)

Lewdness is Hateful to Human Nature and is Disapproved by Society

On account of the monstrosity of lewdness human natu abhors it and human life is never ready to accept it. The Quran syas:

Women impure are for men impure,
And men impure for women impure
And women of purity
Are for men of purity,
And men of purity
Are for women of purity (XXIV-26)

Let no man guilty of
Adultery or fornication marry
Any but a woman
Similarly guilty, or an Unbeliever:
Nor let any but such a man
Or an unbeliever
Marry such a woman:
To the Believers such a thing
Is forbidden (XXIV-3)

It is not the purpose of these Verses to lay down any law; their purpose is to underscore the revulsion of human nature and of society against lewdness. *Roohul Ma'ani* comments by saying that this amounts to the expression of extreme disapproval of the act of lewdness. It goes on to say that the incompatibility of the act has been substituted for the absence of the act.[5]

It is evident that both the male and the female lewd persons are not worthy of marrying a chaste partner because of the stain of corruption they bear. Therefore marital relation between the chaste and the unchaste is forbidden. In the literature of the Arabs descriptions like the following are used for indicating the ugliness of some act:

A king never tells lies. Which means that a dirty thing like a lie does not become an honourable man like a king.

Marrying A Lewd Person is Forbidden by Some Jurists

Some scholars of Islamic jurisprudence have argued for the taboo of marriage between the lewd and the chaste. Others have advised separation between the partners after the act of lewdness has been committed inside wedlock:

There are some people who do not differentiate between the beginning and the middle of a course. What we imply is that just as it is not lawful for a believer to marry a lewd woman in the same way if the woman commits the act of lewdness after marriage it is not lawful to keep her as a wife. Some scholars have given the verdict of unlawfulness in the case of the beginning or entry into marital career; but if the act is committed in the middle of the marital career they have not given the verdict of unlawfulness or taboo. (Razi, *Tafseer-i-Kabeer; Tafsir-i-Noor*)

This is supported by the following Traditions: The Holy Prophet once said:

The adulterer who has been punished with public flogging should marry a woman like himself. (*Abu Daud*, Kitabul Nikah)

Murthid b. Abi Murthid Ghanawi once requested the Holy Prophet to get him married to a woman of Mecca (She was Ghasaq, the notorious adulteress). The Holy Prophet kept silent for some time, till the above metioned Verse (XXIV-3) was revealed, and then he said: "Do not marry her"

The following episode connected with the life of Ali is also enlightening:

A man married some woman. The woman committed adultery. She was punished for it. When the matter was brought to the judgement court of Ali he gave the verdict of separation between them and told the woman to marry somebody like herself.[6]

All these punishments do not amount to any prescription of law; the government is authorised to give whatever punishment it likes in accordance with the exigencies of contemporary laws of the shariah.

Capital Punishment for Lewdness and the Government Acting as Prosecutor

On account of the monstrosity and seriousness of the offence of lewdness this punishment is capital punishment. The state itself acts as a plaintiff for carrying out the sentence. Which means that even if the wronged party Forgoes its claim the state takes upon itself the duty ('the rights of God) to execute the punishment. In Islamic Jurisprudence it is observed:

> The rulers are justified to punish for this offence even in the absence of having it established by prosecution and even in the absence of any plaintiff. Similarly it is justified to point witnesses in absence of any plaintiff.[7]

The standard for the establishment of effences for which the punishment is capital and for which the state itself acts as a plaintiff should be high and invulnerable. There is wide possibility of escaping the punishment in this case, and the conditions for punishments are very strict and difficult to be fulfilled. In this case the state is responsible for doing two things: (1) to propose alternative punishments which may be substituted for capital punishment, (2) to establish such courts as would hear to suits cancelled on account of the paucity of firm evidence or the lack of standard witnesses. For such courts there are terms like *Waliul Jaraem and Sahibulrad* in the books of jurisprudence. Such courts were supposed to propose alternative punishments in cases where the suits had been rejected because of lack of evidence. These courts adopted an outlook wider than the ordinary courts of justice (which gave the sentence of capital punishment). They adopted this wider outlook in enquiring into the offence and establishing it.

Modesty And Self-respect

Modesty and self-respect are a natural characteristic of human nature which gives rise to many moral virtures and safeguards chastity. If this virtue is cultivated from childhood it develops and acquires great significance, otherwise it dwindleds away. In western civilization this virtue is not very much valued, nor any arrangement is made for its cultivation. On the other hand, the western way of life tries to eliminate it from the very beginning. But in our scheme of cultural reconstruction it has been commanded to safeguard and cultivate this virtue from the very beginning. For example, the female parts related to sexuality are to be covered; talking of immodest things and looking at them is forbidden; the lowering of glances is commanded; nakedness and nudeness is forbidden, so much that even in bath rooms and bed rooms precautions have to be taken in this regard. All these punishments are there in order to maintain modesty and self-respect.

Modesty and Self-respect are the Qualities of God and His Prophet

Modesty and Self-respect become God and they are amongst His Attributes—

Indeed Allah would be ashamed to disappoint one who begs Him for some good. (*Baihaqi*. 'Kitabul Asma wal Sifat fil Istihya')

At another place it is said:

Nobody is more self-respecting than Allah. This is why He has forbidden lewdness. (*Op. Cit.*, 'Kitabul Asma Wal Sifat fil, Ghairah')

Modesty and self-respect were the qualities of Mohammad (peace be upon him).

The apostle of God was more modest than a parda-observing virgin. (*Bukhari*, 'Kitabul Adab, Babul Haya')

For the same reason the Quran says that the Holy Prophet was ashamed to dismiss people lingering after dinner:

> ... *He is ashamed*
> *To dismiss you,* (XXXIII-53)

Modesty and self-respect is so much involved with the sense of Prophethood that its violation is not to be tolerated even in the childhood of the Prophet. For example, in his childhood Mohammad (peace be upon him) was engaged in carrying bricks for the reconstruction of the Ka'ba. On the advice of his uncle Abbas he loosened his lower garment and put it on his shoulder. But at this incident Mohammad (peace be upon him) fainted out of his sense of modesty.

Modesty and Self-respect are Constituents of Faith and the Basis of Humanity

In the Traditions modesty and self-respect have been emphasised in such a way as to indicate that they are the integral constituents of faith and the very basis of humanity. Thus the Holy Prophet said:

Faith branches of into more than seventy dimensions. The highest dimension is the formulation of *La Ilaha Illah* (There is no deity except Allah), and the lowest dimension is marked by acts like removing troublesome things off the way. Modesty is also a dimension of faith.[8]

Another Tradition says faith and modesty are mutually involved. If one goes off, the other too does not remain.[9]

There is a Tradition according to Ibn-i-Abbas which says: "when one of these is lost the other too is lost."[10] Another Tradition says: "Every religion has a specific temperament, and the specific temperament of Islam is modesty."[11] Then there is a Tradition which says: "Modesty leads only to good."[12] Another Tradition declares that "modesty is itself good incarnate."[13] There is still another tradition which defines the psychological quality of immodesty in a manner of premonition: 'If you do not observe modesty, do whatever you like'.[14]

Honesty and Trustworthiness

Honesty and trustworthiness are the very essence of morality and the very basis of humanity. Without them the affairs of life are not set right, nor can mutual trust be established. This is why the Quran calls the Revelation bearing Angel 'AlAmin' which means one who is 'Faithful to the Trust' or the 'Spirit of Faith and Truth'. For if trust is not reposed in this Angel the authenticity of the Revelation cannot be ascertained —

With it came down
The Spirit of Faith and Truth — (XXVI - 193)
With authority there,
(And) faithful to his trust. (LXXXI - 21)

Almost every prophet nas manifested to his people his quality of trustworthiness. Thus Sho'aib:

I am to you an apostle
Worthy of all trust. (XXVI -178)

And the people of Mecca had nicknamed Mohammad (peace be upon him) as 'Amin' or 'The Trustworthy' before he was invested with Prophethood, which indicates the absolute trust they reposed in him.

Honesty and Trustworthiness Hold Good for Every Sphere of Life

In the scheme of cultural reconstruction honesty and trustworthiness are not confined to any one sphere of life; they encompass the economic, the legal, the moral — in fact every sphere of life. For example, the principle of honesty and trustworthiness demands that one must not come slack in fulfilling one's duties (to God's creatures and to God); must return undamaged what has ben borrowed; must keep a secret for the sake of the other person's honour; must refrain from being a tell-tale; must give the right advice; must be conscientious; must appoint only the deserving etc. The Quran says:

God doth command you
To render back your Trusts
To those to whom they are due;
And when ye judge
Between man and man
That ye judge with justice (IV - 58)

In this Verse the word 'trusts' encompasses all responsibilities and duties—

Amaanaat (trusts) is the plural of *amanat*, and so it includes all the duties incumbent on man, the duties to God as well as to fellow-creatures. (Syed Mahmud Alusi, *Ruhul Ma'ani*, 'Surah Nisa')

Wider Sense of Honesty and Trustworthiness According to the Quran

The Verses of the Quran testify to the wider sense of honesty and trustworthiness. Thus the responsibility of vicegerency has been described as a Trust.

We did indeed offer
The Trust to the Heavens
And the Earth
And Mountains
But they refused
To undertake it,
Being afraid thereof:
But man undertook it; — (XXXIII - 72)

Whatever material goods man possesses are as a trust from God. Thus the Quran:

And spend (in charity)
Out of (substance)
Whereof He has made you
Heirs (LVII-7)

Even man's life is a trust from God

God has purchased of the Believers
Their persons and their goods;
For theirs (in return)
Is the Garden (of Paradise): (IX - 111)

If one lends something to somebody and allows him to keep it, that thing is a trust. It should be returned intact and undamaged:

And if one of you
Deposits a thing

On trust with another,
Let the trustee
(Faithful) discharge
His trust, and let him
Fear his Lord (II - 283)

Duty (in service) is Also a trust. Any slackness in it is the betrayal of trust and dishonesty:

... truly the best
of men for thee to employ is
The (man) who is strong and trusty (XXVIII-26)

Positions and posts are also a trust; to give them to the undeserving is dishonesty and betrayal of trust. Ibn-i-Taimiya while interpreting the Verse: "God doth command you to render back your Trusts ... " (IV - 58) includes Government and all the resources of the State in the word "Trusts".[15] Some exegetes have made the following observations while interpreting this Verse: "The fulfilment of the trusts also means that positions should be given only to the deserving". (Mohammad Shafi Deobandi, *Magala Dastur-i-Qurani*)

Qazi Sanaullah Panipati says:

The fulfilment of the trusts is not confined to giving things that are due because of birth and inheritence; it includes all the duties of man. Whatever is due to somebody should be paid. (*Tafsiri Mazhari*, Vol.II, p. 48)

The Wider Sense of Honesty and Trustworthiness according to the Traditions

The Holy Prophet has included in the term "Trust" many subtleties and particularities of life. For example he includes advice in this term: 'One who is asked for an advice has been consigned with a trust." (*Bukhari*, Al Adabul Mufrad, Al Mustasharo Motaminun)

It means that the adviser must give the right advice. Matters related to conferences should be treated as trust: "conferences are held on trust."[16] It means that the deliberation of one conference should not be reported in another.

From such report are excluded those intrigues that are made for the purpose of torturing or dishonouring anybody. One should convey the reports of such intrigues to the person concerned, otherwise one would incur a sin.[17]

The greatest trust is the secrets between husband and wife, which one does one's duty to hide and honour. The Holy Prophet says:

On Doom's Day the greatest violation of trust in the eyes of God would be the exposing of secrets about a man's wife before others.[18]

Secret or private affairs are also trust. The Holy Prophet said; "When a man talks to somebody and then turns to the other side this talk is a trust.[19]

All these remarks go to indicate how wide a sense the word "trust" has in Islam.

The Value of the Honesty and Trustworthiness

The value of honesty and trustworthiness and the harm of its violation are brought out by the following saying of the Holy Prophet:

He who is not trustworthy has no faith. He who does not pray has no religion. In religion prayer has the same status as the head has in the body. (*Kanzul, Ummal*, Vol.II, Al Amanat)

Another Tradition says:

Trustworthiness makes one achieve his sustenance: dishonesty produces poverty. (*Ibid.*)

Still another Hadith says:

Trustworthiness is wealth. (*Ibid.*)

Trustworthiness is not something externally impossed. It is something related to the inner most being of man:

Trustworthiness is related to the very roots of the hearts of the people (it is related to man's inner most nature). People have learnt it from the Quran, and then from the Sunnah. (*Mishkat*, Kitabul Fitan, Falt I)

The loss of trustworthiness is the first thing that happens when a community degenerates. Prayer is retained and is the last thing that is lost. A Tradition says:

(By this community) trustworthiness will be lost first; and the thing that is retained in its religion till the very end will be prayer (namaz). But there are many worshippers (namazis) who will have no reward in the eyes of God. (*Kanzul 'Ummal,* Vol. II, p.15)

Another Tradition says:

The first thing that you will lose in your religion is trustworthiness. (*Baihaqi,* Vol.VI, p.289)

Thus in the scheme of cultural reconstruction every duty and every responsibility which has been entrusted is a Trust. Man's status is that of a Trustee, and without fulfilling his Trust he cannot hope to achieve well being.

The other sub-category of Distinctive Attributes, one related to the welfare of human beings, has the following implications:

JUSTICE

Justice is one of those attributes of God that pervades the whole universe. In fact the cosmos rests on it. It is the principle of life and the guarantee for its sustenance, progress and survival. Without it develops neither the character of the individual nor of the community. According to etymology of word for justice '*Adl* means dividing something into two equal halves.'[20]

The Quran Uses the Word 'Mizan' (Balance)

In the Quran the reality of justice is brought home to us by the word *Mizan* which means Balance. If one pan of the balance is tilted, disorder results instead of order, and so the Quranic emblem is of tremendous significance —

And the Firmament has He
Raised high, and he has set up
The Balance (of Justice). (LV - 7)

We sent aforetime
Our apostles with clear Sings
And sent down with them
The Book and the Balance
(Of Right and Wrong), that men
May stand forth in justice; (LVII - 25)

Definition of Justice According to Al Ghazali, Plato and Others

Al Ghazali has defined justice as follows:

It is controlling energy, desire and anger to such an extent that they may function according to Right Reason and the *Sharia.* (*Ahya*, Vol. III, P. 48)

Shah Waliullah offers the following conception:
Justice is, as it were, a Queen, from whom issue forth the actions that make for the smooth management of cities and villages. (*Hujjatullahil Baligha*, p. 58)

To Plato the essence of justice is the inner or the spiritual reality. Which means that the inner life should be so well-organized that every person does his work in a proper or responsible way, and does not meddle in the work of another. Dewey, James and Rogers see justice as the cream of morality and the crown of essential virtues. If this virtue is lacking all other virtues lose their significance and purpose.

Basis of Justice in Western Culture

In Western culture the basis of justice is nationalism and patriotism, which are adopted on a nation-wide scale for the sake of extolling the nation and its progress.

Basis of Justice in the Scheme of Cultural Reconstruction

In the Islamic scheme of cultural reconstruction the basis of justice is piety and spiritual purity. It comes into being through the concept of universal welfare and general mercy, as proclaimed by Islam—'All creatures are the children of Allah'[21] — 'All men are brothers'.[22]

The Standard of Justice

Owing to such an outlook the standard of justice in our scheme is extremely high, one which would not allow for any discrimination between the close and the distant in relation, the enemy and the friend, the rich and the poor etc. Thus the Quran says:

O ye who believe!
Stand out firmly
For justice, as witnesses
To God, even as against
Yourselves, or your parents,
Or your kin, and whether
It be (against) rich or poor:
For God can best protect both.
Follow not the lusts
(Of your hearts), lest ye
Swerve... (IV - 135)

O ye who believe!
Stand out firmly
For God, as witnesses
To fair dealing, and let not
The hatred of others
To you make you swerve
To wrong and depart from
Justice. Be just: that is
Next to Piety: and fear God. (V-9)

Once a gentle-woman of the clan of Makhzoomia committed a

theft. When appeals regarding her reached the Holy Prophet he said:

> People before you were destroyed (by God) simply for the reason that if a person of high status among them committed a theft he was allowed to go scot free but if a weak person committed a theft he was punished to the utmost limit. By God, if my own daughter Fatima committed a theft her hand would be cut off. (*Bukhari, Muslim, Mishkat*: Babul Shafaat fil Hudud)

Justice is of two kinds: (1) personal, and (2) societal.

Personal Justice

Personal justice implies a harmony between rights and duties. The Quran speaks of it in various contexts. Thus regarding orphans it is said:

That ye stand firm
For justice to orphans (IV - 127)

Regarding women:

But if ye fear that ye shall not
Be able to deal justly (with them),
Then only one, (IV - 3)

Regarding witnesses and verdict and mutual agreement:

Whenever ye speak, speak justly,
Even if a near relative
is concerned: (VI - 152)

Make peace between them
With justice, and be fair: (XLIX - 9)

Regarding buying and selling and other affairs and transactions:

... give measures
And weight with (full) justice; — (VI - 152)

Let a scribe write down
Faithfully as between
The parties (II - 282)

Let his guardian
Dictate faithfully. (II 282)

Societal Justice

By societal justice is meant a system of justice which provides for considerations to everybody and everything. Everything should remain within its proper context and confines, and everybody should have equal opportunities according to his capabilities. This is possible only when the powers of thought and action are held in balance, and everybody, realizing that God watches him, fulfils his duty towards establishing justice. Let us turn to what the Quran says:

God doth command you
To render back your Trusts
To those to whom they are due
And when ye judge
Between man and man
That ye judge with justice: (IV - 58)

In this Verse the address is made to the rulers. The term 'Trusts' includes, as pointed out above, all kinds of responsibilities, positions and ranks. Ibn-i-Taimiya rightly points out that the 'Rulers themselves are the cause of the revelation of this Verse'. (*Al Jawame' fil Siyasatil Ilahiya*)

The Quran speaks more of justice:

but say: 'I believe
In the Book which
God has sent down;
And I am commanded

To judge justly between you. (XLII - 15)

If thou judge, judge
In equity between them,
For God loveth those
Who judge in equity. (V - 45)

The Opposite of Justice is Wrong-doing

The opposite of justice is wrong-doing, whether on the level of individual life or that of community life. In either case its consequence is destruction. Etymologically, the Arabic word for wrong-doing, *Zulm*, means 'putting something in the wrong place'. (Ibn-i-Taimiya, *Al Jawame' fil Siyasatil Ilahiya*)

Wider Sense of the Word According to the Quran

The word Zulm has been used in the Quran in a variety of implied senses — blasphemy, joining partners with God, sinfulness, injustice, doing wrong to others, and oppression being some of them. But all these imply senses which are related to the etymological, root-meaning of the word. Regarding blasphemy the Quran says:

Who, then, doth more wrong
Than one who utters
A lie concerning God,
And rejects the Truth
When it comes to him.
Is there not in Hell
An abode for blasphemers? (XXXIX - 32)

Who is more unjust
Than one who invents
A lie against God (VII - 37)

Concerning the joining of partners with God it is said: 'Indeed joining partners with God is great wrong-doing'. Regarding sinfulness it is said:

But there are among them
Some who wrong their own
Souls; (XXXV - 32)

When they have done wrong to their own souls'—'Whomsoever does such a thing, verily he will do wrong to his own soul'. Then, regarding the doing of injustice and wrong to others it is said:

Say: The things that my Lord
Hath indeed forbidden are:
Shameful deeds, whether open
Or secret; sins and trespasses
Against truth or reason. (VII - 33)

The blame is only
Against those who oppress
Men with wrong-doing
And insolently transgress
Beyond bounds through the land,
Defying right and justice: (XLII - 42)

Besides the above Verses there are others dealing with the subject of *Zulm* and its agents and victims.

Condemnation of Wrong-doing in the Traditions

We refer to certain Traditions below, which indicate the condemnation of wrong-doing in the Islamic scheme of cultural reconstruction. Once the Holy Prophet said:

Wrong-doing will take the shape of Darkness on the Day of Judgement. (*Bukhari, Muslim, Mishkat:* Babul Zulm)

Once the Holy Prophet happened to pass by Hijr—the ruins of the habitations of the Thamud, the people of the Prophet Saleh. He said:

'You should enter weeping the (ruined) houses of those who did wrong to their own souls, lest the same punishment of God seize you as it seized them'. Then the Holy Prophet bowed his head and hurriedly passed through that valley (of archaeological ruins). (*Ibid.*)

On another occasion the Holy Prophet said:

'Help your brother, be he the agent of wrong-doing or the victim'. The Companions asked: 'O Prophet of Allah, if he is a victim he can be helped; but if he is an agent of wrong-doing, how can he be helped?'. The Holy Prophet replied: 'He must be prevented from doing wrong'. (*Muslim,* Nasrul Akhi Zaliman au Mazluma)

Once the Holy Prophet asked his companions: 'Who is poor?' The Companions replied: 'One among us who has no money and material goods'. At this the Holy Prophet said:

In my *ummat* (religious community) the poor person is one who carries (the testimony of) all the (theological) virtues like prayers (namaz), fasting and charity (zakat) on the Day of Judgment, but he is the one who has abused somebody, has falsely accused somebody, has devoured the goods of somebody, has shed the blood of somebody, and has beaten somebody. All his virtues shall be given over to these victims. If his virtues fall short of providing compensation for the rights of his victims, the vices of the victims will be taken off and laid on him. And then he shall be thrown into Hell. (*Muslim, Mishkat:* Babul Zulm)

MERCY

Mercy is the greatest Attribute of God. The Quran says:

But My Mercy extendeth
To all things. (VII - 156)

Our Lord! Thy Reach
Is over all things,
In Mercy and Knowledge. (XL - 7)

For Thou art the Best
Of those who show mercy! (XXIII - 109)

Mercy has been regarded as the greatest quality of Mohammad (peace be upon him).

We sent thee not, but
As a Mercy for all creatures. (XXI - 107)
... to the Believers
Is he most kind and merciful (IX - 128)

Mercy or compassion has been emphasized even in the character of the Companions:

Compassionate amongst each other. (XLVIII - 29)

No Redress for Mankind Without Mercy,

There can be no progress and prosperity of mankind without mercy. The Holy Prophet said:
Mercy is lacked only by the unfortunate (*Tirmizi, Mishkat,* Al Shafqa wal Rahma 'alal Khalq, Fasl II).
In the Islamic scheme of cultural reconstruction there are certain Traditions concerning the importance of, and insistence on, mercy. Here are some of the sayings of the Holy Prophet:

Mercy is a branch which is entwined with the Merciful One.[23]

He who does not take mercy on others is not taken mercy on.[24]

Take mercy on earthly beings, and the Heavenly Beings will take mercy on you.[25]

He who has not taken mercy on our juniors and has not respected our seniors is not of us.[26]

Mercy is not confined to human beings; it encompasses the animals too. On one occasion the Holy Prophet said:

There is reward for showing mercy to every animal. (*Bukhari, Muslim*)

On another occasion he said:

If a person shows mercy to a slaughtered animal, God will show mercy to him on the Day of Judgment. (*Bukhari,* Al Adabul Mufrad, Bab Rahmatil Bahaim)

Disapproval of Hard-heartedness

The Holy Prophet has condemned hard-heartedness and lack of compassion and mercy in various ways. For example, a bedouin told him that while the Holy Prophet kissed children his own folk did not do so. At this the Holy Prophet said: 'What can I do if Allah has taken away compassion from your hearts?' (*Bukhari*, Kitabul Adab; Bab Rahmatil Maulud)

The Holy Prophet forbade the various cruel sports of making the animals fight (*Abu-Daud*, Kitabul Jihad).

Mercy and justice do not contradict each other, unlike what some people think. On the other hand it is mercy that implicates justice between the good and the evil, the oppressor and the oppressed, the treacherous and the loyal, the pious and the vicious. Treating them in the same way would be a travesty of mercy.

DOING OF GOOD

It means meting out such treatment to the other person as would give him happiness and relief. The Quran has repeatedly mentioned Allah as the 'Doer of Good'. The good works. He does have been mentioned in various contexts, and His Servants have been ordained to do good likewise. Thus we have the following Verse:

> *God commands justice, the doing*
> *Of good ...* (XVI - 90)

Justice dispenses to every person what his due is. But with the spirit of doing good one feels concerned about the distress and comfort, misery and happiness of the people. In other words, the matter does not end with justice; doing good is also commanded for the sake of bringing redress and comfort to people.

Various Forms of Doing Good:

The Quran speaks of various forms of doing good. For example, giving financial help —

> *but do thou good,*

As God has been good
To thee ... (XXVIII - 77)

Rescuing somebody from affliction:

He was indeed
Good to me (says Joseph) when He
Took me out of prison ... (XII - 100)

Forgiving wrongs etc. In this context it is said:

For God loves those
Who do good: — (III - 134)

Synonymous to 'doing good' some other terms have also been used in the Quran—for example, *fazl*, *'Urf*, *ma'roof* and *bir*. If we consider all their contexts it becomes evident that 'doing good' is not confined to any one particular form; it encompasses all forms of virtue. Hence the Holy Prophet said:

God has made it encumbent on you to do good with every being. Even if you have got to kill somebody, do it with good. If you want to slaughter an animal, do it with good; sharpen your knife well and let your slaughtered animal have quick relief (let it not linger in pain and agony). (*Muslim*, Kitabul Said Wal Zabaih)

Doing good is not commanded merely in return for the good done to you. It is also commanded in return for the wrong somebody does to you. The Quran says:

Is there any Reward
For Good—other than Good? (LV - 60)

Once a person asked the Prophet of Allah (peace be upon him): When I pass by a man he does not offer me any hospitality. If he passes by me, should I do the same?' The Holy Prophet replied: 'No, you must offer hospitality to him.' (*Tirmizi*, Bab Ma Ja-e-fil Ahsan wal 'Afv)

Forgiveness

Forgiveness is also one of the most important Attributes of God. If it were not there this sinful world would have been destroyed. Divine Names like *Ghaffar, Ghaafir, Ghafoor*—which imply forgiveness—keep recurring in the Quran. Forgiveness has been mentioned in several places. It is an important quality of the Beliveres:

> *And, when they are angry*
> *Even then forgive;* (XLVII-37)

> *Let them forgive and overlook,*
> *Do you not wish*
> *That God should forgive you?*
> *For God is Oft-Forgiving*
> *Most Merciful.* (XXIV-22)

The Quran makes special mention of those situations which call for forgiveness.

Situations Calling for Forgiveness

People are very touchy in matters of religion. They may give rise to hot disputes and enraged feelings; but in such situations forgiveness is commanded:

> *But forgive and overlook,*
> *Till God accomplish*
> *His purpose;* (II-109)

When a man's honour is assaulted, he is enraged. In this situation too the command is forgiveness.

> *Let not those among you*
> *Who are endued with grace*
> *And amplitude of means*
> *Resolve by oath against helping*
> *Their kinsmen, those in want*
> *And those who have left*

Their homes in God's cause:
Let them forgive and overlook. (XXIV-22)

The historical occasion for the revelation of this Verse is significant. Mistah was a Kinsman of Abu Bakr who used to support him with financial assistance. But when Mistah took part in hurling slanders against Aisha, in connexion with Ifk, (slander) Abu Bakr withdrew his support. At this the above Verse, which commands forgiveness, was revealed.

Once a person asked the Holy Prophet: 'O Prophet of Allah, How many times should I forgive the offences of my servant?' The Holy Prophet kept silent for sometime, and then said: 'Seventy times every day'. (*Tirmizi,* Abwab AlBirwal Sila) Here the number is not meant to be taken literally; it means 'most frequently' according to the Arabic idiom.

Forgiveness Taught to Maintain Self-respect

In the existing New Testament forgiveness is taught in such a way as to engender feelings of meekness and lowness in the individual. But in the Islamic scheme of cultural reconstruction it is taught in a manner which does not injure self-respect; nor does it upset the social system. Thus even revenge is sanctioned in the face of oppression and wrong-doing; but forgiveness is seen as the better policy, one which is loved by God and is worthy of reward in his eyes—

The recompense for an injury
Is an injury thereto
(In degree): but if a person
Forgives and makes reconciliation,
His reward is due
From God: for God
Loveth not those who
Do wrong. (XLII.40)

To be able to forgive even when one is entitled to take revenge is a matter of great courage and moral nobility.

Sacrifice

Sacrifice means giving priority to the needs of others over one's personal needs. It is an image of the Divine Attribute of Independence. The spirit of sacrifice manifests the very essence of humanity and exalts man to higher modes of being. Thus the Quran:

By no means shall ye
Attain righteousness unless
Ye give (freely) of that
Which ye love; (III-92)

The spirit of sacrifice was an outstanding quality in the character of Mohammad (peace be upon him), of which many instances are on record.

The greatest Moral Virtue of the Ansars

Among the Companions the Ansars (Helpers of the Holy Prophet) had the spirit of sacrifice as their greatest moral quality. It helped to strengthen Islam, and its range became wider and wider after the Holy Prophet had reached Medina. The Quran speaks of it in highly commendable terms:

But those who
Before them, had homes
(In Medina)
And had adopted the Faith,—
Show their affection to such
As came to them for refuge,
And entertain no desire
In their hearts for things
Given to the (latter),
But give them preference
Over themselves, even though

Poverty was their (own lot).
And those saved from
The covetousness of their own
Souls,—they are the ones
That achieve prosperity. (LIX.9)

Once a hungry man came to the Holy Prophet. In his house there was nothing except water on that occasion. So the Holy Prophet said: 'To him who offers hospitality to this man for tonight God will show his Mercy'. At this an Ansar took him to his house. On enquiring from his wife if there was any food in the house he was told that only the food meant for the children was there. The Ansar said to his wife: 'Calm the children to make them sleep. Give the food to our guest, and put out the light so that he may not know that we ourselves are not taking our meal.' The wife did as she was told. Next morning the Ansar came to the Holy Prophet and reported how he had treated the guest. The Holy Prophet told him that Allah was exceedingly pleased with him because of what he had done. (*Muslim,* Kitabul Ashriba, Bab Ikramil Zaif wa Fazl wa Ithar).

When Bahrain was conquered the Holy Prophet called the Ansars and said that he wanted to distribute the territory among them. They said they would not accept it unless their Mahajir (those who migrated with the Holy Prophet) brethen shared it with them equally. At this the Holy Prophet said: 'If you cannot accept the offer, have patience. For after me you will be afflicated by the fact that people will grab things and will not without offer you (in consideration of your right)'. (*Bukhari,* Vol. I, Bab Manaquibil Ansar)

Qualities Emanating from Constructive Attributes

The following qualities emanate from Constructive Attributes. There is a sense of man's superiority in creation, which impels him to strive. This is an image of the Divine Attribute of being the Lord of the Worlds and the Irresistible—

Say: 'O God!
Lord of Power (and Rule)
Thou givest power
To Whom Thou pleasest,
And Thou strippest off Power
From whom Thou pleasest:
Thou enduest with honour
Whom Thou pleasest,
And Thou bringest low
Whom Thoa pleasest:
In Thy hand is all Good. (III-26)

He is the Irresistible (watching)
From above over His worshippers;
and He is the Wise,
Acquainted with all things. (VI-18)

Awful Grace

This virtue makes for self-manifestation. Actually this is an image of the Divine Attributes of being the most Exalted One and the Greatest One etc. —

To Him be Glory
Throughout the heavens
And the earth, —
Lord and Cherisher
Of all the worlds! (XLV-36)
... Whose will be
The dominion on the Day?
That of God, the One,
The Irresistible (XI-16)

Glory and Power

These qualities go to make the personality impressive and also insulated from the interference of others. These qualities are actually the image of the Divine Attributes of being The Irresistible and the Supreme—

Blessed be the name
Of Thy Lord, full of majesty,
Bounty and Honour (LV.78)

All that is on earth
Will perish:
But will abide (over other)
the Face of that Lord, —
Full of Majesty
Bounty and Honour. (LV.26-7)

Industry and Rigorousness

These qualities go to engender the spirit of industry and hard work in man. He is unable to take challenges and perform difficult tasks. These qualities are the image of the Divine Attributes of being the Powerful and the Firm One and of being One Who Hath a Long Reach—

And hath a Long Reach
(In all things) (XL-3)
Truly strong is the Grip
(And power) of thy Lord (LXXXV.12)

Motivation for Progress

Owing to this virtue a man does not sit contented with one state but goes on striving continually to advance from state to state. This is an image of the Divine Attributes of the Ever Developing One —

Raised high above ranks
(or degrees),
(He is) the Lord
Of the Throne (of authority): (XL.15)

Every day in (new) splendour
Doth He (shine); (LV.29)

Subjection of the Universe to Man

This quality enables man to subject the universe to him, to exploit it in his interest, to enquire into the reality of things and to control nature. This is an image of the Divine Attribute of being The All-Conquering One. In the Quran we have many Verses in this connection:

It is He who has made
The sea subject, that ye
May eat thereof flesh
That is fresh and tender,
And that ye may extricate
Therefrom ornaments to wear; (XVI.14)

He has made subject to you
The Night and the Day;
The Sun and the Moon;
And the Stars are in subjection
By His Command... (XVI-12)

Glory to Him Who
Has subjected these
To our (use), for we
Could never have accomplished
This (by ourselves) (XLIII-13)

Control Over Beneficial And Harmful Things

This quality enables man to have control over beneficial and harmful things in nature so as to establish his supremacy. This is an image of the Divine Attributes One Who of Directs to Good, Restrains and Dispenses Harm. Thus the Quran says :

If God do touch thee
With hurt, there is none
Can remove it but He:
If He had designed some benefit
For thee, there is none
Can keep back his favour: (X.107)
If God touch thee
With affliction, none
Can remove it but He;
If He touch thee with happiness,
He hath power over all things. (VI-17)

Avenging Wrongs and Punishment

These qualities make for the power of resistance, for avenging of wrongs and for acting as a scourge. They bring about the eradication of evils. They reflect the Divine Attributes of the Avenger and the Punisher. The Quran says:

And God is swift
In taking account. (XXIV-39)
And verily thy Lord
Is (also) strict in punishment. (XIII.6)
Then shall anyone who
Has done an atom's weight
Of good, see it!
And anyone who

Has done an atom's weight
Of evil, shall see it, (XCIX—7-8)

Thus from the Divine Attributes of Glory emanate constructive qualities that bring about discipline in life and manifest man's stature of vicegerency. In the scheme of cultural reconstruction the Attributes of both Beauty and Power must have scope for manifestation. If any of these is neglected life would become lop-sided and man would fail to achieve his proper status.

Virtues Emanating From Complementary Attributes

From the Complementary Attributes the following virtues emante:

The Quality of Sustaining

In Arabic language *Rabubiat* means sustaining somebody or something according to various needs. It means: sustaining and cultivating something according to various needs and in such a way as to make it reach perfection (Raghib Asfahani, *Mufridatul Quran)*. From this virtue the emotion of parental care emanates. Man is able to sustain, bring up and look after things and persons with love and affection. The Quran says:

Praise be to God,
The Cherisher and Sustainer of the worlds (I.1-2)
(When this message was delivered),
(Pharaoh) said: 'who, then,
O Moses, is the Lord
Of you two?
He said: 'Our Lord is
He Who gave to each
(created) things its form
And nature, and further,
Gave (it) guidance." (XX.49-50)

All sustenance, life and death come from God
Such is God, your real
Cherisher and Sustainer (X-32)

Power of Supporting

The Self-subsisting One is He who subsists not only Himself and in His own right but also supports the subsistence of others. Etymologically, 'the self-subsisting One is he who subsists by himself, guards and takes care of everything and provides for everything the support that it needs for its subsistence.' (Zubaidi, *Tajul 'Urus*)

At another place it has been observed:

Along with the permanent or eternal support of His own Self He should also make for the subsistence of everything that exists, so much so that it is not possible to imagine the existence and subsistence of anything without the Self-Subsisting One. *(Ibid).*

When this virtue is reflected in human life it engenders endurance and independence from all that is not God. It enables man to help others and to support them with all courage and fortitude. The Quran says:

God! there is no god
But He—the Living,
The Self-Subsisting, Eternal.
No slumber can Seize Him
Nor sleep. (II.255)

God! there is no God
But He, —the Living,
The Self-Subsisting, Eternal.
It is He Who sent down
To thee (step by step),
In truth, the Book, (III.2-3)

Knowledge of the Reality of Things

This virtue also leads man to discovering the reality of things. It is the reflection of the Divine Attribute of The Knower of Invisible Things. Regarding Adam it is said in the Quran:

And He taught Adam the names
Of all things; (II.31)

Here the word names (*Asma*) is preceded by the Definite Article 'the' *(Al)*.This implies particular names which are mentioned here generically.[27] The word *Al-Asma* has been explicated as follows:

God revealed to Adam knowledge regarding the Essential nature of things, their names, the modes of knowing, the principles operating behind created things, and the knowledge of tools. *(Baizawi)*

In Razi's Tafseer-i-Kabeer it is said God taught Adam the nature of things and their properties. In *Kashshaf* it is said that God taught Adam the names by which things should be called. When Adam recounted the Names and when the angels could not do so God said:

.... "did I not tell you
That I know the secrets of heavens
And earth, (II-33)

Discovery And Invention

Man has the ability to enquire into the reality of things, to make researches and inventions. Thus he goes on progressing. This virtue is a reflection of the Divine Attribute of the Originator and the Inventor. The Quran says:

To Him is due
The primal origin
Of the heavens and the earth:

When he decreeth a matter,
He sayth to it: "Be",
and it is (II - 117)

To Him is due
The Primal origin
Of the heavens and the earth:
How can He have a son
When He hath no consort? (VI - 101)

Artistry

The virtue of making artifice inclines man to craftmanship and works of artifice. This whole system of creating artifice and artifacts is running because of the image of God's attribute of the Maker in man. Man, according to his capabilities, assimilates this attribute of God and creates his own work. The Quran says:

(Such is) the artistry of God,
Who dispenses of all things
In perfect order: (XXVII - 88)

Knowledge of Secret Realities and Wisdom

Man has the ability of prying into secret realities and into the causes of things. With this ability he is able to analyse situations, to have knowledge of individual and social life, and to put everything in its proper place and proper context. This is a reflection of God's Attribute: the Possessor of Knowledge and Wisdom. Thus the Quran speaks again and again of God as the Knower and the Wise and the Knower of the Secrets of the Hearts

He granteth wisdom
To whom He pleaseth;
And he to whom wisdom

In granted receiveth
Indeed a benefit overflowing; (II - 269)

All-Encompassingness

This virtue enlarges the horizons of the mind. It helps man to understand things and to extend his grasp and reach. It is a reflection of God's Attribute of being All-Encompassing in Knowledge. The Quran says:

Nor shall they compass
Aught of His Knowledge
Except as He willeth. (II - 255)

Uniqeness

Owing to this virtue the individual develops his unique individuality, which makes him like nobody else. This is a reflection of God's Absolute Uniqueness, and Attribute about which the Quran says:

there is nothing
Whatever like unto Him, (XLII - 11)

The above argument indicates the measure of human character in the Islamic scheme of cultural reconstruction; it indicates the kind of human character which should be regarded as the essential and the ideal one.

INSTITUTION OF THE FAMILY

Disintegration of the Family in the West

Individual life is constructed in the context of social life, and social life begins in the family which is its units. In western culture the institution of the family has been disintegrated, resulting in the freezing of feelings of affections, love and sympathy. There, every person feels that nobody is his or hers, and that he is alone in an alien world.

Insistence on Affection Through Family in Cultural Reconstruction

In the scheme of cultural reconstruction the institution of the family is the basis of the life of the community. For maintaining this institution mutual love, affection and sympathy have been insisted on. The Quran speaks of these things in various ways:

> *Reverence God, through Whom*
> *Ye demand your mutual (rights),*
> *And (reverence) the wombs*
> *(that bore you)* (IV - 1)

The Meaning of Reverence to the Wombs

Al Arham (wombs) is the plural of the Arabic word *Rahm* womb which literally means the womb of a woman. But figuratively it means family relationship and bounds of kindship—the English word 'kindness', in its original and wider meaning is the closest synonyms for the Arabic terms. *Tajul 'uroos* says:

> *Rahm* means the womb of a woman. Since the various members of family come from the same womb the term has been used in the sense of kinship. The figurative meaning of *rahm* is kinship. When an Arab says that such and such persons have *rahm* between them he means they are very closely related.

Rahm includes close relations which may be both intimate and non intimate: "*Rahm* is the term used for all relations, without distinction whether they are intimate or non-intimate"(Qurtubi).

The above Quranic verse (IV - I) insists on rewarding kinsfolk and condemns the rejection of kinship bonds, Abu Bakr Jassas says: 'the Verse insists on the right of familial relationships and prohibits their severence'. (Jassas Razi, *Ahkamul Quran*) Ibn-e-Hayyan says: Juxtaposing God with the 'womb' indicates that violation of the bonds of kinship is a great sin (*Al Bahrul Muheet*).

Importance of Bonds of Kinship in Other Quranic Verses

The implications of Sympathy for, and doing good to, one

another because of familial bonds of kinship are not confined to this life. They extend beyond this life too. The distribution of inheritance is based on such an idea:

But kindered by blood
Have prior rights
Against each other
In the Book of God. (VII-75)

The bond of kinship is so strong that even differences of religion do not break it; and the claim for affection and love remains inspite of them. Thus the Holy Prophet said to his kinsfolk:

Say: 'No reward do I
Ask of you for this
Except the love
Of others near to kin. (XLII-23)

Those who violate the bond of kinship have been regarded by the Quran as transgressors:

But He causes not to stray,
Except those who forsake (the path),
Those who break God's Covenant
After it is ratified,
And who sunder what God
Has ordered to be joined,
And do mischief on earth: (II-26-27)

Interpretation Given By the Holy Prophet

The Holy Prophet has interpreted the reverence to kinship or wombs in various ways. He always spoke of the excellence of this virtue and insisted on the importance of maintaining it. For example he says:

God said: 'I am Allah, I am the One. I created mercy and derived it from my own name. He who joins the bond of mercy, I shall join him (with blessings).

He who breaks this bond, I shall break him (into damnation) (*Abu Daud, Mishkat,* Babul Birre Was-Sila)

Mercy is a twig entwined with the Merciful One. Allah said: 'He who joins it, I shall join him. He who severes it, I shall severe him. (*Bukhari, Muslim,* Kitabul Birre Wal-Sila)

Allah created all the creatures. After He has finished this work Mercy stood up and got hold of the Merciful One by the waist. The Merciful One said: 'Stop! Mercy said: 'This is the place of him who seeks refuge with thee. The Merciful One said: 'Art thou not satisfied with the decree that I burnt him who burnt thee and I severed him who severes thee? At this Mercy replied: 'I am satisfied'. (*Mishkat,* Babul Birra Wal-Sala)

Rahm or Mercy is related to the throne of God. Mercy says: 'He who joins me, Allah shall join him; and He who servers me, Allah shall severe him (*Op cit.*).

In the West Children and Parents are not Responsible for Mutual Care

In Western culture parents and children have become burdens on one another. The relation between them has been broken down and so have the bonds and rights of kinship. The childrei are brought up in nurseries and the old parents are taken care of by houses for the old, which are separately and specially built for them. Eventually in such a position the natural feelings which are related to blood kinship are suppressed and vitiated. Feelings of affection and love should not be looked for or expected in such a situation.

Natural Feelings and Rights in the Scheme of Islamic Cultural Reconstruction

In the Islamic scheme of cultural reconstruction due consideration is given to natural, family feelings. The bond of kinship between persons has been emphasised very much and the rights and duties associated with it have been spelled out and insisted on. Various Verses of the Quran insisted on doing good to parents. Often this command comes after the command regarding faith in one God and His workship, which, perhaps, implies that the efficient cause of man's birth (God) and the material cause (parents) both must be considered and one must give what is due to both of them. The difference is only with regard to what is primary and what is secondary. Here are some

Verses of the Quran:

The Lord hath decreed
That ye workship none but Him,
And that ye be kind
To parents. Whether one
Or both of them attain
Old age in thy life,
Say not to them a word
Of contempt, nor repel them,
But address them
In terms of honour.
And, out of kindness, lower to them the wing
Of humility, and say:
'My Lord! bestow on them
The Mercy even as they
Cherished me in childhood'. (XVII - 23.24)
Serve God, and join not
Any partners with Him:
'Do good — to parents, kinsfold (IV - 36)
Say: 'come, I will rehearse
What God hath (really)
Prohibited you from; join not
Anything as equal with Him;
Be good to your parents; (VI - 151)

Since in bringing up children the mother has to suffer more of trouble priority is given to her in the matter of doing good to parents. The Quran says:

Any We have enjoined on man
(To be good) to his parents:

In travail upon travail
Did his mother bare him,
And in years twain
Was his weaning: (hear
The command), 'show gratitude
to Me and to thy parents:
To me is (thy final) Goal. (XXXI - 14)

We have enjoined on man
Kindness to his parents:
In pain did his mother
Bare him, and in pain
Did she give him birth (XLVI - 15)

Regarding doing good to parents there are certain Traditions. Once a man asked the Holy Prophet: 'What duty is enjoined on children towards their parents,' The Holy Prophet said: 'both of them are thy paradise or hell'.[29]

Another Tradition says: 'The pleasure of God depends on the pleasure of the parents, and the displeasure of God is the displeasure of the parents.[30] Still another Tradition says: 'May his nose be laid in the dust! May his nose be laid in the dust! May his nose be laid in the dust! (May he suffer abjection and humiliation). The audience asked: 'Whose nose, O Prophet of Allah?' The Holy Prophet replied: 'He who finds his parents or one of his parents and does not enter paradise'.[31]

The traditions, like the Quran, also command the giving of priority to the mother. Once a man asked the Holy Prophet who was most worthy of his good treatment. The Holy Prophet said: 'Thy mother'. He asked: 'Who next?' The reply was: 'Thy mother'. He once again asked: 'Who next?' The reply was 'Thy Mother'. At this he asked for the fourth time: 'Who next?' This time the reply was: 'Thy father'. Another Person asked the Holy Prophet about the treatment to the memory of the parents after their death. The Holy Prophet said: 'pray for their salvation; fulfil their vows and pacts; do good to your kinsfolk, keeping the parents in mind; and respect the words of your parents'.

Doing good to parents is commanded even if their religion is different. When Abu Bakr's daughter Asma asked the Holy Prophet regarding her infidel mother, the Holy Prophet advised doing good to her out of human kindness. (*Bukhari, Muslim,* Kitabul Birre Wal Silah).

Cherishing Is the Foremost Duty of Parents towards Children

In the scheme of cultural reconstruction, just as there are the duties of children towards parents in the same way there are the duties of parents towards children. Among them the foremost duty is that of cherishing and bringing up the children. The Quran speaks of the desire and the prayers of parents before the birth of the child as follows:

And if Thou givest us
A goodly child,
We vow we shall
(ever) be grateful' (VII - 189)

By the word 'goodly' are meant particular traits of character. But the word keeps changing its meaning according to the context.[32] In this context 'goodly' has been explained by exegetes as follows:

A healthy child, one whose body should be alright;[33] healthy in the sense that his limbs should be intact;[34] perfectly healthy in the sense of having the capability to do good deeds for the benefit of humanity.[35]

Children should be brought Up According to Their Needs

The bringing up of children should be done in such way as to ensure their proper development and to provide them with the things they need according to their age. Thus the Quran speaks of breast-feeding the child as follows:

> *The mother shall give suck*
> *To their offspring*
> *For two whole years,*
> *If the father desires*
> *To complete the term* (II - 233)

The relation established by giving suck to a child is reverenced so much that if another woman gives suck to the child instead of the mother the child and that woman have the same relation between them as would obtain in the case of the real mother. This relation is Holy and not to be violated. Hence the Quran prohibits marriage with:

> *foster-mothers*
> *(Who gave you suck), foster sisters:* (IV - 23)

The father is entrusted with supporting the woman who gave suck to the children, be she a real mother or a foster mother:

> *But he shall bear the cost*
> *Of their fooding and clothing*
> *On equitable terms* (II-233)

Several Traditions speak of the affection of the Holy Prophet for children. Once a rustic Arab said to the Holy Prophet: 'Do you kiss your Child? I have never done it myself.' At this the Holy Prophet said: 'If Allah has taken off all mercy from your heart, what can I do'.[36] In another Tradition the name of this rustic arab is mentioned as Iqra'b. Habis. He saw the Holy Prophet kissing the child Hasan and said: 'I have ten children. I never kiss them'. At this the Holy Prophet said: 'He who does not show mercy is not shown mercy'.[37] Still another Tradition observes: 'He who does not show affection to our juniors and respect to our ancestors is not one of us.[38]

In showing affection it is necessary to act on the principles of equality, that is no distinction should be made between superior and inferior in this regard—it is not proper to give some gift to one person and to deprive the other person from it on the basis of any distinction. There is the story of No'man. Once his father give him some gift. The Holy Prophet asked the father: 'Have you given such a gift to all your sons?' He said: 'No'. The Holy Prophet said: 'withdraw the gift you have given'.[39] Another Tradition reports this incident as follows: 'Do you like that all your children should receive equal treatment from you? He said 'Yes'. The Holy Prophet said: 'Then do not do such a thing (do not observe partiality."[40] Still another Tradition gives the following advice: 'Fear Allah, and mete out equal treatment among your children'.[41]

Special Attention to Bringing up of Daughters

Among Arabs the daughters had no importance. For this reason the Holy Prophet has drawn special attention to their character. He said: 'He who gets a daughter and lets her live, does not dishonour her and does not prefer her to the son—Allah will send him to paradise'. (*Abu Daud, Mishkat,* Babul Shafqa Wal Rahma 'alal Khalq). Another tradition says: 'He who has daughters and who metes out good treatment to them, his daughters will become a block against the fire of hell in his case. (*Bukhari, Muslim, Mishkat*)
Still another Tradition says:

> He who brings up two daughters till they come of age, he and I shall be together like two fingers of the hand on the Day of Judgment. (*Muslim, Mishkat*)

Family Planning for the Sake of Proper Bringing Up of Children

If poverty comes in the way of the proper bringing up of children child births should be properly spaced through various methods. Even birth control is permitted if it becomes necessary.

The various methods of birth control that are used in modern times were not there in the day of the revelation of the Quran. So it is not fair to look for some command in the Quran and the Sunnah regarding birth control and to reject birth control on not finding the command there. The basic consideration in this regard is that the fundamental principles of Islam are not violated. If they are violated birth control should be rejected. But if they are not violated then it is not fair to insist on opposing it. The possibility of both supporting and rejecting it should be kept open, subject to the demands of the circumstances. Just as there may be circumstances which demand the increase of population, in the same way there may be circumstances which demand birth control. Perhaps it is for this reason that the Quran and the Sunnah have not given any definite command regarding this matter.

Birth Control in Islam According to Circumstances

Here we give some evidences which suggest that Islam is not inimical to the policy of family planning and birth control. The Quran says:

If any of you have not
The means wherewith
To wed free believing women,
They may wed believing
Girls from among those
Whom your right hands possess (IV - 24)

Let those who find not
The wherewithal for marriage
Keep themselves chaste, until
God give them means
Out of His grace. (XXIV - 33)

Argument From The Quranic Verses

In the above Verses poverty is recognised as undesirable for marriage. It is therefore amenable to reason that if circumstances demand it the size of the family should be restricted through birth control. At the time when the Quran was revealed a birth control method, the *coitus obstructus* (not allowing the semen to go inside the women), was in vogue among Arabs. But it is significant that the Quran did not forbid it. Jabir has taken the silence of the Quran for permission: 'We practised *coitus obstructus* when the Quran was being revealed [42] Sufian says: 'If *coitus obstructus* was something to be prohibited, the Quran would have prohibited it'.[43] Regarding women the Quran says:

> *Your wives are*
> *As tilth unto you,*
> *So approach your tilth*
> *When and how ye will;* (II - 23)

In connection with interprettion of this Verse Ibn-i-Abbas, Ibn-i-Umar and Abu Haneefa provide the following comment: 'How ye will means practising *coitus obstructus* or without it'.[44] Another Verse of the Quran says that only one wife or slave-girl will be more suitable,

> *To prevent you*
> *From doing injustice* (IV - 3)

With regard to the interpretation of this Verse Zaid b. Aslam, Jabir b. Zaid (Successors of the Companions) and Imam Shafa'i offer the following comment: 'Being contented with one wife or slave-girl implies that you should not have many children'.[45] Sufian b. Ainia has offered the following interpretation: 'To prevent you from doing injustice' (IV - 3) comes close to the suggestions that you should not become isolvent and needy'.[46]

Argument From the Sayings of Saints and Scholars

There are various Traditions regarding the number of children. Some of them encourage big family, others encourage small family. In the same way there are many Traditions regarding *coitus obstructus.* Some of them imply permission, others imply prohibition of the practice. A study of all these Traditions indicate that in this matter the Holy Prophet had a liberal outlook and was moulding his outlook according to the demands of the circumstances. Otherwise he would have no difficulty in giving a commandment for or against birth control.

In the days of Caliph Omar the Conqueror and the ruler of Egypt Amroo b. Al-as gave the following lecture to the people. This lecture was moulded according to the Demands of the circumstances and it can be called a declaration of the government policy of that time:

> O my people! avoid four bad habits, for they cause distress after confort, misery after prosperity and degradation after honour: (1) Avoid having a great number of children (2) Avoid low standard of life, (3) Avoid wasting your goods through profligacy, and (4) Avoid wasting time in unnecessary and pointless discussion.[47]

This lecture has been quoted by Ibn-i-Hakeem in his history of Egypt (*Futuh-i-Misr wa Akhbaruha*, Vol.I, p.139)

Imam Ghazali and Shah Abdul Aziz have also permitted *coitus obstructus* as a method of birth control in view of poverty and destitution.[48]

After seeking religious sanction for birth control it does not remain important whether the man uses some device or the woman. But the sanction that has been suggested is conditional and applies only to critical cases. If a general sanction for birth control were given its consequence would be dangerous, as western and westernised cultures testify.

Education Regarding Both Man and the Universe Necessary

In addition to bringing up children education is also the responsibility of the parents. Undoubtedly the West has made great progress in matters of knowledge regarding the Universe, but as regards knowledge about man it is still very much backward. It is successful in understanding the mysteries of the universe but unsuccessful in understanding the mystery of man. David C. Marsh admits that our knowledge of the physical universe has become very wide. We have been able to control and harness the powers of nature to a great extent; but we are ignorant regarding innumerable aspects of man and his affairs to an unfortunately great extent.[49]

A.W. Haslet says that a scientist is not more helpless in other matters of knowledge than he is in the matter of knowledge about man. He can split the atom; can analyse the composition of the farthest star;can harness the power of electricity—but tne same scientist is confronted with difficulties when he wants to understand the nature of life and even his own or man's nature. For neither life nor man can yield to any experiment under controlled conditions.[50]

Both Kinds of Education Recommended By the Quran

In the Islamic scheme of cultural reconstruction so much knowledge about man is available that there is no problem in solving human problems. As regards Universe, it has been insisted not only that man should acquire all kinds of useful knowledge but should also maintain progress or evolution of human knowledge, otherwise the survival of the human species will be endangered. Hence the very beginning of the revelation of the Quran is by the commandment: 'Read' (*Iqra*) the very first Verse of the Quran points to the fact that man is originally a clot of blood. He does not deserve any exaltation on the basis of this origin, but it is only through knowledge that he is exalted to higher and higher stages:

Proclaim! (or Read!)
In the name
Of the Lord and Cherisher,
Who created—
Created man, out of

The (mere) clot
Of congealed blood:
Proclaim! and thy Lord
Is Most Bountiful,—
He Who taught
(The Use of) the Pen,—
Taught man that
Which he knew not. (XCVI—1-5)

Similary immediately after the creation of man (Adam) this truth was revealed, through a competitive test with the angles, that supremacy is determined by knowledge. The angels themselves has to acknowledge it—

'Glory to thee: of knowledge
We have none, save what Thou
Has taught us: in truth it is Thou
Who art perfect in knowledge and wisdom (II-32)

The episode of Talut also brings out the truth that supermacy is determined not by wealth, family, or racial or tribal religion, but by knowledge and physical prowess. The Quran relates the episode as follows:

Their Prophet said to them:
'God hath appointed
Talut as king over you.
They said: 'How can he
Exercises authority over us
When we are better fitted
Than he to exercise authority,

And he is not even gifted
With wealth in abundance?'
He said: 'God hath
Chosen him above you,
And hath gifted him
Abundantly with knowledge
And bodily prowess (II-247)

Conformity to Contemporary Standards of Prowess and Knowledge

It is not enough to have knowledge and physical prowess. Knowledge and physical prowess should be acquired in conformity with the standards of a particular age. For example the modern age is an age of science and technology, so in this age the measure of supremacy should be according to modern standards of knowledge and prowess.

The words 'power' (Quwwat) and 'iron' (AlHadid) have been used in the Quran in a manner that indicates that the equipment of power and technological potentialities of man shall go on increasing day by day. Without keeping pace with this progress no community can survive—

Against them make ready
your strength to the utmost
Of your power, (VIII-60)

And We send down Iron,
In which is (material for)
Mighty war, as well as
Many benefits for mankind, (LVII-25)

Both Kinds of Education Recommended By the Traditions

The Holy Prophet has drawn attention to knowledge in various ways. For example he says: 'I have been sent as a teacher'.[51] Regarding the Pen (which is a means of knowledge) he says: 'Allah created the Pen first'.[52]

The effects of knowledge have been recognised by the Holy Prophet: They are progress and exaltation: undoubtedly 'wisdom' adds to the nobility of the noble person and exalts the low persons to make them sit in the company of the King.[53]

Knowledge has been described by the Holy Prophet as the cause of the leadership of the nations and also of their influence over other people:

Knowledge is a weapon against enemy and an embellishment for the sake of friends. Allah raises nations through knowledge and exalts them to the position of leaders. They are followed by other nations and their opinions become decisive for other nations.[54]

God has made knowledge capable of infinite development. He has not confined it to any one (religious or worldly) sphere-- 'wisdom or knowledge is the lost property of the knower; he has a right to it wherever he finds it.[55]

The Holy Prophet has Recommended Long Journeys for the Sake of All Useful Knowledge:

The Holy Prophet has recommended that we should undertake journeys to very remote places for the sake of all kinds of useful Knowledge—and without any prejudice too: A Tradition says 'Aquire Knowledge even if you have to go to China'.[56] This Tradition has been regarded as 'weak' in terms of the degree of authenticity.[57] But its import is very much in line with the spirit of Islam, and it does not say anything fantastic either. China and Arabia are to antipodes. But the ports of Arabia were visited by the merchant ships of China in those days, and Chinese goods were sold in some Arabian towns. Masudi writes that 'Chinese ships visited the ports of Amman, Seraf, Fars and Bahrain'.[58] About the port of Daba in Amman Ibn-i-Habib writes: 'There was a port called Daba. On the last day of the month of Rajab a big market or fair was set up there. In this fair came merchants from Sindh, Hindustan, China and from various places of the east and the west'.[59]

The Holy Prophet Used the Most Important Modern Weapons of His Time

The most important weapons of the days of the Holy Prophet were as follows:
Dabbaba: It was a special kind of armoured car, made for protection against arrows by coating it with layers of thick skin. It was used for the purpose of battering fortresses.[60]
Zabr: It was made in the shape of an umbrella from skin mounted on wood, and was used for protecting the back against arrows'.[61]
Minjaniq: It was a weapon of offence, and was a kind of sling by which heavy stones were thrown at the enemy. (*Lissanul Arab*)
Hasak: It was a kind of thorny shrub which was spreas around the fortress and around the enemy army so as to make the way dangerous for the enemy. (*AlQamusul Muhit*)

The Holy Prophet was the First to Use Minjaniq and Hasak

The Holy Prophet imported *Minjaniq* and *Hasak* for deployment in the Battle of Taif.[62] In fact, he himself was the first to use *Minjaniq* and *Hasak*. Ibn-i-Hisham says:

> A trustworthy person reported to me that in Islam the Holy Prophet himself was the first to use *Minjaniq* against the army of Taif. (*Al Siyarul Nabuwiyah,* Zikr Ghazwatul Taif)

Miqraizi says:

> The Holy Prophet installed the Minjaniq on the fortress of Taif.[63]

Another report says:

The Holy Prophet spread Hasak around the fortress of Taif.[64]

There are various accounts regarding the *Minjaniq* that the Holy Prophet used. Some reporters say it was imported, while others say it was made by Salman Farsi.[65] After the conquest of Taif, in the year 9 H., Urwabin Masud Thaqafi and Ghailan bin Salma Thaqafi adopted Islam and went to Jarsh and acquired skill in the use of the above-mentioned weapons:

Urwa bin Mas'ud Thaqafi and Ghailan bin Salma Thaqafi were not present in the siege of Hunain and Taif. They had gone away to Jarsh to learn the art of using *Dababa, Manjaniq* and *Zabr.* (Ibn-i-Hisham, *Al Siyarul Nabuwiya,* Vol. III, Ghazwatul Taif: *A Rauzul' Unuf,* Zikr T'alim Ihlil Taif)

Arms Factory at Jarsh

Jarsh was a town in the suburbs of Damascus. It was under the power of Rome, which was second in greatness in those days. This town had big arms factory. It was conquered by Sharjil bin Husna in the days of Omar's Caliphate:

(The town) was under the suzerainty of Rome, Sharjit conquered it in the days of Omar bin Khatab. (*Imta'ul Asma',* Nazala Rasulullah bil' Araj, Hashiya 366)

The Holy prophet's Command to Develop the Science of Weaponry

When, after the conquest of Jarsh, the arms factory fell to the hands of Muslims they developed it further. The Holy Prophet incited his people in various ways to learn the arts of warfare. For example he said: 'He who gives up archary after learning it is not one of us'.[66] On another occasion he said: 'By the virtue of one arrow Allah sends three persons to paradise: the maker of it who wants to earn a reward (from God), the archer who shoots it, and the helper who picks the arrow and gives it (to the archer)'.[67]

The above agrument should make it clear that the Islamic system of education encompasses all spheres of life.

Special Attention to Character-building

Along with the acquiring of knowledge and skill special attention is drawn to character-building in the commandments of Islam. The commandments in this regard are addressed to parents and teachers first. In western culture there is no standard of character. In the Islamic scheme of cultural reconstruction the standard is there: It is the Attributes of God Himself. These Attributes are related not only to Beauty but also to Glory (and Power) and Perfection. The qualities of character that emanate from these Attributes have been discussed above. All the qualities are needed, in due proportion, for the development of a balanced character. By innate dispositions certain qualities may be increased or decreased; but such a thing should not be allowed to happen by human design.

Both the East and the West have Failed Here

Here, in the matter of character-building both the East and the West have failed. About the West, it can be said that it aimed at worldly gain only, and therefore it gave importance only to those qualities of character which are related to the acquisition of worldly gains. But how about the East? The East has not been able to achieve any success in character-building beyond a few moral reforms, and this in spite of its spiritual trumpeting.

The Pattern of Balanced Personality is the Holy Prophet

In the scheme of cultural reconstruction the pattern of balanced personality is the Holy Prophet. As the Quran puts it:

We have indeed
In the Apostle of God
A beautiful pattern (to conduct) (XXXIII. 21)

That the Apostle may be
A witness for you, and ye
Be his witness for mankind! (XXII. 78)

Thus have We made of you
An Ummat justly balanced,
That ye might be witnesses

Over the nations,
And the Apostle a witness
Over yourselves (II. 143)

Those who are perceptive know how perfect and comprehensive the life of the Holy Prophet was.

The Life of the Companions As A Pattern Of Character-Building

After the life of the Holy Prophet the life of his companions is a pattern of character-building. These Companions performed in every sphere of life such feats as have no equal in human history. If their activities had been confined to any one particular sphere Islamic civilization would not have come into existence. Nor would it have survived.

Adjacent to Masjid-e-Nabwi there was an institution called Saffa. This institution trained the companions in character-building. Its activities encompassed all spheres of life in those days. The products of Saffa exemplified a particular way of life. They undertook responsibilities of earning livelihood, education and other responsibilities of citizenship, and along with these the responsibilities of participating in battles voluntarily. Some eminent products of the Saffa institutions were: Abdullah b. Masood, Saad b. Abi Waqqas, Huzaifa b. Yamaan, Abdullah b. Omar, Salman Farsi, Abu Darda, Abu Huraira, Salim, Abu Zar Ghifari, Hanzala, Bilal Habshi and Suheb Roomi. *(Tabaqati Ibni-i-S'ad*, Vol. I, II; *Musnad; Ibn-i-Hambal, Vol. I)*. Their deeds testify to the education for character-building that the Holy Prophet initiated.

Fundamental Principles of Character-building

From the Quran the following fundamental principles of character-building can be derived. They are : (1) gnosis, (2) Utility, (3) Trustworthiness, (4) Responsibility of Care taking,

(5) Justice and (6) Application. We shall discuss them below:

(1) *Gnosis:* It means the realization of the self and the realization of God. On the one hand it would inculcate virtues like self responsibility, liberal outlook, boldness, contentment and freedom from wants, and on the other virtues like humility, hope, piety, resignation, discipline and fortitude. —

As also in your own
Selves : will ye not
Then see (LI-21)

Because God will never change
The Grace which He hath bestowed
On a People until they change
What is in their (own) souls: (VIII-53)

Without the realization of the self the realization of God is not possible :

And be ye not like
Those who forget God :
And He made them forget
Their souls (LIX-19)

(2) *Utility:* It means that every individual should become useful: according to his natural abilities. The individual should be equipped with all kinds of accomplishments, material, moral, spiritual, physical etc. The Quran says:

He sends down water
From the skies, and the channels
Flow, each according to its measure:
But the torrent bears away
The foam that mounts up
To the surface. Even so,

From that (Ore) which they heat
In the fire, to make ornaments
Or utensils therewith,
There is a scum likewise.
Thus doth God (by parables)
Show forth Truth and Vanity.
For the scum disappears
Like froth cast out;
While that which is for the good
Of mankind remains on the earth. (XIII-17)

In the above parable the useful things like silver and gold remain, and the useless things which are the scum disappear like froth. The obvious implication is that in this world only the useful things survive and the useless things gradually perish.

In our Muslim society the concept of utility has been confined to moral betterment, and thus material power was left to the worldly people. This has resulted in degradation and lowness. Even if moral betterment is accomplished, progress can not be made without physical power. This fallacy has two reasons behind it: (1) The wrong concept of religion led people to think that only by performing certain religious rituals they would achieve all that the worldy people do by tireless effort and striving. This is against God's law of justic. (2) The wrong concept of miracles led to the notion that things, and even the advancement of a nation, can happen without any physical causality. This is against the law of nature. The property of the fire is to burn. He who puts his hand into it, will necessarily get burnt. If the fire was turned into a garden in the case of Abraham, it was a miracle which has no relation to the common laws of nature. But the world is run by the common laws of nature and not by miracles.

(3) *Trustworthiness*: The notion that trustworthiness is the basis of the good life should be promoted. In this world man is like a trustee (*Ameen*). God has endowed him with a Trust and he is to answer for his deeds before God. The Quran syas :

God doth command you
To render back your Trusts
To those whom they are due; (IV.58)

In the above verse the word 'trusts' has a general meaning; it includes all kinds of responsibilities, be they related to one's duty towards God or to one's duty towards fellow human beings. The Holy Prophet has regarded trustworthiness as the basis of faith. He says : 'He who is not capable of trustworthiness, does not have faith'.[69] Another Tradition says : 'The first thing that you will loose from your religion is trustworthiness, and the last thing that you will loose in prayers (*namaz*). Some people will go on saying prayers but religion will not be with them.[70]

(4) *Responsibility of Care-taking*: Every individual should feel his own responsibility and also the responsibility of others. He should extend whatever kind of help is needed by others, be it moral or material. He should extent this help as a matter of his duty. The Quran says:

O ye who believe!
Save yourself and your
Families from a Fire. (LXVI-6)

At another place the fulfilment of the needs of God's creature has been described as the giving of a beautiful loan to God Himself —

Who is he
that will loan to God
A beautiful loan, which God

Will double unto his credit
And multiply many times? (II – 245)

The Holy Prophet once said: 'listen! everyone of you is the caretaker of others, and everyone will be asked about his responsibility towards those who are under his care. (*Bukhari,* Kitabul Istiqraz) The word *Raa'i* means: 'Guarding the other person according to his Good' (*Baizawi*) hence Raa'i is : 'anyone who is the guardian of somebody else' (*AlMunjid.*). At another place it has been said: 'The creatures are the children of Allah. The person who does good to Allah's children is a dearer to Allah! (*Mishkat,* Bab fil Shafqa' lal Khalq)

The care-taking mentioned above should be carried out in a particular spirit. The Holy Prophet has elucidated it through a parable :

Think, there is a ship having many people on board. The provisions for their needs (water etc.) are kept in the upper storey of the ship. Those who are in the lower storey keep coming to the upper storey for, say, water. If the people of the upper storey allow them to have water out of a spirit of carmaraderie, everything works well, and no untoward incident happens. But if the people in the upper storey deny water to the people of the lower storey just because it causes a little trouble to them, the people of the lower storey will be forced to adopt some other means for getting water. Suppose they decide to make a hole in the bottom of the ship for getting water, and start making this hole. Now if the people of the upper storey neither prevent them from making the hole nor allow them to have water, it is evident that the ship will sink. Then, neither the hole-makers will survive, nor those who ignored their responsibility towards them. (*Bukhari, Mishkat :* Bab Amr bil Ma' ruf)

In the above Tradition life is compared to the situation of being on board a ship and the needs of life to water, The spirit of co-operation, which should not be violated in spite of some trouble, is emphasized in a beautiful way. The violation of this spirit in the ship leads to the sinking of the ship and the destruction of all its inmates, be they of the upper storey or of the lower storey. All these elements of the parable have a significant bearing on the understanding of the human situation and the truths of social psychology.

5. *Justice*: Justice implies balance in all spheres of life, so that everything may have its course without transgression limits and along the way of temperance. We have already discussed Justice. Here we shall reinforce the argument by some quotations from the Quran and the Traditions.

The Quran has prohibited intemperance and excess, and has recommended balance and temperance in every sphere of life :

O People of the Book!
Commit no excesses
In your religion: nor say
Of God aught but the truth (IV-171)

Say : 'O People of the Book!
Exceed not in your religion
The bounds (of what is proper),
Tresspassing beyond the truth,
Nor follow the vain desires
Of people who went wrong
In times gone by, —
Who mislled
Many, and strayed (themselves)
From the even way (V-8)

The Holy Prophet drew attention to temperance, balance and justice. He said :

Do not be harsh on yourselves, otherwise Allah will be harsh on you. For when the people before you were harsh on themselves Allah was harsh on them. Their remnants are now the priests of the worshipping places of the Christians and the Jews.

Once upon a time three companions visited the house of the Holy Prophet in order to find out the truth about his private worship and prayers. When they were told about it they thought that the worship and prayers were not very much. But they also thought that the Holy Prophet was already among the saved and they themselves were sinners, so perhaps no comparison could be drawn between them. On that occasion one of the Companions took a vow to keep awake all night in prayer. The other said that he would always keep fast. The third one said that he would not marry. When the Holy Prophet came out of his house and when he was told about their vows, he impressed it upon them that they should not be so harsh to themselves in matters of religion and that they should adopt a moderate or middle course:

Remember I have more of piety than you, but I sometimes fast and sometimes eat, sometimes say prayer and sometimes I sleep and cohabit with women. He who deviates from my Way or Sunnah is not one of mine. (*Bukhari, Mishkat, Muslim, Abu Daud,* Kitabul I'tisam bil Kitab wal Sunna, Fast I)

6. *Application:* Application means that one's belief and ideals should be translated into one's actions. It means that one's life should be a continuous enactment of these beliefs and ideals. This virtue takes an individual out of the world of self-delusion and brings him into the world of practical life. It puts this Practical life at the very center of his being. The Quran says:

And say: 'work (righteousness):
Soon will God observe you work,
And his Apostle, and the believers: (IX-105)

That man can have nothing
But what he strives for: (LIII-39)
...to them
We shall pay (the price of)
their deeds therein (XI.15)

The following Tradition brings out the significance of application and the life of action:

'Suppose there are three workers. One of them works from morning till noon; the other from noon till sometime in the afternoon; and the third from sometime in the afternoon till dusk. The first two get one carat each as wages, and the third gets two carats each. Then the Holy Prophet said that the first two are the Jews and the Christians and the third one is my 'Ummat'; (this third category worker has such a great efficiency that) in comparatively less time he does the same work to earn double wages. (*Mishkat*, Bab Thawabi Hazihil Ummah)

Punishment for Evil Deeds Postponed In the Case of the Practical

Efficiency is so important that God postpones the punishment of those who are practical. In their case immediate punishment for evil deeds would cause disturbance in the system of the Universe and in the dialectical process of its functioning. Shah Waliullah says:

Indeed, Divine justice does not let any sinner remain unpunished in this world, except that it may be done on consideration of causing disturbance in the functioning of the world. (*Hujjatullahi Baligha*, Al Jazai'alal A'mali fil Dunya).

He goes on to add:

Many times it happens that the commandment in consideration of the system of the universe becomes more urgent than the commandment in consideration of individual's deeds. It is for this reason that the evil doer is given a long rope and the righteous person has to face hardships. The hardships serve the purpose of breaking down his selfish desires. *(Ibid)*.

We See Only One Aspect of Reality

In advanced countires people are not getting punishment for their evil deeds. It is so because their deeds imply dynamism and practical abilities, which make for the dynamic movement of the universe. It is not that evils are not regarded as evils now, in the modern age, or that they have been transformed intc virtues. In fact we human beings have a limited view, and we see only one aspect of reality, whereas Divine Providence sees the total reality. If we were to see all the aspects of reality we would not raise doubts regarding the functioning of Divine Providence.

In Western Culture Woman is Licentiously Free

In western culture the supremacy of man has ended, which has resulted in the disintegration of the unity of the family and given licentious freedom to woman. Behind this kind of freedom the motive is not so much self-reform as of revenge against man. So in every sphere of life woman is pitted against man, so much so that even in the case of immorality of sexual licentiousness woman claims equal rights with man. In the personal affairs of a woman the husband or somebody else is not entitled to interfere. Even marriage is regarded as a restraint because it is supposed to restrict personal freedom and frustrate one's enjoyment. Western civilization does make woman 'equal' to man, and even his rival, but it has failed to fill up the 'vacuum' that woman has left behind her in that particular sphere which was specifically her own. Thus a 'vacuum' has been created in family life and is increasing day by day and causing all kinds of trouble.[71]

What happened was this that the wrong concept of religion and morality kept woman deprived of her natural right for a long time, and now the licentious freedom and feminine revolt that we see is actually a reaction of the age-old suppression of woman's natural right. Thus in the present situation both man and woman are uneasy. But things have gone so far that people are helpless to put any check. If somebody dares to do so he is called conservative, which implies the greatest stigma of our time.

Superiority of Man in the Scheme of Cultural Reconstruction

In the scheme of cultural reconstruction the superiority of man is maintained. Woman has been given her due position and the sphere of her activity has been determined and defined. She can contribute to civilization only by remaining within this natural spheres of hers. In this regard the following considerations are involved: (1) The nature of sexual relations, (2) The safeguarding of sexual relations, (3) The limits of the activities of woman.

(1) *The Nature of Sexual Relations:* The relation between man and woman is one of pairing and of mutual assimilation. The Quran has pointed this out but has not ascribed it specifi-

cally to human beings; it is the general pattern in all living things.

And of everything
We have created pairs;
That ye may receive
Instructions (LI-49)

Glory to God, Who created
In pairs all things that
The earth produces, as well as
their own (human) kind
And (other) things of which
They have no knowledge. (XXXVI-36)

... He has made
For you pairs
From among yourselves,
And pairs among cattle: (XLII-11)

The male-female relation is made firm through wedding. The purpose of sexual relation is not the timely appeasement of sexual desire. This relation is made firm so as to form a basis for the whole life. It ensures the well-wedding and survival of both the sexes. The Quran says:

Wed them with the leave
Of their owners, and give them
Their dowers, according to what
Is reasonable: they should be
Chaste, not lustful, nor taking
Paramours (IV-25)

They are your garments
And ye are their garments (II-187)

The Holy Prophet says: 'The whole world is a means of your benefit, and the best means of benefit is a virtuous wife.[72] Another Tradition says: 'He who has the capability of wedding should wed; for wedding safeguards the eyes (against sinful glances and the private parts).[73]

Wedding Promotes the Spirit of Love And Sacrifice

Wedding promotes the spirit of love and sacrifice between the husband and the wife. It provides solace among hardships:

> *It is He Who created*
> *You from a single person,*
> *And made his mate*
> *Of like nature, in order*
> *That he might dwell with her*
> *(in Love).* (VII - 189)

> *... He created*
> *For you mates from among*
> *Yourselves, that ye may*
> *Dwell in tranquillity with them,*
> *And He has put love*
> *And mercy between your (hearts):*
> *Verily in that our Signs are for those*
> *Who reflect* (XXX - 21)

The Holy Prophet said: 'you should not have seen two lovers like those who are joined in wedding lock' (*Mishkat,* Kitabun Nikah, Fast III).
At another occasion he said:

> Next to piety there is nothing more beneficial for a believer than a virtuous wife. If he commands her she obeys; if he looks at her she becomes happy; if he swears by her, he has got to fulfil his word; if she is not there he wishes well for himself and for her goods. (Ibid.)

Marriage Forms the Basis of the Family Institution

Marriage forms the basis of the institution of the family and acts as a safeguard against promiscuity and the sowing of wild oats. The Quran says:

It is He Who has
Created man from water:
Then has He established
Relationship of lineage
And marriage: (XXV - 54)

Your wives are
As a tilth unto you
So approach your tilth
When or how you will;
But do some good act
For your souls beforehand; (II - 223)

The point of the comparison of the wife to a tilth is that sexual relation is meant, not merely for the purpose of satisfying sexual desire, but for the purpose of ensuring the survival of the human race. As the cultivator has the responsibility of not merely sowing the seed but also of providing what the land needs and of protecting it, so has the husband similar responsibilities towards his wife.

Man as the Head of the Family

It is natural for man to be the head of the family. Owing to the natural differences between the two sexes man is more disposed to being active and tough while woman is more disposed to be passive and soft. Besides, man shoulders the responsibility of earning livelihood for the family. The Quran says:

Man are the protectors

And maintainers of women,
Because God has given
The one more (strength)
Than the other, and because
They support them
From their means. (IV - 34)

The Holy Prophet said:

Man is the care-taker of his wife and children. In this matter he is answerable to God. (*Bukhari, Kitabun Nikah*).

It Makes No Difference to the Rights of Woman

The recognition of the superiority of man makes no difference to the rights of woman, nor does it make man entitled to greater rewards for good deeds and virtuous behaviour. 'Women have rights on men just as men have rights on women', says the Quran. At another place it is said: 'Men will earn their rewards according to their deeds, and women will earn their rewards according to theirs' (IV - 32)

SEX AND THE MAINTENANCE OF CHASTITY

Purity of Mind and Heart

Islam has confined sexual relations to matrimonial life, and has commanded us to have hearts and minds purified of lustful desires as far as possible. For this purpose it has emphasized the notion of answerability to God, which is an effective means of maintaining chastity. Thus the Quran says:

Whether
Ye show what is in your minds
Or conceal it, God
Calleth you to account for it. (II - 284)

Say: 'Whether ye hide
What is in your hearts
Or reveal it,
God knows it all.

(III - 29)

Brazen Stare Prohibited

Men are forbidden to stare at women brazenly, for such stares stimulate erotic feelings:

Say to the believing men
That they should lower
Their gaze and guard
Their modesty: that will make
For greater purity for them:
And God is well acquainted
With all that they do.
And say to the believing women
That they should lower
Their gaze and guard
Their modesty;

(XXIV - 30)

Control Over Speech and Voice

Women have been commanded to exercise control over their speech and voice, for these things too may stimulate erotic feelings.

If ye do fear (God),
Be not too complaisant
Of speech, lest one
In whose heart is

A disease should be moved
With desire: but speak ye
A speech (that is) just. (XXXIII - 32)

Scandal-mongering and Immodest Talk Prohibited

Indulging in scandals and immodest talk has been prohibited.

Those who love (to see)
Scandal published broadcast
Among the Believers, will have
A grievous Penalty in this life
And in the Hereafter (XXIV - 19)

Exhibition of Beauty and Immodest Dress Prohibited

Exhibition of beauty has been prohibited because it stimulates erotic feelings — 'make not a dazzling display, like that of the former Times of Ignorance (XXXIII - 33). Tight and thin or transparent dress has also been forbidden, for it also involves exhibition of the body. Women 'should draw their veils over their bosoms' (XXIV - 31). The Holy Prophet said:

> The women who exhibit their bodies even after dressing up and thus try to attract others to themselves or to be attracted towards others; and the women who walk mincingly with their neck bent like that of a camel — such women will not enter paradise, nor will they catch even its fragrance' (*Muslim*, Babul Nisa Al Kasiyatul' Aariyat).

Coming out wearing some perfume is also prohibited. The Holy Prophet said: 'The woman who passes by people wearing purfumes so that they may be pleased is in fact a woman who is inviting immorality (*Nisai, Abu Daud*)

Prohibition Against Meeting of Man and Woman in Privacy

The meeting of man and woman in privacy has been prohibited because it would give an opportunity for Satan to do his work.

Do not seek to meet those women in privacy who are not your close relations, for Satan circulates in man like blood (*Muslim*, Kitabul Libas wal Zinah)

LIMITS TO WOMAN'S ACTIVITY

If woman is allowed licentious freedom and if she is allowed to take part in every kind of activity (lawful or unlawful) it is going to disturb the institution of the family and the proper relations between the sexes. This is why in the scheme of cultural reconstruction the activities of woman are subject to real needs and the permission of her husband. Bertrand Russel gives two reasons for the social evils of western civilization: the emancipation of woman and the device of birth control. But the real reason is the lack of social control, which has created many subsidiary reasons also. Social control is a way of controling the minds and action of the individuals. Various efforts were made to achieve this social control, but these efforts have not met with any success.

The Best Means of Social Control is Religion

The best means of social control is religion, and this is the means used in the Islamic scheme of cultural reconstruction. Religion has the following bearings on human life:

(1) It induces the fear of God and the idea of answerability to God, which controls human actions and thoughts.
(2) Religion helps man to exercise control over his thoughts and feelings, which makes for balance for individual life on the one hand for social stability and solidarity on the other.
(3) It makes for peace of the soul and for the reform of inward and outward life.
(4) It determines the standard for sexual morality and social character and sets up a watch on human relations.
(5) The noble principles of religion make for the control of social evils and protect society against anti-social elements.

The above features of religion have been recognised in every age. All Sociologists affirm the constructive role played by religion in human history. Even Bertrand Russel admits that the fear of hell-fire and of pregnancy were the two factors that guaranteed the preservation of the modesty of woman in the past. Now that the influence of religion has declined and anti-pregnancy devices have emerged both these restricting factors have disappeared and the situation has become what it is.

Possibility of Change in the Sphere of Woman's Activity

The sphere in which woman can play her role and the sphere in which she cannot are matters related to the permission of the husband and the real needs of the community. It is obvious that these determining factors are subject to change in accordance with the change of the circumstances. However, two things must be considered before a particular task is delegated to woman. First, it should be seen that no disturbance is created in the status of woman and in the family institution. Secondly, the laws related to both these subjects should be respected. With these precautionary measures it is not necessary that the woman should cover her face or hands when she comes out to work. The Quran says:

> *... that they*
> *Should not display their*
> *Beauty and ornaments except*
> *What (must ordinarily) appear*
> *Therein.* (XXIV - 31)

'Except what (must ordinarily) appear therein' has been interpreted in various ways by exegetes. Here we quote a preferable interpretation. This has been reported by Aisha:

Once the daughter of Abu Bakr, Asma came before the Holy Prophet wearing a thin dress. The Holy Prophet turned away and said: 'when a woman comes of age it is not proper that any part of her body except the hands and the face becomes visible. (*Abu Daud*)

Walking out is of less importance as compared to the face and the body. Perhaps for this reason it has not been mentioned separately. But if a society is corrupt and if the modesty of woman is in danger when she comes out, special precaution is needed. This is testified by the following Verse:

> *O Prophet! tell*
> *Thy wives and daughters,*
> *And the believing women,*
> *That they should cast*
> *Their outer garments over*
> *Their persons (when abroad):*
> *That is most convenient,*
> *That they should be known*
> *(as such) and not molested* (XXXIII - 59)

'that they should be known (as such) and not molested' testifies to the consideration of the circumstances and the change in the law accordingly. Certainly Traditions indicate that before the days of the Holy Prophet and even in later times in Arab society there was the custom of covering the face. We need not go into details here. But the reader can refer to the following works for his own benefit: (*Alminar* by Rashid Raza Misri, Vol. X, Chapter 11 and Vol. xiii., Chapters 9-10-11; *Hijabul Maratul Mussallema Fil Kitabe Wal Sunna* by Mohammad Nasiruddin Al Yani (Cairo and Beirut).

SOCIAL SYSTEM

Western Culture Could Not provide a Firm Basis for Society

The basis of social life is the family. The condition of the family determines the social system. In western culture the disruption of the family, the invention of new philosophies and the lust for money have precluded the formation of a firm basis for social life.

Consequently, life has become mechanical; every person feels himself or herself lonely and uprooted; and even the daughter of a millionaire has to work for her living by doing an ordinary job, for her father abandons the responsibility of supporting her.

Human Society as the Family of God

In the Islamic scheme of cultural reconstruction the basis of social system is the family. The family is the unit of social system and a miniature society. Just as affection, rights and duties are organizing principles of the family, in the same way they are organizing principles of the society as a whole, which is conceived as a larger family or the family of God. The members of this larger family are brothers and sisters to one another. Thus the Holy Prophet said:

"All creatures make the family of God. God loves him more who treats His family folks well".[74] Another Tradition says: 'All human beings are brothers (and sisters) to one another'.(*Muslim, Abu Daud*).

In order to understand a social system knowledge of three things is needed. They are: the nature of the family, the nature of human life, and the duties of man in life.

NATURE OF THE FAMILY

A. God has created all human beings from a single pair of common parents:

O mankind! We created
You from a single (pair)
Of a male and a female, (XLIX - 13)

The Holy Prophet said: 'All human beings are the children of

Adam, and Adam was created out of clay'. (*Tabri*)

B. All men are sinless and holy by birth. The Quran speaks of "God's handiwork according to the pattern on which He has made mankind" (XXX - 30). The Holy Prophet says that 'every child is born according to the original pattern of nature'. According to this original pattern every man is sinless and Holy.

C. Human beings are superior to other creatures

> *We have honoured the sons*
> *Of Adam* (XVII - 70)
>
> *We have indeed created man*
> *In the best of moulds,* (XCV - 4)

There is a Hadith-i-Qudsi which says:

> The creature (man) whom I have created with my own Hands and breathed of my Spirit unto him — I shall never put him on a par with those creatures for whom I merely said: 'Be I' and they came into being (*Mishkat,* Bab Badil Khalq)

D. All human beings have been addressed by the Word of God (revelation)

> *... and to every people*
> *A guide* (XIII - 7)
>
> *And there never was*
> *A people, without a warner*
> *Having lived among them*
> *(in the past)* (XXXV - 24)

E God has provided equal opportunities for all.

'God has created all that is there on the earth for the benefit of all of you', says the Quran. The Holy Prophet says:

'Except three things man does not have a right on anything else: (1) A house to live in, (2) Garments to cover the body and (3) Water and pieces of bread.'

NATURE OF LIFE

(A) The Lord of life is, not man, but God

God hath purchased all the Believers
Their persons and Their goods (IX-111)

(B) Life is not a futile activity; it is trust

Did ye think
That We had created you
In jest, and that ye
Would not be brought back
To Us (for account)? (XXIII - 115)

(C) Life is not absolutely independent or free; there are certain laws governing it.

Does Man think
That he will be left
Uncontrolled, (without purpose)? (LXXV - 36)

MAN'S DUTIES IN LIFE

Man has two kinds of duties in life: (1) duties related to the universe and (2) duties related to man.

Duties Related to the Universe

(A) It means making use of human faculties to deploy the things of the universe for man's use:

It is We Who have
Blessed you with authority
On earth, and provided
You therein with means

For the fulfilment of your life (VII - 10)
Say: work (righteousness):
Soon will God observe your work,
And His Apostle, and the Believers (IX - 105)

(B) The means of subsistence should be developed so much that nobody may remain deprived of his living:

And We have provided therein
Means of subsistence, — for you
And for those for whose subsistence
Ye are not responsible (XV - 20)
It is He Who has
Spread out the earth
For (His creatures): (LV — 10)

(C) Through labour and striving man should develop the things of nature:

That man can have nothing
But what he strives for (LIII - 39)
... to them
We shall pay (the prize
Of) their deeds therein (XI - 15)

The means of human power keep changing according to circumstances. For example, in modern times we have weapons like the rifles, the missiles, the machine gun, the tank etc. and then we have technology, industry, modern trade and commerce, journalism, literature and modern arts and science. All these things go to make up modern civilized life.

The Centrality of God in Matters of Duties

In matters of duties towards the universe and in all affairs of human activity God should have a central place, and subordination to him should be recognised. Otherwise dreadful consequences may follow, and such dreadful consequences may follow, and such dreadful consequences can be seen in the materialistic civilization of our times. This is why in those verses of the Quran where attention is drawn towards the order of the Universe and man is encouraged to subject the universe to himself God has been mentioned or suggested in some way. This indicates that for man's activity in the Universe God has a central place and man must subject himself to him. Only then his reason and experience can guide him properly and further instruction may not be necessary.

Duties Related to Man

It must be recognised that all human beings are involved with one another, so that if one human being is unjustly killed, it is as if the whole people were killed, and if one human being has been saved from destruction, it is as if the whole human race were saved from destruction. The Quran says that if anyone slew a person

It would be as if
He slew the whole people:
And if anyone saved a life,
It would be as if he saved
The life of the whole people. (V - 35)

Every individual must be deemed responsible for taking care of the other. This care-taking may be material as well as moral and spiritual. The individual will specialise in that sphere of responsibility with which he is more conversant.

Material Responsibility

Regarding material responsibility the Quran says:

Serve God and join not
Any partners with Him,

And do good ——
To parents, kinsfolk,
Orphans, those in need,
Neighbours who are near,
Neighbours who are strangers,
Companions by your side,
The wayfarer (ye meet),
And what your right hands possess (IV.36)

And render to the kindred
Their due rights, as (also)
To those in want,
And to the wayfarer:
But squander not (your wealth)
In the manner of a spendthrift. (XVII.26)

As regards subordinates and juniors the Holy Prophet says:

They are your brothers. Allah has made them subordinate or junior to you. He to whom makes his brother subordinate must give him to eat what he himself eats, give him to wear what he himself wears, and must not have assign him any work which he himself cannot do, or if he assigns him such a work he must himself helf him, as a co-worker. (*Bukhari,* Kitabul Iman).

Special commandment is given regarding treatment towards women:

On the contrary live with them
On a footing of kindness and equality.
If ye take a dislike to them
It may be that ye dislike
A thing, and God brings about
Through it a great deal of good. (IV.19)

Let the man or means

spend according
To his means:
And the man
Whose resources are restricted,
Let him spend according
To what God has given him. (LXV - 7)

In his sermon on the occasion of his last Haj the Holy Prophet said:

In your dealings with women fear God. You have made a convenant with them that God has a witness. (*Muslim; Mishkat,* Bab Jajjatul Wida)

Regarding treatment with human beings in general the Holy Prophet said: 'He who is engaged to fulfil the need of his brother, his need Allah is engaged to fulfil.'[75] At another place he said: 'The human creature does not become a complete Believer until he chooses for his brother what he chooses for himself.'[76]

Moral and Spiritual Duties

Regarding moral and spiritual duties the Quran says:

O ye who believe!
Save yourselves and your
Families from a Fire
Whose fuel is men
And Stone. (LXVI-6)

Help ye one another
In righteousness and piety. (V-3)

The Holy Prophet said: 'Listen everyone of you is a care-taker (or (or a shephered); and everyone of you will be asked about his care-taking of those who are put under his care'. (*Bukhari,* Kitabun Nikah)

Giving Priority to the Needs of Others Over One's Own Needs

One must always give priority to the needs of others over one's own needs. The Quran says:

By no means shall ye
Attain righteousness unless
Ye give (freely) of that
Which ye love. (III-92)

What has been recognised as the greatest virtue of the Helpers (Ansars) is the spirit of sacrifice. Attention is drawn to it in the following Verse of the Quran. It is said that the helpers

Give them (refugees) preference
Over themselves, even though
Poverty was their (own lot). (LIX-9)

Commandment to Overlook the Defects of Others

One must meet out good treatment of others in spite of their defects, shortcomings and wrongs. The Quran says:

Let not those among you
Who are endued with grace
And amplitude of means
Resolve by oath against helping
Their kinsmen, those in want,
And those who have left
Their homes in God's cause,
Let them forgive and overlook;
Do you not wish
That God should forgive you?

For God is Oft-Forgiving,
Most merciful. (XXIV-22)

The historical context of the revelation of this Verse is as follows. Some people made a false accusation against Aisha. Among them were some relations of Abu Bakr, whom Abu Bakr supported financially. After the innocence of Aisha had been established Abu Bakr felt bad about the relations whom he supported. He took an oath not to support them. Seeing him do it other companions also did the same regarding their relations. In the context of this situation the above Verse was revealed. It says that the bad deeds of others are for them. You must not change your good behaviour towards them. The reward is with God; always have hope of getting it from him and pleasing Him.

Things Necessary for the Maintenance of Social System

The following things are Necessary for the maintenance of the social system:

(1) The standard of honour should be such as to encompass all the people and to be equal applicable to all of them.
(2) The idols of the dinstinction of race, family colour and nationality should be broken down.
(3) There should be equality and amity regarding human relations on the level of practical life.

These factors have been given great attention in the Islamic scheme of cultural reconstruction. Some details in this regard would bring them home.

The Right Standard of Honour

Instead of the family, wealth, race etc. the standard of honour is character and moral behaviour. This standard can be acquired voluntarily and it is also acceptable to all human beings. The Quran says:

verily ...verily
The most honoured of you

In the sight of God
Is (He who is) the most
Righteous of you. (XLIX-13)

The Holy Prophet said: 'One person earns excellence over the other only on the basis of righteousness and piety'. (*Mishkat,* fi Sho'abil Iman)

Distinction of Family etc. Dissolved

It is very difficult to demolish the idols of race, family etc. Various efforts to do so were made in every age, but without leading to much success. But the Prophet of Islam (peace be upon him) adopted such devices in domestic and social life that people, both of inferior and superior status, began to feel that these men-make distinction of "high" and "low" had no validity. Islam first compaigned for the reform and purification of the minds and then it declared that the distinctions mentioned above were invalid and insignificant.

And made you into
Nations and tribes, that
Ye may know each other
(not that ye may despise each other). (XLIX-13)

The Holy Prophet said:

No Arab excels over a non-Arab, nor does a non-Arab excel over an Arab (*Mishkat,* Khutba Hajjatil Wida')

About colour and language the Quran says: 'And among the signs of God are the creation of the heavens and the earth and the differences of language and colour'

The above distinctions emerge more prominently in matters of marriage, and involve many complexities and subtleties. For this reason the Holy Prophet and his Companions began the charity at home and broke the idols of these distinctions. The Holy Prophet got his cousin Zainab married to a freed slave, Zaid

b. Harisa. Omar got married his son Asim to a milk-seller's widowed daughter. Both these evidences are famous in Islamic history. After reforming his own home Omar gave verdict in favour of marriage without the consent of the guardians, which is called 'marriage without sufficient conditions' (*Ghair Kafu*). The following incident bears it out. A rich man Mawali, who was one of the freed slaves, sent a proposal for marrying the sister of a Quraish. The Quraish refused saying: 'We are people of a high family. The man does not suffice for my daughter' When Omar came to know of it he sent for the Quraish and said that the man was well to do as well as righteous. If his sister was willing he should wed her to him. The Quraish asked his sister and she expressed her willingness, and the wedding was performed. (*Siyasat—i—Farooq-i-A'zam,* Izalatul Khifa, Maqsad II)

Jurists have discussed at length *Kafu* or sufficient conditions for marriage, but in modern times it need not be a subject of discussion. The discussion of the jurists is guided by considerations of compromise with the circumstances. It is not a verdict of the Shariah. The subject came up for discussion after the time of the Holy Prophet and his Companions and stirred up great controversy among the jurists. Among the conditions considered sufficient for marriage are bravery, good family, vocation, financial status, age and religion (moral character). But except religion all the other requisites are subject to controversy. The fact that all the jurists agree on the point of religion and disagree on all other points itself goes to prove that only religion is the condition laid down by the Shariah. The other requisites or conditions are there only for making matrimonial life comfortable. In modern times the other requisites for 'sufficiency' are obstructions to marriage and become a blot an Islamic culture. Hence in our scheme of cultural reconstruction we would consider religion *plus* social status as sufficient conditions for marriage, which were considered so in the era of Prophethood, too. In our scheme education and the ability of earning livelihood should become more important since these are the demands of our time. These factors certainly go to make matrimonial life comfortable.

Equality and Amity in Human Relations

The equality and amity in human relations has been emphasised by Islam. This is brought out by an incident in the life of the Holy Prophet. Once the Holy Prophet was talking to the Jews of Mecca on Islam. On that occasion a ragged, blind man (Ibn-i-Umme Maktum) came in and expressed his desire to know something. The Holy Prophet did not like this interruption. At this the following Verse was revealed:

(The Prophet) frowned
and turned away
Because there came to him
The blind man (interrupting).
But what could tell thee
But that purchance he might
Grow (in spiritual understanding)?—
Or that he might receive
Admonition, and the teaching
Might profit him?
As to one who regards
Himself as self-sufficient,
To him dost thou attend;
Though it is no blame
To thee if he grow not
(in spiritual understanding).
But as to him who came
To thee striving earnestly,
And with fear
(In his heart),
Of him wast thou unmindful (LXXX-1-10)

Abolition of Distinctions for the Sake of Equality

When there is slight corruption in society ordinary reforms will do, but when the corruption is so deep that it seeps into the very fibres of a community strict measures are required and 'high' and 'low' have got to be inverted.

Once Sohail b. Amr, Haris b. Hissham, Abu Sufian and other dignitaries of the Quraish came to Omar. At the same time Sohaib, Bilal and other freed slaves also came. Omar gave priority to these slaves in giving an audience. At this Abu Sufian angrily said: 'I never saw such an outrage. These slaves get permission for audience (to the Caliph) and we keep standing at the door, and no attention is paid to us' Sohail was more He said: 'it is true; but we should complain, not against Umar, but against ourselves. Islam called equally to all, with one voice. Those of us who lagged behind out of their own negligence deserve to remain behind even today. (*Usudul Ghaba*, Vol. III, Tazkira Sohail b. Amr)

Purgation of Socially Disordering Elements in Oneself

It has been commanded that one should purge in oneself those elements that would cause disturbance in the social order. The Arabic word for purgation or purification is *tazkiya*. Etymologically, it means cleansing something so as to make it capable of growth or development. The *tazkiya* of land means purifying it of weeds, levelling it, manuring, and irrigating it in order to make it capable of growing seeds. In the same way, the *tazkiya* of the self should mean purifying it of evil motives of thought and action in order to make man capable of moral and spiritual growth in accordance with the original, God-made, pattern of his nature. *Tazkiya* of the self has its analogue in medicine. Just as medicine deals with the diseases of the body and their purgation or cure, in the same way *tazkiya* deals with the diseases of the soul and their purgation or cure. *Tazkiya* is needed in all spheres of life, and thus the main mission of the Prophet of Islam (peace be upon him) was *tazkiya*. Many are the Verses of the Quran that speak of it and words like *yuzakkikum* or *yuzakkihim* occur at many places. But here we are concerned with the purification of those motives and tendencies which cause disorder in social relations. In the Islamic scheme there are commandments for their purification. We give some examples below:

Prohibition against Riducule Slander etc.

Riduculing somebody, slandering him, taunting and calling him by bad nicknames, conceiving and propagating evil notions about him, picking up his faults, back-biting him or prying into his secrets—all such things are prohibited in Islam. The Quran says:

O ye who believe!
Let not some men
Among you laugh at others:
It may be that
The (latter) are better
Than the (former):
Nor let some women
Laugh at others:
it may be that
The (latter) are better
Than the (former):
Nor defame nor be
Sarcastic to each other,
Nor call each other
By (offensive) nicknames...

O ye who believe!
Avoid suspicion as much
(As possible): for suspicion
In some cases is a sin:

And spy not on each other,
Nor speak ill of each other
Behind their backs. Would any
Of you like to eat
The flesh of his dead
Brother? Nay, ye would
Abhor it ... But fear God: (XLIX—11-12)

Prohibition Against Rejoicing at Another's Degradation etc.:

Islam prohibits rejoicing at another person's degradation and debasement. The Holy Prophet says: 'Do not rejoice at the degradation and debasement of your brother. Allah will take mercy on him and make you suffer in his place'. (*Tirmizi, Mishkat, Hifzullisan,* Fasl II)

Making somebody ashamed at his wrong or sin is also prohibited. The Holy Prophet says: 'The man who makes somebody ashamed of the sin he has repented, he will be involved in that sin himself before death comes to him'. (*Ibid.*) Behaving as a tell-tale is prohibited. The Quran says:

and heed not...
A slanderar, going about
With calumnies (LXVIII-2)

Tradition says: 'Those who behave as tell-tales create mischief among friends'. (*Musnad-i-Ahmad,* p. 459)

Breaking of Engagements, Duplicity and Violation of the Bonds of Kinship Prohibited

Breaking of engagement is prohibited. The Quran says:

For (every) engagement
Will be enquired into
(On the Day of Reckoning). (VII-34)

The Holy Prophet has regarded the breaking of engagement as a sign of hypocrisy. He condemns the man who makes some engagement or promise and then breaks it and does the opposite. (*Bukhari, Muslim*)

Duplicity is also prohibited. A Tradition says: 'On the Day of Judgment the Double dealer will be in the worst plight—he is the man who shows one face to some person and another face to other person. (*Bukhari,* Kitabul Adab). Another Tradition says: 'He who is a double dealer in this world, his tongue will be of fire on the Day of Judgment. (*Abu Daud,* Kitabul Adab)

Violating the bond of kinship and showing inconsiderateness to kinsfolk has been prohibited. The people who do it have been regarded as mischief-makers by the Quran:

Those who break God's covenant
After it is ratified,
And who sunder
What God has ordered to be joined,
And do mischief on earth:
These cause loss (only) to themselves. (II-27)

Pride, Jealousy and False Accusation Prohibited

Pride was first manifested by Satan when he said:

. . . 'I am better
Than he' (Adam) (VII-12)

Pride hardens the heart or seals it up and insulates it

Thus doth God seal up
Every heart—of arrogant
And obstinate transgressors. (XL-35)

Pride deprives man of God's love. The Quran says:

For God loveth not
The arrogant, the vainglorious: (IV-36)

Pride or arrogance shuts the doors upon courtesies, which doors are actually the means to enter paradise. The Holy Prophet says: 'He who has a single atom of pride in his heart he will not enter paradise'. (*Abu Daud,* Kitabul Libas)

Jealousy is the source of all social evils and it is something very dangerous. God has commanded the Holy Prophet and every Muslim to seek refuge with God from jealously—'I seek refuge'

From mischief
Of the envious one
As he practises envy. (CXIII-5)

The Holy Prophet says:

Beware of jealousy and avoid it, for jealousy eats the virtues just as fire eats wood. (*Abu Daud* Kitabul Adab, Bad Fil Hasad)

False accusation, that is, imputing some evil to the other person, which is not there in him, is condemnable (even if the evil is there in him talking about it is back-biting). The Quran says:

And if anyone earns
Sin, he earns it against
His own soul; (IV-111)

And those who annoy
Believing men and women
Undeservedly, bear (On themsleves)
A calumny and a glaring sin. (XXXIII-58)

Rage, Malice and Abusive Language etc. Prohibited

Working oneself into anger or getting enraged has been condemned by Islam. Those who overcome their anger are regarded as pious ones by the Quran. Those 'who restrain anger' (III. 134) are the righteous ones according to the Quran. They are those who forgive even 'when they are angry'. (XLII. 37). The Holy Prophet said: 'the heroic warrior is not one who flings down the other person, but one who controls himself in anger'. (*Bukhari,* Kitabul Adab, Babul Hazr Minal Ghazab). Another Tradition says: 'Anger is from Satan, and Satan is made of fire. The fire is killed down and extinguished by water, therefore, he who gets anger must perform ablution.' (*Abu Daud,* Kitabul Adab)

Malice and rancour are condemned because they hamper the fulfilment of one's duties towards God's creatures, just as joining partners with God hampers the fulfilment of one's duties towards God. We are commanded to pray to God for freedom from malice:

And leave not, in our hearts,
Rancour (or sense of injury)
Against those who have believed (LIX-10)

The Holy Prophet says: 'Do not have rancour and malice against one another; do not be jealous of one another; live like brothers and sisters'. (*Bukhari, Muslim*)

Regarding showing off and exultation it is said:

And be not like those
Who started from their homes
Insolently and to be seen of men. (VIII-47)

And how many populations
We destroyed, which exulted
In their life (of ease and plenty); (XXVIII-58)

Use of abusive and obscene language, whether charged with sexuality or rage, has been strictly prohibited.

Let there be no obscenity,
Nor wickedness,
Nor wrangling
In the Hajj. (II-197)

The Holy Prophet said: 'It is a sacrilege to speak ill against a Muslim, and to murder him is infidelity'. (*Bukhari,* Kitabul Adab). In this regard another Tradition says: 'A Believer never indulges in taunts and slanders, ill language and obscenity'. (*Tirmizi,*Adwabul Birri, wal Sila). In fact any behaviour, gesture, speech or action that creates disturbance in social life has been strictly prohibited.

Some Commandments Regarding Eating and Drinking, Dress etc.

In the Islamic scheme of cultural reconstruction the social order has been given so much importance that etiquettes have been laid down in respect of eating and drinking, dress and appear ance. Obviously, the purpose is to prevent the social evils that arise from bad form. With regard to eating and drinking the following commandments have been given:

1. You must eat with your right hand.
2. You must have an attitude of reverence towards food.
3. You must eat sitting. (If you eat standing, or if you sit on some high place and put your food on some low place, it is against the Islamic way of life.
4. Eat only as much as to cause no indigestion.
5. You must not eat unlawful things or things about which you have doubts as to their lawfulness.

Similarly, there are commandments regarding dress and appearance. For example:

1. You must not imitate or try to resemble any particular community in matters of dress and appearance.
2. It must not be the dress and appearance of those who are proud or indecent.
3. Silken dresses are forbidden for men.
4. The dress must not be such that it does not cover your shame—the parts that decency demands to be covered—or such as is likely to stimulate erotic feelings.
5. Women must be specially careful to maintain modesty in their dress and appearance.

Prohibition Against Profligacy and Show-off

One must take care of two things in matters of spending money and goods:

1. There must be no extravagance, both in terms of appropriateness and quantity of the expenditure.
2. The purpose of the expenditure must not be show-off or impressing the people of poor means with your wealth and position. This is no occasion for going into the details of the subject which has been discussed at length in various books dealing with the Islamic way of life.

4 ECONOMIC SYSTEM

Western Civilization Based on the Mechanistic View of Life

Western civilization is based on the mechanistic view of life, which is confined to man's physical life and his personal gain. In it only those things are considered which have a bearing on man's physical needs. Regarding these things it has been understood that the guidance of reason is enough. For satisfying these material needs reason first gave rise to the capitalistic system, and when it failed to socialism and communism, which are still in the experimental state.

Islamic Scheme of Cultural Reconstruction is Based on A Divine View of Life

The Islamic scheme of cultural reconstruction is based on A Divine view of life. This view divides life into material and non-material and insists that both are necessary for the perfection of humanity. For this reason in the economic system of the Islamic scheme both these factors are considered, and it has been understood that the guidance of reason alone is not sufficient.

In the context of the perfection of humanity the transcendental part of life is nonetheless important. Rather, it is more important because it is this part of life that manifests Divine Attributes and embodies the higher values of life. If it is neglected man is reduced to a mere lump of flesh.

Reason Protects Personal Interest, Revelation Protects Values

The qualities which emanate from Divine Attributes are called ultimate values of life. They do not change with the changes of time and place. They begin where reason ends, and, therefore, something higher than reason is required for their maintenance and promotion. This thing is revelation. Thus, in the Islamic scheme of cultural reconstruction personal interests are looked after by reason and the ultimate values by revelation. Evidently, a system which looks after both can guarantee human well-being.

When ultimate values are maintained, every individual will remain safe from the exploitation of the other. Rather, every individual will consider the interest of the other as important as his own interest and the loss of the other as bad as his own loss—if need arises he will not hesitate to bear loss himself for the sake of the benefit of the other person. Thus, the Quran says that the Ansars are those who give the needs of the refugees preference to their own needs:

> *But give them preference*
> *Over themselves, even though*
> *Poverty was there (own lot).* (LIX-9)

The Holy Prophet says:

The creature of God does not become a full Believer unless he chooses for his brother the same as he chooses for himself. (*Bukhari, Muslim, Mishkat*)

End of Capitalism Through Promotion of Ultimate Values

Through promotion of ultimate values the course of capitalism will come to end, and man will be freed of economic exploitation. Marx was unable to find any scheme of ultimate values and therefore he had to take recourse to the concept of historical necessity. As L. Laurel says, Marx and Engels did not base their socialistic aspirations on moral foundations. They said that communism is a historical necessity, which means that history testifies to the fact that no order remains unchanged for long; from one order another order emerges which contradicts the former order to a great extent.

But historical necessity could not provide any firm foundation for the communistic scheme. This is why Lenin and, after him, Stalin have brought about important changes in communism. This is not the occasion to go into details. In the Islamic scheme the government has more powers.

Values and Powers of Government

The maintenance of ultimate values is a subject which is concerned not merely with preaching and sermonizing but also with the laws of the government. It means that the government has the business of controlling the production and the means of production in such a way that the ultimate values are maintained in every sphere of life. In the Islamic scheme of cultural reconstruction only the real purpose of life is insisted upon, which is that God's creature should secure lawful living, and their needs according to the changing circumstances should be fulfilled with justice. In this scheme we are not concerned with the details of administration and distribution. These things keep changing according to the circumstances. The emphasis is on Trust and Vicegerency as fundamental principles. According to these fundamental principles the real Lord of everything, on the individual as well on the social level, is God. Man is his vicegerent and he has been given various things as a trust from God. The Quran says:

> *God doth command you*
> *To render back your Trusts*
> *To those to whom they are due.* (IV-58)

> *And spend (in charity)*
> *Out of the (subsistence)*
> *Whereof he has made you*
> *Heirs* (LVII-7)

Questions and Answers Related to Administration and Distribution

After giving some commandments regarding administration and distribution the Quran says about the distribution of wealth:

> *In order that it may not*
> *(Merely) make a circuit*
> *Between the wealthy among you.* (LIX-7)

To the question about spending, the following answer is recorded in the Quran:

> *Say: 'What is beyond*
> *Your needs'.* (II-219)

On another occasion we have the following answer:

> *Say: whatever*
> *Ye spend that is good,*
> *Is for parents and kindred*
> *And orphans*
> *And those in want*
> *And for wayfarers.* (II-215)

The difference between these two answers indicates the difference in the spending of wealth according to the demands of different circumstances. Say: 'What is beyond your needs' goes to the extent of indicating that when the demands of circumstances are more pressing the owner has no right on his superfluous wealth: he must spend the whole of it.

Besides the above Verses there are some other Verses of the Quran prompting the believers to spend out of whatever they have. The Quran has also spelled out the various people who deserve to receive charity. But it has not specified the quantity of the wealth and the mode of its distribution, which indicates that commandments in regard to these matters are subject to continual change in accordance with the changing circumstances.

Laws of Justice Must Keep Changing

Economic life cannot be the same in every age, and therefore the laws of creating and maintaining justice and economic balance cannot be the same for every age. In modern times the community is involved in class struggle; wealth has accumulated in the hands of a small class while the other, and bigger, class is deprived of the means of livelihood and is so destitute as to want even loaves of coarse bread—in such a situation the laws of creating and maintaining justice and economic balance must be different from those that are obtained when the community is not prosperous and so economically debalanced as to have some class deprived of the means of livelihood. In view of such a situation if the Quran had fixed a particular mode of administration and distribution or had regarded the established private and social property as basis, it would have fallen short of its universal significance and its purpose of completion of Guidance would not have been fulfilled.

The Establishment of Justice—Whatever be its Mode

Ibn-i-Qaiyam says:

> The purpose of God behind the Shariah is to establish justice amongst God's creatures. In whatever mode the justice is established that mode will be regarded as religion (*Din*); it will not be regarded as something contradictory to religion. (*Al Turuqul Hikamiya,* p.14)

The same thing has been said by him in a different way at another place:

> The basis of the Shariah is wisdom and the welfare of life in this world and in the hereafter. It is all justice and mercy and wisdom and consideration for welfare. Any issue which makes you move from justice to injustice, from mercy to cruely, from consideration for welfare to corruption and from wisdom to acts of futility will not be a commandment of the Shariah, though polemical attempts may be made to push it into the realm of the Shariah (*I'lamul Mowaqq'ein,* Vol. III, p.37)

The norm must be the Middle way of Life

Standards of living are of three levels according to which the laws of justice may differ. The three levels are: (1) Ordinary, (2) middle and (3) higher.

The ordinary level is one in which the basic needs of life, those regarding clothes, house, and marriage etc. are available so that people can make do and get on in life. The higher level is one in which nice food, nice clothes, posh house and means of marrying beautiful women are available. The middle level is between these two which means that life is not so prosperous as to reach the higher level, nor is it so hard as to remain bogged down on the ordinary level.

The norm of justice in economic life must be set on the ordinary level of living; the laws should be made according to this norm. Jurists have called this norm of needs *hajat.*

Equality and justice in the distribution of wealth should be maintained according to *hajat.* Which means that the norm for the fulfilment of the needs of the people should be according to the middle level of living. It is not necessary that all the people should have wealth in equal amount. For regarding the distribution of wealth and control of expenditure the purpose of the Shariah is to secure the middle level of living. (Abu Mohammad Izzudin bin Abdul Aziz, *Qawaidul Ahkam,* Vol. I, p. 28)

Liberal Outlook Regarding Legislation

For the purpose of achieving the middle way of living whatever administrative and distributive mode is adopted and whatever laws are made will be according to the Shariah and Islamic spirit. It is not necessary that the mode should have its sanction in the Quran and the Sunna. As the mode must keep changing in accordance with the changing circumstances any one particular mode should not be stuck to. Ibn-i-Qaiyam says:

In whatever mode the signs of Truth are manifested it will be all Shariah and Religion (*Din*). In it will be the will of God and his commandment. (I'lamul Mowaqqe'in, Vol.III, p. 543)

Economic Responsibility of Government

We shall now quote some instances regarding the economic responsibility of the government. They also indicate the liberal power of the government in legislation.

Omar has explained the economic relation between the government and the people by means of a parable:

We the (Caliphate) and the people can be likened to the following situation. There are people who are on a journey. Some of them entrust their money to a fellow traveller asking him to spend it on themselves (according to needs). In such a situation, is the trustee entitled to any kind of preferential treatment or privilege? Never, answered Omar himself. (Ibn-i-Jauzi, *Tarikhi Omar,* Chap. 29)

While breaking the news of the conquest of Qadisiya, Omar

spoke of the responsibility of the Caliphate in the following words:

As long as people have sufficient capacity to fulfil one another's needs I shall fulfil your needs. When this capacity decreases we shall be frugal till all become equal in respect of what is needed for each. I wish you knew how much concerned I am for all of you. I can make you comprehended it only through my deeds. By God I am not a king to treat you as servants (subjects). I am myself the servant of Allah; and goverment has been assigned to me as Trust. If I regard it as a Trust and render it back to you according to what is your due and walk behind you for rendering service to you until you are able to eat your food securely and to your heart's fill, I should hope to earn blessings and welfare through this government. But if I regard it as may personal property and compel you to come after me and to come to my house (for the demands of your rights) I shall come to a woeful end. (*Al Bidaya wal Nehaya,* Vol. VII, p. 46)

To the Governor of Basra, Abu Musa Ash'ari, Omar gave the following instructions:

Listen to me! You must provide for the comfort of the people in their homes and you must feed the members of their family. (Tar Tusi, *Sirajul Muluk,* p. 109).

When Omar bin Abdul Aziz became Caliph he began to weep because of his sense of responsibility and his beard was soaked with tears. His wife Fatima asked the reason and said: 'Has any untoward thing happened?' Omar b. Abdul Aziz said:

I have taken the responsibility of the whole community. In this community there are all kinds of people: the hungry, the beggars, the destitute, the sick, the people of no means, the *mujadics* (warriors in the cause of God), the helpless, the oppressed, the poor, the captives the extremely aged and decrepit, and the people who have a big family to support with scant means; then there are other needy people belonging to various regions—on the Day of Judgement I shall be enquired about all these people and their suits will be pleaded by the Apostle of God. I am afraid I shall break down in this Trial, and so I am weeping out of self-pity (*Tarikhul Kamil,* Vol. V, p. 24; *Kitabul Khiraj* by Abi Yusuf, p. 10)

Government is responsible for Two Kinds of Administration

In the Islamic scheme of cultural reconstruction the government is responsible for two kinds of economic administration: (*a*) that which seeks to fulfill the needs of the people (according to the norm of the middle level of living), (*b*) that which seeks to make the nation economically self-sufficient.

(A) Administration that Fulfils the Needs of the People

Among the needs are included both the basic and non-basic needs. Various Traditions mention the responsibility of government regarding basic needs like food, clothing, house, medical treatment, education, supporting of one's family, fulfilment of one's duty, marriage and servants (when needed). The Holy Prophet addressed a letter to the Tribe of Hamir. It says:

> O Tribe of Hamir, I enjoin on you the doing of good. Do not betray trusts, do not oppose one another in feuds. Indeed the Apostle of Allah (as heard of the governments) is the caretaker of the rich as well as the poor. (*Kitabul Amwal* by Abi Obaid, p. 21)

On another occasion the Holy Prophet said: 'The ruler is the guardian of him who has no guardian' (*Tirmizi,* Abwabul Faraizfi Mirathil Mal). On still another occasion he said:

> Allah and His Apostle (Government) are the Care-takers of him who has no care-taker for himself. (*Abu Daud,* Kitabul Nikah)

On one occasion Omar said in his speech:

> O people! God has burdened me with the responsibility that I should prevent the prayers that are sent to God. (*Ibid.*)

Commenting on it Azizuddin Abdul Aziz, the famous Shafa'i jurist says:

> The prevention of prayers means that a government should do justice with the oppressed, so that they need not ask for justice from God. The government should fulfil the needs of the people, so that people do not ask God for the fulfilment of their needs. (*Qawaedul Ahkam Fi Masalehu Anam,* Vol. 1, p. 147) .... How appropriate these words of Omar are, and how inclusive of all the human rights! (*op. cit.*)

Food, Clothing and House

Besides general principles and tenets the Traditions also discuss the basic needs of man. The Holy Prophet says:

> Except three things man has no right on anything else. The three things are: (1) a house to live in, (2) clothings for covering the body and (3) water and the loaf of bread. (*Tirmizi*)

Ibn-e-Qayyam says:

Food, clothing etc. are related to the common welfare of the people. On these nobody has any special right; all the people have an equal right to share them. (*Al-Turuqul Hikamiya,* p. 262)

Medical Treatment and Education

Regarding medical treatment and education Omar once said:

If a scabies-striken goat is left to roam along the bank of a canal in a condition in which oil is not rubbed on its body (by way of treatment), it is feared that on the Day of Judgement God will enquire Omar about it. (Quoted by Ghazali in *Al tibrul Masbook,* p. 17)

Man is more important than an animal; and the possibility of enquiry about human beings is something more terrifying. The government which feels its responsibility with regard to the treatment of even the animals, how much responsible should it feel with regard to the treatment of human beings?

Regarding education there were various organizations, which may be modified and extended according to the modern conditions. In the Traditions the acquisition of knowledge has been given great importance; it is supposed to be the duty of every Muslim. The Holy Prophet appointed Saeed b. Al 'Aas for the purpose of teaching, reading and writing. (*Al Iste'ab Fi M'arefital Sahaba,* Vol. 1, p. 393). Zaid b. Thabit was commanded by the Holy Prophet to learn the Syriac language from the Jews (*Abu Daud,* Kitabul 'Ilm). The Holy Prophet also sent various companions to the countryside for imparting education to people. (*Bukhari,* Kitabul Maghazi)

Omar adopted very wide-ranging means for the propogation of education. He established many *Madrsas* (institutions or universities) and appointed salaried teachers (*Kanzul Ummal,* Vol. 2, quoted in *Musnadi Ibn-i-Abi Shaiba*). Omar b. Abdul Aziz appointed teachers in rural areas. (*Op. cit,* Vol. 1, p. 217)

There is also the evidence of scholarships granted for the purpose of education. Abu Obaid in his *Kitabul Amwal* has quoted many Traditions on this subject. The Traditions say that scholarships were granted for the learning of knowledge and of Quran (p. 261). Islamic scholars have written many books on the importance of education and on the educational system. The books that deserve mention are *Jame'o Bayanul Ilm Wal Ulama* by Ibn-i-Abdul Bar Undlasi and *Tazkiratul Sam'e Wal Motakallim* by Shaikh Badruddin. History gives evidence of the great service of Islamic governments and Islamic scholars in respect of education, science and arts.

Supporting the Family and Paying of Debts

There are many Traditions on the subject of supporting the family and paying of debts. For example, the Holy Prophet said: 'He who has left property and wealth after him the property and wealth are for his family but he who has been left without support, for supporting him it is my responsibility (as Head of the Government). (*Kitabul Amwal* by Abi Obaid, p. 261)

Tirmizi explain the phrase 'left without support' by saying that it means somebody who is provided with nothing and the phrase 'it is my responsibility' means: 'I will support him, and spend on him'. (*Tirmizi,* Abwabul Faraiz)

One Tradition says:

> He who leaves a burden of liabilities, all his liabilities are with Allah. Many times the Holy Prophet said the liabilities are with God and his Apostle. (Abi Obaid, *Kitabul Amwal*, Al-Farz Lil Zurriyah Min Alfai)

Abu Obaid has explained the word 'all' by saying that it includes children and all those persons for whom the deceased had the responsibility of supporting. (*Op. cit.*)

Another Tradition says:

> My relation to the believers is stronger than their relation to their soul. He who leaves debts after his death, the payment of those debts is my responsibility; and he who leaves wealth it is for his inheritors to inherit. (*Bukhari,* Kitabul Nafqat)

One tradition substitutes 'my' by 'Allah and His Apostle' (which means government) (*Abi Obaid, Op.cit.,* p. 220).

Omar also included the subject of the payment of debts under financial support. He said: 'Every debtor shall be freed of his debts (*Sharh Shar'atul Islam* by Syed Ali Zade) Omar b. Abdul Aziz promulgated an ordinance for the payment of debts. It says: 'Behold! you should pay all the debts of every debtor who is of poor means and who is not a spendthrift'. (*Kitabul Amwal*)

Marriage and Servants

Marriage and servants have also been mentioned in the Traditions. For example the Holy Prophet said:

Allah undertakes the responsibility of helping three types of people: (1) he who fights for the cause of Allah, (2) he who wants to pay for the copying of some book and (3) he who weds with a view to lead a pious life. (*Ibn-i-Majah,* Abwabul 'Itq, Al-Mukatab).

Omar b. Abdul Aziz issued the following promulgation:

'Behold! the young man who wants to marry and has no means, you must get him married. (*Kitabul Amwal,* p. 251)

Omar saw a man eating his food with the left hand and asked him for the reason. He came to know that the right hand of the man was lost in the battle of Mauta. On hearing this Omar kept weeping for sometime, and then asked the man how his various personal works were done and who does them for him. He commanded that the man 'should be provided with a servant and other provisions. Also he was gifted an animal for riding'. (*Kitabul Aathaar,* Fazaelus Sahaba, Tradition no. 852)

Thus government, through a particular system or organization, is responsible for fulfilling the above mentioned needs or for creating facilities for their fulfilment. The system for this purpose does not encourage the life of intemperance and the system itself keeps changing according to changing circumstances.

(B) Economic Administration to Make the Nation the Nation Self-sufficient

On the subject of making the nation economically self-sufficient the following observations occur in Islamic literature. The Quran says:

It is He Who hath produced you
From the earth and settled you
Therein: (XI-61)

Abu Bakr Jassas says: 'The argument of the Verse is that it is incumbent (upon the government) to inhabit the earth, with cultivation, gardening and the construction of buildings'. (*Ahkamul Quran*, Vol. II, p. 165). In this discussion on Vicegerancy, Baizawi writes: 'Similarly God has appointed every prophet as His Vicegerant for the purpose of the inhabitation of the earth, for organizing the body-politic, for the completion of their selves, and for the execution of the commandment of God'. (*Baizawi*, p. 52). There is a Hadith-i-Qudsi which says: 'Inhabit My land, so that My servants may lead a prosperous life' (Sarakhsi, *Al Mabsut*, Vol. xxiii, p. 15). A Tradition says: 'Seek your sustenance in the wide stretches of the earth' (*Ibid.*). Abu Huraira reports the following Tradition:

When people spoke ill of the non-Arabs in presence of the Holy Prophet, he said: 'Do not speak ill of them, for these people have inhabited the land of God, which enabled God's creatures to lead a prosperous life'. (*Mawardi: Adabul Din wal Duniya*, p. 82)

Recounting the responsibilities of the government Mawardi says: 'The third responsibility is to keep the country inhabited and prosperous by taking care of the means of transport, of the high-ways and of all other arrangements (according to the needs of the times)' (*Al Ahkamul Sultania*). Amadi says: 'That without which a duty cannot be fulfilled also becomes a duty of the same status'. (*Usulul Akham*, Vol. I, p. 158). Ibn-i-Taiyimia says: 'That without which a duty cannot be fulfilled is also a duty'. (*Al Jawam'e fil Siyasatil Ilahiya*, p.16).

Wider Powers of Government in Administration

Concerning both the above-mentioned kinds of administration the government is authorized either to establish some new organization or to make use of the old organization; to have the organization under its direct control, or to allow the people to establish it by their own free choice. But two considerations are necessary, whatever mode is adopted: the organization should be more useful, and its criterion of benefit and harm should be a moral one.

1. The Organization should be More Useful

Comparatively speaking, the organization should be more useful, otherwise there would be no justification for its existence. The Quran testifies to this requirement by saying:

> *God commands justice, the doing*
> *of good,* (XVI-90)

The terms 'justice' and 'the doing of good' are very comprehensive terms. Through them people ar persuaded to achieve all that is good for the society and to eschew all that is harmful. The obvious implication is that in the context of contemporary conditions and circumstances a comparatively more useful organization should be adopted. (*T'alilul Ahkam*, p. 287)

At another place the Quran says:

> *We sent thee not, but*
> *As a Mercy for all creatures.* (XXI-107)

'Mercy for all creatures' also encompasses a more useful socio-economic organization in the context of the contemporary condition and circumstances. Such an organization must be an open system, admitting all possible modes of operation for the sake of doing justice and good to all. If any one particular, exclusive, mode of operation is stuck to people will be unhappy. Which would contradict mercy for all creatures (*T'aleelul Ahkam*, p. 287).

The Criterion of Benefit and Harm must be Moral

The Quran provides the following evidence for the principle that the criterion of benefit and harm must be moral:

> *They ask thee*
> *Concerning wine*
> *And gambling.*
> *Say: 'in them is great sin,*

And some profit, for men;
But the sin is greater
Than the profit'. (II.219)

In Arabic literature the word *ithm* (sin or wrong) is used for moral and spiritual harm and also for physical and material harm. For this reason this word has been used in the above Verse instead of a word implying mere 'harm'. This goes to show that for justified and unjustified deeds or for lawful and unlawful deeds the criterion is moral and spiritual harm, according to the Quran, and not mere physical or material harm. The Quran also gives the story of Joseph and tells us how in the time of famine he stored food to distribute it among the people according to their needs. Once again this indicates that the government is authorised to adopt the more useful mode of organization in view of contemporary conditions.

Organization under the Direct Control of the Government:

In the era of Prophethood there was no established, official, socio-economic organization for the distribution of state income. The Holy Prophet used to distribute then and there whatever income was obtained. However, Abu Huraira was appointed to bring the needy, the hungry and the destitute to the Holy Prophet himself, and the Holy Prophet used to arrange for their food and other needs. (*Al Sunanil Kubra,* Kitabul Wikalah, Bab Al Taukil fil Mal; *Al Taratibul Idariah,* Vol. II)

Abu Bakr also followed the same method. He distributed the income among the people. Thus, the income of the first year of his Caliphate was distributed, without distinction, among men, women, the old, the young, the free and the slaves, so that each got 10 Dirhams. Similarly from the income of the next year each got 20 Dirhams. (*Tabaqat-i-Ibn-i-Sa'ad,* Vol. II, Qism I)

Omar established an official organization called 'Baitul Mal'. Among the expenditures of this institution was included the giving of aid, without any distinction, to Muslims, non-Muslims and to all the poor and the needy. The details about this institution are found in the books of Traditions and Jurisprudence. Omar made a general proclamation which said: 'Through the wealth of the state every needy person must be provided for; the debt of every debtor must be paid off; help must be extended to every third person; every oppressor or exploiter must be prevented from oppression or exploitation; every unclothed person must be provided with clothes etc. (Syed Ali Zade, *Sharh Shar'atil Islam*). M'aawia appointed a high official at the governmental level for looking after the welfare of the people. (*Tirmizi*, Abwabul Ahkam)

Free Organization

The evidence of a free organization of the people is provided by the fact that the Holy Prophet retained all sensible people's organizations of the Days of Ignorance. He also made the people responsible for helping and supporting one another, which indicates the sanction for establishing a new organization. The Holy Prophet said:

> 'He who has means of riding and other goods in excess of his needs must give them to the person who is without them; and he who has food in excess of his needs, must give it to the poor and the needy'. According to Abu Sa'eed Khadri 'the Holy Prophet used to mention various kinds of excessive goods and insist on distributing them among others till people began to understand that they had no personal right on goods that are in excess of their needs. (Ibn-i-Hazm, *Al Muhalla*, Vol. VI, p. 158)

On one occasion Ali said:

> God has made it incumbent upon the rich to fulfil the needs of the poor. If they are hungry and unclothed or if they are hard up financially, it is because the rich have not given away their surplus goods. On the day of Judgement God has the right to call them to an account and punish them. (*Ibid.*)

These are general instructions which encompass individual charity and also its mode of organization.

Both Public and Private Property Allowed

Unfortunately, in modern times the subject of property has been given the greatest importance in the context of the distribution of the means of production. A wrong notion of property has resulted in very bad consequence. Thus in the modern world a particular class is leading the life of luxury without doing any labour, while the other class is suffering from poverty and destitution in spite of doing labour. On the one hand a few persons are masters of the means of production, and on the other the country is in need of foreign aid for procuring ordinary things. In such a situation the Islamic scheme of cultural reconstruction would give no importance to the controversy about property, nor would it restrict socio-economic organization into a 'public' or a 'private' category to produce hardship for the common people. It would allow both 'private' and 'public' sectors and distribute the means of production according to the needs of circumstances and under the following sections:

Distribution of the Means of Production

(1) The section which is concerned with public property, in which case the government would exercise direct control.
(2) The section which is concerned with gradual nationalisation of property.
(3) The section which is concerned only with private property.

Items Under the First Section

Under the first section will be included government controlled basic industries etc. For example:

(a) Iron and Steel — mining and heavy industry.
(b) Arms — industries related to Defence.
(c) Electricity — industries related to electric power.
(d) Atomic Energy.
(e) Industries related to coal mining, petroleum and natural gas.
(f) Industries related to raw mangnese ore.
(g) Industries related to minerals — gems, gold, silver, copper, zinc, lead etc.
(h) Departments and industries related to railways and air and sea transport.

(i) Telephone, telegraph, wireless and other means of communication.
(j) Cloth mills and big factories and post offices.

Items under the Second Section

(a) Aluminium and tin industry.
(b) Coal and Carbon manufacturing industry.
(c) Small tools and machines.
(d) Plastics and dyes.
(e) Medicine, pesticides and germicides.
(f) Road transport.
(g) Cement factories.
(h) Paper mills.
(i) Tea and coffee.
(j) Other industries.

Items under the Third Section

Under the third section are included small scale industries and cottage industries:

(a) Small scale industries will be controlled by private and public committees, or they will be looked after by individual enterprises. Rules and regulations for controlling them will be formulated in the light of the Shariah, and the government will be authorised to assign a definite amount in the budget for them according to requirements. This will intimate the process of the emergence of these industries from the private sector into the public sector.

(b) For cottage industry the capital will not be subject to limitation, for in these industries members of a family rather than outsiders are often engaged. For this reason working hours are not specified, nor any official organization is set up. The government will extend loans for small scale industries and cottage industries and encourage them in all possible ways.

Thus, on the one hand there will be an experiment of nationalization and on the other individuals will get opportunities for work. In this matter there will be no final form of organization, nor will any form of organization be maintained for the sake of anybody's personal glorification so that he may grab the means of sustenance to force the creatures of God to slavery.

The Right Concept of Property in the Islamic Scheme

In the Islamic scheme of cultural reconstruction controversies of private and public sectors will not be stirred up, but instead the right concept of property will be translated into actual practice. Of course, for this purpose education will get its due emphasis.

The right concept of property is that God is the real Owner of everything, and man is in charge of things only as a 'trustee' (*amin*). It does not matter who is in charge of the means of production; it may be individuals or it may be the nation: but the status of the in-charge is only that of a 'trustee', who has the right to make use of the property according to the wish of the Owner. Individuals and society have this right as long as they help the government in the realization of the aim of 'trusteeship', which is the welfare and progress of all God's creatures, and create the proper conditions for this realization.

In the Islamic scheme of cultural reconstruction the right of property is nothing but 'the right to make use of property for the good of all God's creatures'. Thus, concerning land Shah Waliullah observes: 'The right of property (in the case of land) simply means that the owner has the right of greater benefit than the others'. (*Hujjatullahil Baligha*)

Moral Climate and Correspondence of Law to Morality

Through education the proper moral climate will be created and maintained, and a mutual correspondence established between law and moral sense. Without such a correspondence no human organization can work to any desirable ends. If through a mere change of the state organization the solution of the economic problems of the society is achieved, the other, psychological and social problems will emerge, in the absence of moral reform, in all their disturbing intensity, and there will be almost no real solution for them.

The above list of various organizations is not final, nor, for that matter, can any list be final. The government of the time has every right to change it or replace it by a new list according to the needs of the time. With the exception of a few subjects, the government is also authorized to shift any subject from the private sector to the public sector and vice versa. But the concept of answerability to God is essential both for the individual and for the government; and duties shall have greater emphasis than rights.

5 POLITICAL ORGANIZATION

Democracy an Advanced Form of Government

Western civilization has made great advances in the matter of political organization. Democracy is its most advanced form, which has been reached after a very long struggle and experience. For the time being a better political organization cannot be possibly conceived. But in spite of a long period of democratic experiment the concept of democracy has not been clearly defined, nor has it been properly translated into actual practice. It is interesting to note that the enquiry committee on democracy set up by the cultural assembly of the U.N.O. in 1947 raised the following basic questions.

Basic Questions on Democracy

These basic questions are: (1) What is the meaning of democracy? and (2) Is the decision of the majority always and necessarily right?

In replying to the first question most people admitted that 'democracy' is a vague term whose meaning has not been definitely determined. As to the second question it was replied that to regard the decision of the majority as free of mistake was itself a big mistake. Man is after all man, whether he acts as an individual or as a community; he cannot be free of all those weaknesses or frailties which are characteristic of the human species. *(Democracy in a World of Tension,* p. 504)

Perennial Requirements for which Guidance of Reason is of Reason is insufficient

Since the form of government is determined by the development of consciousness and the changes of circumstances, the guidance of reason and experience works in this matter to a great extent. This is why in the Islamic scheme of cultural reconstruction the form of the government is not discussed. Rather, those fundamental, perenial requirements are discussed concerning which the guidance of reason is insufficient. They are in need of definition in every age. They are, for example: the concept of sovereignty, the nature of government, the criterion of good and evil, the aesthetic values, the right of legislation, and the concept of rights and duties.

Machiavelli's View

In the political philosophy of the west we lack the concept of a Being which is perfect in every sense and free of all weaknesses and frailties. Hence, willy-nilly, man has been considered the guide in respect of the above-mentioned requirements. What man can achieve on his own can be comprehended by looking into Machiavelli's views. For Machiavelli the national state is the highest reality of the universe and the ultimate end of human striving. For the sake of power Machiavelli adores the development of power. He is not concerned with the direction in which power will operate. In his view the state is neither moral nor legal; it is merely political. He thinks that all the functions of the state should be judged only by political standards; considerations of religion, morality and law are not necessary. He is of the opinion that for the establishment of the government and its continuation the ruler should often act against the demands of pacts, of sincerity, of humanity, and of religion. When the existence of the state or the kingdom is in danger, considerations of justice or injustice, of mercy or cruelty, or of commendable or shameful acts do not apply. None of these should come in the way. And only that way or course should be adopted which secures the existence and the integrity of the state or kingdom. He who cannot shake off moral scruples had better confine himself to the sphere of individual life; he should not venture to become a ruler.

Man's Natural Weaknesses

The Islamic scheme takes into account the following weaknesses of man, which everybody recognizes and are testified by everybody's experience:

1. Man is capable of being impatient or weak of heart:

> *Truely man was created*
> *Very impatient.* (LXX-19)

2. He is weak:

> *For man was created*
> *Weak (in flesh).* (IV-28)

3. He is prone to be hasty:

> *For man is given to*
> *Hasty (deeds).* (XVII-11)

4. He is prone to be fretful:

> *Fretful when evil*
> *Touches him;* (LXX-20)

5. He is likely to become arrogant and niggardly in prosperity:

> *And niggardly when*
> *Good reaches him;* (LXX-21)

6. Very often, he is contentious:

> *But man is, in most things*
> *Contentious.* (XVIII-54)

7. He is prone to an inordinate love of wealth:

And ye love wealth
With inordinate love! (LXXXIX-18-25)

God says that man's wealth and wife and children are a trial for him.

Your riches and your children
May be but a trial: (LXIV-15)

8. Woman is man's greatest weakness. Thus the Holy Prophet said: 'I have seen none other than you, O women, having greater power to reduce the wisdom of a wise man'.

In view of the above natural weaknesses it is evident that man cannot be a reliable guide where the above mentioned requirements are concerned. This is why in the Islamic scheme of cultural reconstruction God, who is perfect and free of all weaknesses, has been recognized as the guide. Let us consider the matter in relation to these requirements:

Sovereignty is with God

As regards the concept of sovereignty, in the west sovereignty is supposed to lie in the will of the people. The perverse influence of this concept on human life and on society is something that a sensible person is not unaware of. In the Islamic scheme the Sovereign is God, to whom everybody is answerable — and this sense of answerability prevents man from doing any wrong even in a condition of privacy. Regarding the sovereignty of God the Quran says:

It is He Who is God
In heaven and God on earth;
And He is Full
Of Wisdom and Knowledge. (XLIII-84)

... O God!
Lord of Power (and Rule),
Thou givest Power
To whom Thou pleasest
And Thou strippest off Power
From whom Thou pleasest: (III-26)

He is the Irresistible, (watching)
From above over His worshippers;
And He is the Wise,
Acquainted with all things (VI-18)

... and God
Hath full power and control
Over His affairs; but most
Among mankind know it not. (XII-21)

... blessed
Be God, the Cherisher
And Sustainer of the Worlds! (VII-54)

Denying the authority of any other than God Joseph spoke to his Fellow prisoners in the following words and invited their contemplation:

'O my two companions
Of the prison! (I ask you):
Are many lords differing
Among themselves better,
Or the One God,
Supreme and Irresistible? (XII-39)

Nature of Government and Changes in It

The recognition of the sovereignty of God implies certain changes in the nature of Government.

(A) The real government is that of God; man is authorised to rule only as a 'trustee'. The Quran says:

O David! we did indeed
Make thee a vicegerent
On earth: so judge thou
Between men in truth (and justice):
Nor follow thou the lusts
(of thy heart), for they will
Mislead thee from the Path
Of God. (XXXVII-26)

And spend (in charity)
Out of the (substance)
Whereof He has made you
Heirs (LVII-7)

God doth command you
To render back your Trusts
To those to whom they are due;
And when ye judge
Between man and man,
That ye judge with justice; (IV-58)

Explicating this verse Zaid b. Aslam says: In this verse God has addressed the rulers, asking them to provide properly for the ruled and to make them follow the dictates of religion and the Shariah. 'Rendering back the trusts' also means that positions should be given only to those who deserve. (Ibn-e-Taimiya, *Al Jawame' Fil Siyasatil Ilahiya*, p. 3)

(B) In accordance with the commands of God the mode of government should be parliamentary, though its form does keep changing with the changes of circumstances and of human consciousness. The Quran commands the Holy Prophet as follows:

> *... and consult*
> *Them in affairs (of moment).* (III-159)

> *... who (conduct)*
> *Their affairs by mutual Consultation.* (XLII-38)

(C) In every law or organization of the government the wisdom of God is reflected. Which means that like the all-benefitting rain the laws of governmental administration and distribution are for the good of all:

> *God commands justice, the doing*
> *of good.* (XVI-90)

This Verse encompasses all the spheres of life as regards doing justice and doing good. Mohammad Mustafa Shibli comments: 'This verse encourages us to achieve all kinds of good and to condemn and reject all kinds of evil. In this sense it is most comprehensive. (*T'aleelul Ahkam*)

(D) The concept of answerability to God emerges in relation to every department of governmental administration. This concept enhances the sense of responsibility and acts as a safeguard against many evils. The Quran says:

> *... for*
> *Every act of hearing,*

Or of seeing
Or of (feeling in) the heart
Will be enquired into
(On the Day of Reckoning). (XVII-36)

Then shall anyone who
Has done an atom's weight
Of good, see it!
And anyone who has done an atom's weight
Of evil, shall see it.

(E) The purpose of the government is the safeguarding of values, the elimination of evils and the enhancement of good:

(They are) those who
If we establish them
In the land, establish
Regular prayer and give
Regular charity, enjoin
The right and forbid wrong;

(F) The Government transcendends the limitations of nationality and race and enters the international sphere of humanity, which makes every act of the government acquire universal implications. This is why the Attributes of God as mentioned by the Quran and the implications of these Attributes, transcend all limitations and boundaries.

Good and Evil

The subject of good and evil is very sensitive. If the manipulation of good and evil had been assigned to men the lustful desires would have turned good into evil and evil into good and human intellect would have tried to justify this change. Thus, in western civilization the standard of good and evil is personal likes and dislikes. Since personal likes and dislikes are subject to change, what was good in the morning turns into evil in the evening and vice versa.

Book of God as the Criterion

In the Islamic scheme of cultural reconstruction the criterion of good and evil is the Book of God, which book speaks for itself and is true and final in its judgment. It does not yield to any changes in any age. The Quran says:

> *For he commands them*
> *What is just and forbids them*
> *What is evil; he allows*
> *Them as lawful what is good*
> *(and pure) and prohibits them*
> *From what is bad (and impure);* (VII-154)

> *Tha word of Thy Lord*
> *Doth find its fulfilment*
> *In truth and injustice;*
> *None can change His Words*
> *For He is the One Who*
> *Heareth and knoweth all.*
> *Wert Thou to follow*
> *The common run of those*
> *On earth, they will lead*
> *Thee away from the Way*
> *Of God. They follow*

Nothing but conjecture: they
Do nothing but lie. (VI-115-16)

About the Quran the Holy Prophet said: 'It is a judge between truth and falsehood; it is not a joke; it cannot bend to human desires'. (*Mishkat,* Fazailul Quran).

Values

Values are of three kinds: (1) spiritual, (2) moral, and (3) aesthetic.

Aesthetic Values

What we have said so far is related to spiritual and moral values. But aesthetic values, too, are equally important in life. Under aesthetic values we have considerations of beauty and good form, grace and perfection; balance, proportion, harmony etc.

No Co-ordination among Values in the West

In Western culture there is no co-ordination among the various values; on the other hand there is clash. Thus aesthetic values do not correspond to moral values, or even defy them. Efforts are made to keep art alienated from morality; let alone spirituality which would get a secondary importance. And so, in western culture all forms of obscenity and immodesty go by the name of 'art'. P.A. Sorokin rightly observes that modern art has ignored all religious and moral values, for these values would not have provided entertainment like the one provided by wine and women. Consequently art has become devoid of morality; it has become immoral and unsocial, and very often it appears in a form inimical to the religious, the moral and the social sense. Sorokin goes on to say that now-a-days sexuality and crime are central to 70—80% of the films. They dominate sculpture and painting, too. The fine arts are particularly engaged in parody, ridicule and satire. It is usual with them to slight and make fun of everything, from God down to the Devil.[1]

Aesthetic Source in Divine Attributes, and Values:

In the Islamic scheme of cultural reconstruction aesthetic values, like all other values, emanate from the Attributes of God, which partake of mutual harmony and not of mutual contradiction. Indeed in and through that Divine Source all the three kinds of values grow in harmony, due proportion and balance, and within set limits.

Certain Verses and Traditions Regarding Aesthetic Values:

The Quran speaks of aesthetic values in the following Verses:

And (God has given you shape
And made your shapes
Beautiful, (XL-64)

We have indeed created man
In the best of moulds (XLV-4)

Him Who created thee,
Fashioned thee in due proportion,
And gave thee a just bias; (LXXVII-7)

We have indeed decked
The lower heaven with beauty
(In) the stars (XXXVII-6)

That which is on earth
We have made but as
A glittering show for the earth, (XVIII-7)

He Who has made
Everything which He has created

Most good: (XXXII-7)

And ye have a sense
Of pride and beauty in them (cattle)
As ye drive them home
In the evening, and as ye
Lead them forth to pasture
In the morning. (XVII-5)

The Holy Prophet said: 'Verily Allah is Beautiful and loves Bea-duty'.[2] On another occasion he said: 'He is Pure and loves Purity'.[3] 'Verily, Allah is Wholesome and loves Wholesomeness; On still another occasion said the Holy Prophet: 'What I particularly appreciate in the world is women and fragrance'[4].

Besides these there are some other Verses and Traditions which testify to the appreciation of aesthetic values in Islam.

Right of Legislation and God

For legislation two considerations are essential : (1) perceptiveness into subtleties and egalitarianism, (2) safeguarding of dignity and sanctity.

Without these two considerations a law cannot safeguard human rights and welfare, nor can it make the transgressor bow before its verdict. Western culture where legislation comes from man himself has not been able to accommodate these two considerations, in spite of all the advances it has made.

In the Islamic scheme of cultural reconstruction the right of legislation actually belongs to God, Whose law, because of His egalitarian and all-perceptive view of things, can safeguard man's material and spiritual welfare on the one hand, and can make everybody bow before its dignity and sanctity on the other. Listen to the Quran:

The Command
Rests with none but God: (VI-57)

...nor does
He share His Command
With any person whatsoever. (XVIII-26)

Fellow (O men!) the revelation
Given unto you from your Lord,
And follow not, as friends
Or protectors, other than Him. (VII-3)
Say: 'Shall I seek
For Judge other than God?—
When He it is
Who hath sent unto you
The Book, explained in details'. (VI-114)

Two Kinds of Laws

Laws are of two kinds : (1) primary, and (2) secondary. 'Primary laws' are those that have been promulgated by God for permanent execution. They cannot be changed, though their relevance is determined by the context of contemporary circumstances. 'Secondary laws' are those that are promulgated from time to time by the legislative authority for the purpose of enforcing 'primary laws'.Of course, they keep changing with the changing circumstances .It is for two reasons that 'secondary laws' are needed:(1) because 'primary laws' are not observed on account of social corruption;(2) because the high level of society necessary for observing the 'primary laws' does not exist.

Principle of Prescription

Whether it is a matter of the formulation of law or that of the determination of the relevance of law, the principle of prescription is made use of. Through this principle the legislative authority acquires power according to the conditions that prevail, to prescribe the law in both the matters. The powers are as follows:

1. To determine the priority or otherewise of the implementation of the law.
2. To make the law specific if it is general in its implications.
3. To subject it to conditions if it is unconditional or absolute.
4. To delimit it if it is indefinite or wide
5. To exclude from it certain things as exceptions.
6. To add some condition for the implementation of the law.
7. To add some new feature to the law for its implementation.

From our predecessors, specializing in jurisprudence, we get, with reference to their concept of prescription, the following testimony of the powers of the legislative authority:

What we call 'prescription' is the lifting of validity from certain terms which are general, absolute or apparent in their implications. That is, the general is delimited by certain specifications, and the absolute by certain conditions or limitations; or the absolute is transferred to the conditional in order to interpret and explicate it. Thus exception, condition and feature also come within the purview of 'prescription'; for through these, too, the validity of the apparent is lifted off and the purpose (behind it) is states. In the terminology of the ancients 'prescription' means the statement of purpose, and this statement is also implied by the antonym of this term and even by an extraneous imperative[5].

At another place it is observed:

Ignoring the apparent bearing or implication in view of certain specifications, limitations, conditions or preclusions is what the ancients usually called 'prescription'[6].

It was by virtue of the above-mentioned powers that Omar, acting as legislative authority, determined the contemporary relevance of many of the 'primary laws' and devised many new ('secondary') laws—which is evident by the books of Islamic jurisprudence.

Ijtihad: A Comprehensive Term

In every age the legislative authority or its deputy, the group of the '*ulema*' has had the right to devise "secondary laws' or to determine the contemporary relevance of the 'primary laws'; so that, on the one hand, the 'primary laws' do not stagnate, by becoming mechanical imperatives, and, on the other, a dynamic relation is maintained between life and law. But it has not been permitted to use this right freely and arbitrarily. That it may be used properly a comprehensive term, ***Iitihad,*** has been devised: only within the purview of this term can it be used. In fact *Ijtihad* is the highest effort employed to bring law into harmony with dynamic and ever-growing life—with the provision that the correspondence of law to morality be maintained. This is not the place to go into a detailed discussion on *Ijtihad;* but the subject comes under full discussion in my other books *Fiqah-i-Islami Ka Tarikhi Pas-i-Manzar* and *Masala-i-Ijtihad par Tahqiqi Nazar,* to which interested readers may turn.

Rights and Duties of Citizenship

The question of determining the rights and duties of citizenship is none the less important. The West has not been able to determine them on a firm and definite basis for the simple reason that it regards values as relative and seeks their source and their criterion in human society. In the Islamic scheme of cultural reconstruction the basis of rights and duties is moral values; which are perennial. On this basis every citizen, without any distinction of religion, community, caste or creed etc., has the following rights.

1. Every Human Being is Entitled to Respect

Every human being, *qua* human being, is entitled to respect. In this matter distinctions of race, language, religion, family, richness or poverty, vocation, caste, colour, creed etc. do not apply. It is, in fact, the duty of the government to eliminate these distinctions and the very tendency of making these distinctions by various efforts. The Quran proclaims:

We have honoured the sons
Of Adam, (XVII-70)

To all are degrees (or ranks)
According to their deeds: (VI-132)

...verily
The most honoured of you
In the sight of God
Is (he who is) the most
Righteous of you. (XLIX-13)

2. Everybody Has a Right for the Protection of His Life and Honour

Everybody has the right of having his life and property and honour safeguarded. The question of the sacrosancity of man and his life was so important that in his last sermon the Holy Prophet insisted on it. He said:

Like the Sacrosanct day (Youme 'Arfa) the life, property and honour of everyone of you is sacrosanct for others. (*Mishkat*, Bab Hajjatul Wida'e)

Ali once said:

The property of these people (Non-Muslims) are like our property; and their lives are like our lives **(they are eqully sacrosanct)** —(*Nasbul Raya*, Vol. 3, Kitabul Siyar).

3. The Laws of Justice and Doing Good are Common for All

The laws of justice and doing good are common for all and everybody has equal right to benefit from them, even if he is an enemy:

...and let not
The hatred of others
To you make you swerve
To wrong and depart from
Justice. Be just: that is

Next to Piety : (V-9)

4. Equal Right to Benefit From the Good Things Of Life

All human beings are equally entitled to benefit from the things of the universe.

It is He Who hath created for you
All things that are on earth; (II-29)

And We have provided therein
Means of subsistence, —for you
And for those for whose sustenance
Ye are not responsible. (XV-20)

5 Everybody Has the Right to Participate in the Government :

In the government everybody has the right to participate (of course in accordance with his or her ability). In the Parliamentary system of government this consideration is important as ony other considerations are. Verses concerning the parliamentary mode have been quoted above.

Some episodes may be mentioned here. For example Omar wrote to the people of Kufa, Basra and Syria instructing them to elect competent persons from among themselves competent so that they may be inducted into the government[7]. Similarly after various countries had been conquered, it happened that the Non-Muslim officials were kept in the administration by way of status quo. In this regard Maqraizi says that with the change of the temperament of the government these officials gave up their own practice of oppression and injustice—'the mode of administration and collecting revenue in the case of these officials was oriented according to the justice'. (Miqraizi, *Kitabul Khutat,* p. 120)

6. Everybody has the Right of Religious Freedom

In matters of belief, religion, creed and cult everybody has equal freedom—

> *Let there be no compulsion*
> *In religion* (II-256)

Various Forms of Freedom

On the same basis Mohammad (peace be upon him) proclaimed that the followers of different religions are brothers (and sisters) to one another and they form a single grand community. He said: 'All human beings are brothers to one another' (Muslim; *Abu Daud*) On another occasion the Holy Prophet said: 'They are all of One Community'. (Ibn-i-Hisham, *Seerat*, Vol. 1; Abi Obaid, *Al-Amwal*, pp. (204-5)

In the days of the Holy Prophet the worshipping places of every religion, their respective modes of worship and their respective religious chiefs were guaranteed protection. Thus the command was:

> The places of worship of the Jews and Christians should not be demolished. These people should not be prevented from blowing their conchs, taking out their crosses and other signs on their festival days. (*Kitabul Khiraj*, p. 72)

At Another place it has been proclaimed:

> The worshipping places of the Jews and the Christians should not be demolished. At any time of the day or night, whenever they like these people can blow their conchs, but, of course, the timings of Muslim prayer are exceptions. These people are free to take out their crosses and other signs on festival days. (*Ibid.*)

Besides freedom for worship, freedom was given in all religious matters to each and every citizen. After giving an account of various conquered countries Abu Obaid says: 'All these countries were conquered by force, and their natives were allowed to continue following their respective religions and rituals'. (*Al Amwal*, p.101)

Safeguarding of everybody's personal law and culture have

been guaranteed. It has been proclaimed that 'the non-are Muslims free in matters of witnesses, wedding, laws of inheritance and in all other matters related to their personal affairs.' (*Al-Amwal*, p. 140)

Everybody was given full freedom to propogate his religion. This is evident from the following command:

Nothing should be interposed between them (the Non-Muslims) and their religious rituals and rights. (*Tabari*, Sec. 4)

At another place it is proclaimed:

Let there be no coercion of any king in matters of their religion. (*Tabari*, Fath Baitual Maqdis)

Rights and Duties Related to Both Government and people

Just as every citizen has the above rights, in the same manner he has duties towards the government; he should obey the government in matters concerning common welfare and the doing of good. He must cooperate with the government in these matters and be its well-wisher.

The government also has certain duties towards its citizens. It must make every effort to have the rights of every citizen looked after. In this matter it must not be negligent or slow. It must undertake all troubles for the sake of the comforts of the citizens.

Thus, we can say that in the Islamic Scheme of Cultural Reconstruction ghts and duties have been determined properly from both sides. If these rights and duties are properly observed the problems of the government and of the people can be easily solved and chaotic situations, like the one that prevails now, can be prevented.

NOTES AND REFERENCES

CHAPTER ONE

1. See William Mc Dougall, *Social Psychology,* Chapter III.
2. See William Mc Dougall, *An Outline of Psychology,* Chapter VII.
3. *Social Psychology, Op.cit.*
4. *Risala Ganjul Asrar* (MS), July - August, 1968.
5. Shah Ismail Shahid, *Abqat,* Abqah I, p.4.
6. Jassas, Ahkamul Quran, Vol. I, p. 33; Qazi Thanaullah, *Tafsir-i-Mazhari,* Vol. I, p.5.
7. Qazi Thanaullah, *Op. cit.,* p. 51.
8. For an elaborate discussion on the subject see Mohammad Taqi Amini, *'Uruj-o-Zawal ka Ilahi Nizam.*
9. History of Arabia, p. 107.
10. Percy Board, *The Laws of War between Belligerents* (Chicago).
11. Quoted by Hamidulla in *'Ehd-i-Nabwi men Nizami-i-Hukmrani,* p. 148
12. *Op.cit.,* p. 51
13. *Ibid.*
14. See *Social Psychology,* Chapter IX.
15. For example, *Jallain.*
16. Abul Kalam, Preface to *Tarjumanul Quran.*

CHAPTER TWO

1. Quoted by Ibn-i-Taimiya in *Risala Baghiatul Murtad,* p. 33.
2. *Ahyau 'Ulumil Din,* Vol. I, Haqiqatul Aql.
3. Baghiatul Murtad, Kitabul 'Aql.
4. *Hujjatullahil Baliqha,* Vol. II, Al Maqamat wal Ahwal.
5. Shah Ismail Shahid, *'Abqat,* Abqah IV.
6. Mohammad Taqi Amini, 'Al Faqih fi Mustalahil Shariah' in *Al Ba 'ithul Islami,* Feb. 1978.
7. *Hujjatullahil Baligha,* Al Hujbul Man 'ia.
8. *Altaful Quds,* Chapter V.
9. *Op.Cit.,* Chapter IV.
10. Preface to *Critique of Pure Reason.*
11. For a detailed discussion on the subject see Mohammad Taqi Amini, La Mazhabi Daur Ka Tarikhi Pas-i-Manzar. The English translation (Delhi, 1986) is also available.
12. Al Ghazali, *Ahyau 'Ulumil Din,* Vol. III, discussion on 'Nafs' etc.
13. Ibn-i-Taimiya, *Sharhul Qasidatil Asfahaniah; Al Munqiz minal Zalal, Qaul* Fi Sabab-i-Nashril 'Ilm, p. 38.

14. Al Ghazali, *op. cit.*, Mithalul Qalb.
15. Al Ghazali, *op. cit.*, Ausaful Qalb.
16. *Ibid.*
17. *Ibid.*
18. Al Ghazali, *Al Munqiz minal Zalal.*
19. Mulla Jiwan, *Nurul Anwar*
20. Al Ghazali,*Op. Cit.*, Vol. III, Al Lafzul Awwal wal Rab'e.
21. Shaikh Ahmad Sarhindi, *Maktubat-i-Imam-i-Rabbani,* Vol. I, Maktub. 253.
22. *Ibid.*
23. Al Ghazali, *op. cit.*
24. *Ibid.*
25. *Ibid.*
26. Qazi Thanaullah Panipati, *Irshadul Talibin,* Khwariq-i-Aadaat.
27. *Ibid.*
28. *Risala Ganjul Asrar,* Chapter III (Sindh University MS).
29. *Awaariful M 'aarif.*
30. Al Ghazali, *op. cit.*, Al Farq Bainal Maqamain
31. Mohammad Taqi Amini, 'Al Faqih fi Mustalahil Shari 'ah' in *B 'athul Islami,* Feb. 1968.
32. *Ibid.*
33. *Aqrabul Mawarid al Wahi.*
34. Rashid Raza Misri, Al Wahiul Mohammadi, Chapter I.
35. Sabhiul Saleh, *'Ulumul Hadith; Kulliyat Abil Baga.*
36. Mohammad Siddique Afghani, *Zubdah Tartilil Quran.*
37. *Ibid.*
38. Ibn-i-Sina, *Al Risalatul 'Arshia Haqiqatul Wahi,* M.S. Maulana Azad Library, Aligarh Muslim University.
39. *Ibid.*
40. *Al Maznunul Saghir,* Fasl Qila lahu, p. 91.
41. *Hallo Masail-i-Ghamiza,* p. 3-36.
42. *Hujjatullahil Baligha,* Haqiqatual Ruh.
43. *Op. Cit.* Asrsrul Salat
44. *Op. Cit.* Min Abwabil Zakat

CHAPTER THREE

1. *Tafsir Azizi,* Nawadirul Usul.
2. *Mufridatul Quran.*
3. *Tehzibul Akhlaq.*
4. Mohammad Taqi Amini, *'Uruj-o-Zawal ka Ilahi Nizam,* p. 48.
5. Syed Mahmud Alusi, *Ruhul M 'aani,* Tafsir Surah Nur.
6. *Ibid.* Also Saeed b. Mansur and Ibnul Munzar.
7. Syed Mahmud Alusi, *Op. Cit.,*
8. *Bukhari; Muslim; Mishkat:* Kitabul Iman.

9. Baihaqi, Fi Shu.'bil Iman; *Mishkat,* Fil Rifq wal Haya.
10. *Ibid.*
11. *Ibn-i-Majah; Mishkat:* Fil Rifq wal Haya.
12. *Bukhari; Muslim; Mishkat:* Fil Rifq wal Haya.
13. *Ibid.*
14. *Ibid.*
15. *Al Jawame' fil Siyasatil Ilahiya,* p. 3.
16. *Abu Daud,* Fi Naqlil Hadith
17. *Ibid.*
18. *Ibid.*
19. *Ibid.*
20. Raghib Asfahani, *Al Mufridat fi Gharibil Quran.*
21. *Mishkat,* Al Shafqah wal Rahmah 'alal Khalq.
22. *Muslim; Abu Daud.*
23. *Bukhari,* Kitabul Adab.
24. *Op. Cit.,*Bab Rahmatul Nas wal Bahaim.
25. *Op. Cit.* Abwab Al Bir wal Silah.
26. *Tirmizi; Mishkat,* Al Shafqah wal Rahmah 'alal Khalq, Fasl II.
27. Amin Hasan, *Tadabbur-i-Quran.*
28. The *American Way of Life,* p. 694.
29. *Ibn-i-Majah; Mishkat,* Babul Bir wal Silah.
30. *Tirmizi; Mishkat,* Babul Bir wal Silah.
31. *Muslim; Mishkat,* Babul Bir wal Silah.
32. See Mohammad Taqi Amini, *'Uruj-o-Zawal ka Ilahi Nizam.*
33. Qazi Abdullah Baizawi.
34. Sheikh Suleiman, Hashia *Jalalain:* Al Jamalul Jamal
35. Rashid Raza Misri, *Al Manar,* Vol.9.
36. *Bukhari; Muslim; Mishkat,* Babul Shafqah wal Rahmah.
37. Bukhari, Kitabul Adab, Bab Rahmatul Walid.
38. *Tirmizi; Mishkat,* Babul Shafqati 'alal Khalq.
39. *Bukhari; Muslim; Mishkat,* Babul 'Ataya.
40. *Ibid.*
41. *Ibid.*
42. *Muslim,* Vol. I, Bab Hukmul 'Azl.
43. *Ibid.*
44. Jassas Razi, *Ahkamul Quran,* p. 416.
45. *Lissanul 'Arab,* Vol.XI-IV, 'Aul; *Ruhul M 'aani,* Part IV, p. 197; Zamakshari, *Al Kashshaf,* p. 226.
46. *Ruhul M 'aani,* Part IV, p. 197.
47. Yusuf Ibn-i-Nusri, *Al Nujumul Zahira fi Akhbar Misr wal Qahira,* Vol. I, p. 72.
48. See, for example, Ghazali, *Ahya,* Vol. II, Adabul M 'ashira.
49. David C. Marsh, *The Changing Social Structure* (London) p. 263.
50. *Unsolved Problems,* p. 195.

51. Ibn-i-Abdul Bar, *Jame' Bayanil 'Ilm,* Vol.I; *Mishkat,* Kitabul 'Ilm, Fasl III.
52. *Mishkat,* Babul Iman bil Qadr, Fasl III.
53. Ibn-i-Abdul Bar, *Jame' Bayanil 'Ilm,* Vol. I, Babul Hasad.
54. *Ibid.*
55. Ibn-i-Abdul Bar, *Jame' Bayanil 'Ilm,* Bab Jame' fi Fazlul 'Ilm.
56. *Tirmizi, Ibn-i-Majah, Mishkat,* Kitabul 'Ilm; Ibn-i-Abdul Bar, *Jame' Bayanil 'Ilm,* Bab Talabul 'Ilm.
57. *Baihaqi,* Madkhal.
58. Masudi, *Murujul Zahab,* p. 308.
59. Ibn-i-Habib, *Al Muhabbar,* Aswaqil 'Arabil Mashhura.
60. Abul Qasim Abdul Rahman, Suhaili AlRuzul Unf, Fasl Zikr T'alimi Thlil Taif.
61. *Ibid.*
62. Taqiuddin Ahmad b. Ali Miqraizi, *Imtaul Asma' Hisnul Taif.*
63. *Ibid.*
64. *Ibid.*
65. *Ibid.*
66. *Muslim, Mishkat, Bab I'dadi Altil Jihad.*
67. *Tirmizi, Ibni-i-Majah, Mishkat,* Bab I'dadi Altil Jihad.
68. *Tabaqat-i-Ibn-i-S'ad,* Vol. I, II; Musnad-i-Ibni-i-Hambal, Vol.I.
69. *Baihaqi,* Fi. Sho'baul Iman, *Mishkat,* Kitabul Iman, Fasl II.
70. *Baihaqi,* Vol. VI, p. 289.
71. Bertrand Russel, *Marriage and Morals,* pp.65, 69, 91; See also the *American Way of Life,* pp. 649, 654.
72. *Mishkat,* Kitabul Nikah, Fasl I.
73. *Ibid.*
74. *Baihaqi,* Fi Sho'bul Iman, *Mishkat,* Babul Shafqah wal Rahmah 'alal Khalq, Fasl III.
75. *Bukhari, Muslim, Mishkat,* Babul Shafqah wal Rahmah 'alal Khalq, Fasl III.
76. *Ibid.*

CHAPTER FIVE

1. *Crisis of Our Age,* pp. 52-75.
2. *Muslim,* Kitabul Iman, Bab Tahrimil Kibr.
3. *Tirmizi,* Abwabul Adab Majaae fil Nazafah.
4. *Nasai,* Kitab 'Ishratil Nisa, Bab Hubbul Nisa.
5. *'Ilamul Mowaqqe' in,* Faslul Murad bil Naskh 'inda 'Aammatil Salaf.
6. *Ibid.*
7. *Kitabul Amwal,* Bab fi Taqbilil Sawad wa Ikhtiyaril Wolat.